"Aubrey Bergauer's book has given arts organizations a bold and special road map to becoming successful, sustainable, relevant, and transformative. Many have identified the myriad challenges facing today's orchestras and performing arts organizations. Few, if any, have identified the problems, using data and a transformative vision to effectively address them. Aubrey does. She walks her talk. Her data-based, customer-centric, financially viable, artistically exciting, and inclusive approach works. Aubrey dared to challenge the existing orthodoxies and paradigms. Dared to embrace the wonder, beauty, and majesty of classical and orchestral music and make it accessible for everyone. Dared to expect the most from our constituencies. She tried on her vision and it worked. You should try it on. It will work for you, too."
—Pamela Carter, board chair of the Nashville Symphony

"In *Run It Like a Business*, Aubrey Bergauer brilliantly weaves the heart's passion with strategic pragmatism. You can feel on every page that she has lived what she's writing. The dedication and fervor poured into this book is nothing short of inspiring. She really put everything there in a simple and very well-mapped way to connect with your audience for real. For every arts leader, this isn't just a guide—it's a testament to what can be achieved when mission meets meticulous planning, discipline, and creativity."
—David Lomelí, chief artistic officer of the Santa Fe Opera

Praise for *Run It Like a Business*

"*Run It Like a Business* is a fresh and modern method for sustaining your not-for-profit. Aubrey Bergauer is an energetic, knowledgeable coach when it comes to sensible business practices for people who hate business."

—Sallie Krawcheck, CEO and cofounder of Ellevest

"Just when arts organizations need it most, here comes an extraordinary book that brings it all together—from programming to marketing, from outreach to development. Bergauer's passion for the arts is complemented by the mind of a brilliant CEO. Here is the playbook for the performing arts of the future."

—Mason Bates, Grammy-winning composer and former composer-in-residence for the Kennedy Center and Chicago Symphony

"*Run it Like a Business* captures exactly what every arts leader needs to lead their organization to success. Aubrey Bergauer cuts to the chase, using her experience and industry data to ground the book in the reality of what is needed to do this work. Astutely weaving strategy, data, and case studies, this text is a must-read for emerging arts leaders enrolled in arts management, leadership, or entrepreneurship programs."

—Dr. Brett Ashley Crawford, associate teaching professor at Carnegie Mellon University

"As someone who performs all over the world, I regularly encounter many challenges facing our industry—and the path through them can look daunting! Luckily, Aubrey Bergauer has brought together a well-crafted plan for how the classical music industry can flourish. Her impressive collection of data on where we are—and what needs to change—will benefit any nonprofit organization that seeks to connect with their community and remain relevant. This is an absolute must-read for leaders looking for inspiration, and it's left me with real hope for a brighter and more inclusive future in classical music."

—Jamie Barton, mezzo-soprano

"Aubrey Bergauer promotes a critical examination of existing business strategies to help arts organizations reclaim their financial acumen and develop generations of loyal supporters. As an artistic consultant, she shares her knowledge so that administrators feel empowered to implement proven business practices and to widen the spectrum of artistic voices in today's digital world. Aubrey's vision is to build an equitable society, increase financial revenue for arts organizations, and inspire humanity all at the same time."

—Germaine Franco, Grammy–winning composer and music producer

RUN IT LIKE A BUSINESS

Strategies for Arts Organizations
to Increase Audiences, Remain
Relevant, and Multiply Money—
Without Losing the Art

AUBREY BERGAUER

BenBella Books, Inc.
Dallas, TX

Run It Like a Business copyright © 2024 by Aubrey Bergauer

BenBella Books, Inc.
10440 N. Central Expressway
Suite 800
Dallas, TX 75231
benbellabooks.com
Send feedback to feedback@benbellabooks.com

BenBella is a federally registered trademark.

Printed in the United States of America
10 9 8 7 6 5 4 3 2 1

Library of Congress Control Number: 2023031661
ISBN 9781637744383 (hardcover)
ISBN 9781637744390 (electronic)

Editing by Alyn Wallace
Copyediting by James Fraleigh
Proofreading by Sarah Vostok and Denise Pangia
Indexing by Amy Murphy
Text design and composition by PerfecType
Cover design by Morgan Carr
Printed by Lake Book Manufacturing

CONTENTS

"Business is not part of the community.
Business *is* the community."
Tom Peters

Introduction

"Can we move this meeting to the restroom?" Sara Blakely brazenly asked a Neiman Marcus executive.

Well before she was a billionaire, Blakely, the Spanx founder and CEO, was shifting her sales approach, emulating a strategy she saw work in other industries: have the decision maker actually try the product firsthand.

The meeting hadn't been going well. The Neiman buyer was distracted and disinterested, and Blakely was watching her window of opportunity slip away—until her abrupt yet savvy pivot to a bathroom stall clinched her big sales break. The executive tried on some Spanx shapewear and was an immediate fan. Neiman Marcus became the first major department store to carry Spanx products. Now, Spanx are in more than 11,500 stores in better than fifty countries and the company is valued at $1.2 billion.[1]

Folks running arts organizations have a lot in common with Blakely. Her task and the moment she seized were critical. Long before Spanx became the Kleenex or Velcro of shapewear, Blakely had to convince someone who didn't know much, if anything, about her product to ultimately put their money into it—all before their attention ran out. Likewise, cultural organizations now face a similarly tall order at a crucial moment. We in the arts are also tasked with getting people who don't know much about our product to buy in, either to purchase something (usually tickets) or also—we hope—donate. Yet, our job is becoming increasingly difficult in the face of challenges like shrinking audiences, donor competition, and labels of elitism and even racism.

Even before the COVID-19 pandemic shut down the world, arts attendance in the United States was falling. The National Endowment for the Arts said in 2015 that their 2002–2012 survey period saw US arts participation across all disciplines and genres decline by nearly 20 percent.[2] By 2014, attendance at classical music events specifically was declining by 2.8 percent a year.[3] Museums similarly were seeing a 2.7 percent annual attendance drop since 2009.[4] For theaters, subscription sales tumbled 28 percent over the fourteen years before lockdown.[5] Other exhibit-based organizations (zoos, aquariums, botanical gardens, science centers, and the like) report their own versions of this issue: pre-pandemic, the average patron visited these sorts of institutions just once every 27 months—not exactly habitual behavior.[6]

Compounding this challenge is that it gets more expensive every year to produce our art. Arts and culture is a labor-based industry, onstage, offstage, in the pit, in the exhibits, in the archives, and in the office. And there are virtually no ways left to save on costs. You can't play Mozart faster; you can't have one actor play Tybalt, Mercutio, and Benvolio in one performance; and Picassos definitely aren't going down in value. Plus the artists—at least the living ones (sorry, Wolfgang, William, and Pablo)—want raises each year, as do as the people supporting them via fundraising, marketing, production, operations, finance, education, et cetera, like just about every other working human.

Producing art simply never gets cheaper.

Ever.

Cutting nonartistic expenses is not a solution either. Most cultural organizations, regardless of size, are already pretty lean. It always feels like we don't have enough people on staff to do all the work, no matter how many zeroes are in the budget—like there's not enough hours in the day or money in the coffers. And there's usually not much fat elsewhere to trim. We trimmed it last year when we needed to balance the ledger, or the year before that when we didn't make our revenue goals, or the year before that when we cut back a few positions, or the year before that when times were tough, or the year before that when . . . you get my drift.

Another "solution" has been to increase prices—a lot. As the above-mentioned theater subscriptions were plummeting by nearly a third from 2004–2017, the average price of a subscription package increased 15 percent.[7] For orchestras, season ticket prices swelled by twice that from 2005–2014. And during that same decade or so, single-ticket prices skyrocketed a whopping 50 percent.[8] By comparison, over that same period, the Consumer Price Index rose by only 25 percent.[9] This means some ticket prices have risen at essentially double the rate of inflation.

First Lady Michelle Obama looked beyond prices for the attendance decline. In a 2015 speech from the steps of the Whitney Museum in New York City, she said,

> There are so many kids in this country who look at places like museums and concert halls and other cultural centers and they think to themselves, "Well, that's not a place for me, for someone who looks like me . . ." In fact, I guarantee you that right now, there are kids living less than a mile from here who would never in a million years dream that they would be welcome in this museum.[10]

These two ingredients make for a bad brew: only a portion of the population believes they belong in a cultural institution, and even for those inclined to attend, their dollar doesn't get them in as easily as it once did.

So, the last major search for a solution has landed on programming. We are scheduling more blockbusters, such as *Harry Potter* in concert, the Egyptian mummies' latest touring exhibit, *La Bohème* and *Carmen* (again), *Our Town*, *Swan Lake*, *Wicked* and *Hamilton*, the immersive Van Gogh show, and on and on. Don't get me wrong, these programs sell! And for all other, less popular programming, selling fewer tickets at higher prices has plugged the budget hole that otherwise would remain. In some ways these "charge more, program bigger" strategies had sort of been working, at least as a stopgap. Until one day in March 2020 when it was all suddenly, completely halted altogether.

Almost overnight, COVID-19 decimated the arts. Performances abruptly shut down. Exhibits closed. Administrative staffs were laid off. Artist paychecks diminished or disappeared altogether. And we were forced to confront all our perennial challenges anew: insufficient cash flow, trailing digital adoption, and lacking alternate revenue streams. Two months later, the spotlight the Black Lives Matter movement had been shining on pervasive inequity and racism in both our country and our field could no longer be ignored. It was all brutal.

The pandemic, according to analysts across multiple industries, didn't create new problems so much as it accelerated existing ones. NYU Stern School of Business professor Scott Galloway says in his book, *Post Corona*, "Take any trend—social, business, or personal—and fast-forward ten years." No matter if the trend was positive or negative, "consumer behavior and the market now rests on the 2030 point on the trend line."

In late 2020, my team mapped out what it would look like if pre-pandemic trends *were* accelerated by ten years. The graph below shows the results in full, but essentially, if COVID really did do what Galloway forecasted, we'd be looking at only 63 percent of audiences returning when we reopened.

ARTS ATTENDANCE—PROJECTION WITH PANDEMIC ACCELERATION

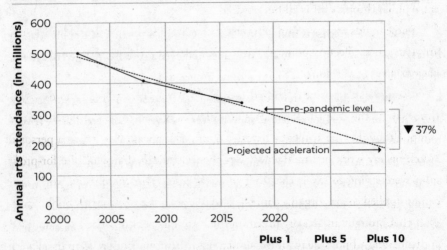

National Endowment for the Arts attendance totals across jazz, classical music, opera, musical and non-musical plays, ballet, and visits to an art museum or gallery[11]

By the 2022–2023 season, we weren't far off from that projection. Nationwide, still only 60 percent to 70 percent of pre-pandemic audiences are back. One research center even calls a 70 percent audience return "the idealized best-case scenario" per their modeling, and another says up to 20 percent of arts patrons are now "long-term non-returners."[12] Some organizations have fared better, but just about none have returned to even their pre-pandemic, already-declining level of sales. Either way, we are in desperate need of a parachute.

Donations offered a potential bright spot, with giving for arts and culture hitting $23.5 billion in the United States in 2021, exceeding pre-pandemic giving totals.[13] However, experts cautioned that this number was propped up by major gifts—the total number of active *small*-donor households was still declining.[14] Sure enough, in 2022, charitable giving "plunged," as *The Nonprofit Times* described, dropping 10.5 percent after adjusting for inflation, led by the continued decline of individual donors.[15] And with recession talk in the air as I write (who knows where the economy will be by the time you're reading this, but what's definitely true is that if we're not in a recession at the moment, we will be again someday), if we don't feed the giving-prospect pipeline with recurring ticket buyers and subscribers, a philanthropic cliff is all but ensured.

These trends are not going to reverse themselves. Arts and cultural institutions are at an acute inflection point: either reclaim relevance in our community and our patrons' lives . . . or don't.

"Run it like a business," board members with for-profit backgrounds sometimes say, to the chagrin of nonprofit employees. I used to be in that chagrined camp. I thought that it meant I wasn't doing enough, or that it was a personal attack on my work or intelligence. But then I realized that what the for-profit folks were trying to say is that there are strategies from the outside world that can be applied to arts organizations—strategies like the ones in this book. Strategies that brought an arts organization I led from its near deathbed to a doubled audience and almost quadrupled donor base, running budget surpluses every year. Strategies that are working for other organizations we'll hear from in these pages, too.

Regaining lost ground is absolutely possible, but just as it was for Sara Blakely, standing in that Neiman Marcus executive's office, it's time for us to change our approach.

There is some good news: The art itself is not the problem. Over the years, the field has sort of collectively summarized our plight as "we need new audiences so we should tinker with the programming." But as I'll discuss in chapters one and two, the arts are actually pretty good at getting new audiences; we're just bad at retaining them. And, as I will cover in chapter five, we do need to work on our programming to produce more inclusive, representative, and thus better art—but at our core, as cultural institutions, we've been making stellar art for hundreds of years.

This enduring strength comes from an incredible asset that professional cultural organizations possess: extraordinary artistic talent across disciplines, geographic regions, and budget sizes. Our artists are so remarkable and their training so rigorous that it's harder to win an audition at a major professional orchestra than it is to get drafted into the NBA.[16] We have an exceptionally strong product, a competitive advantage many brands work a lifetime to achieve. That's why this book is about how to better deliver that product—not sacrifice it—to build a lasting future for the industry.

If you're ready to turn a challenge into opportunity and not simply accept past industry trends, you are in the right place. And if looking at strategies proven to work in other industries, from shapewear to Silicon Valley, seems counter to everything you've previously thought about the arts, welcome.

By way of introduction, much of my background is performance based. Growing up, I played an instrument pretty seriously—the tuba. (If you could see me, you'd say I don't look like a tuba player, and you'd be right. Me breaking down stereotypes, though? Yeah . . . that tracks.) In high school I played in my local youth orchestra, and during my sophomore year, our orchestra changed executive directors. That was when the light bulb went off: *there's a job managing this whole operation . . . and that's the job I want.*

Fast-forward to today, and the focus of my entire career has been not just on the business side of the arts, but also about optimizing that business—growing audiences and donor bases, building relevance and visibility, using technology to elevate and extend the brand, galvanizing staff and community stakeholders, and ultimately generating the revenue we need to sustainably fund the art we produce.

I've worked at a major symphony orchestra in fundraising; a top opera company in marketing; and a multidisciplinary, multigenre festival overseeing both those areas. I've been an executive director at a regional orchestra, a VP at a higher-ed music conservatory, and a founder of industry training programs. Most recently, I've worked as a consultant with all those types of organizations and more. Altogether, I've served dozens of cultural institutions, ranging widely in size, scope, discipline, geography, and budget. The ideas outlined in this book have been vetted, tested, and verified—outside and across the arts—and they're here to serve as your guide.

But before we venture down this path together, you need to know a few more things about me. First, though obviously I'm intimately familiar with classical music, and therefore a lot of the examples and statistics in this book are associated with that knowledge base, these concepts apply to other artistic disciplines (dance, theater, museums) and cultural organizations more broadly (libraries, zoos, art centers—even sports teams). So, I've highlighted other applications from a variety of disciplines and organizations throughout. And, to take it a step further, in each chapter I've included an "Application Box" with examples of how that chapter's subject matter applies to other disciplines. It looks like this:

APPLICATION BOX

Concept: A concept discussed in the chapter you're reading

Organization: Name of an organization nailing the concept

Short summary here of a case study or element of the strategy and how the organization applied it in their own work.

The next thing you need to know about me is I like money. Without it, we don't fund our mission. I also think everyone in this business should be paid more (we'll talk about this more in chapter six). To be clear, I'm not endorsing growth in a profit-at-all-costs, cutthroat-capitalist kind of way, although competing for consumer eyeballs and wallets is the hand we've been dealt given the paltry public funding for the arts in the US. So, we're tasked with paying the bills in other ways.

Said differently, I believe that "nonprofit" is a tax status, not a scarcity mindset or can't-make-money mandate. Just ask the National Football League, which was the largest nonprofit on the planet until 2015 when they gave up the tax exemption to avoid the public scrutiny and accountability that comes with it. (And . . . yeah; they should have.) The point is, love 'em or hate 'em, with $12 billion of annual revenue on the books,[17] they've figured out how to ignite a rabid fan base that eats, sleeps, breathes, and—most important—buys what they offer. We don't have to be the NFL, but we can change the rules of our game.

The third thing to know about me is I come from long-established, traditional institutions. I haven't run one of the smallest companies or the largest, but I have worked in and with organizations ranging in budget size from $300,000 to $300 million, from staffs of one to one thousand. I've had sleepless nights in the CEO hot seat, led large and small teams, worked with internal and external stakeholders, presented to board members across the country and abroad, and demonstrated success that defies industry trends time and again. In this book, I outline strategies I've seen work across budget sizes and disciplines, as well as ways to scale these strategies up and down.

However, since my experience at conventional institutions has been the backbone of my near twenty years in this business, the last thing to know about me is that I don't have experience at organizations created to center historically marginalized populations. While I'm on a mission to dismantle old systems of racism and oppression in the established arts ecosystem, I don't always know how. I have learned, listened, and, honestly, failed, a lot. I'm sharing what I've absorbed and believe in these pages, but want to be explicit about the fact that there's still so far to go toward systemic change with our traditional institutions and with my own journey as well. So, I also hope this book offers some guidance for those on similar journeys and, if you're not yet sure why this work is essential to the future of arts and culture, it also makes the case for you to start that journey.

Note: This book doesn't have a dedicated EDI (equity, diversity, and inclusion)* chapter, and that's by design. I think this work must permeate everything

---

* A note on "EDI" versus "DEI": my understanding is that DEI is more commonly used in general, but EDI is gaining traction. The argument is for equity to be the first consideration, which I personally agree with; hence, I'll use the EDI acronym throughout.

we do, so I've tried to weave it throughout. If you're looking for these subjects particularly, though, we'll hit representation in programming choices in chapter five, fair and equitable hiring in chapter six, and company culture and values in chapter seven. And if you want some specific organizations serving truly diverse and traditionally excluded audiences, you likely don't have to look farther than your own backyard.* The work these organizations do serves communities in meaningful ways I'm not sure legacy organizations ever can—but they absolutely can aspire to.

What I'm trying to say in all this is there's a lot I don't know. But here's what I do know: there's a big body of knowledge we can glean from other business-to-consumer companies. Throughout these ten chapters, I'll share volumes of data, research, and case studies from the for-profit sector combined with the stats from arts and culture that demonstrate how to achieve success across the following areas:

- **The customer experience**: centering the customer and community from their first interaction online to the moment they leave the building, so they feel welcome and unintimidated

- **Patron loyalty**: keeping audiences coming back, not just as one-and-done attendees, but by moving them from new buyers to season subscribers and eventually to donors

- **The subscription economy**: learning and applying what works for Netflix and other brands where the subscription model reigns supreme to reverse that model's decline in the arts

- **Technology and media**: leveraging streaming to attract new customers and lower barriers to entry, by borrowing from how companies like Amazon and Disney use streaming as a vehicle to keep the customer buying what the firm really cares about: their in-person or physical products

---

* Some organizations doing fabulous work here in the San Francisco Bay Area include the Crowded Fire Theatre (whose website features a transparent list of action items to dismantle White supremacy in their own spaces), Deep Waters Dance Theater (exploring issues facing people of color and the environment, like their House/Full of Blackwomen project around displacement, well-being, and sex trafficking of Black women and girls in Oakland), and Sins Invalid (a self-described disability justice–based performance group that incubates and celebrates artists with disabilities, centralizing artists of color and LGBTQ/gender-variant artists, led by disabled people of color, and challenging paradigms of "normal" and "sexy").

- **New revenue**: expanding product offerings beyond the stage, developing high-profit margin activities via our education teams, and seizing opportunity from other sectors ripe for disruption

- **Representation**: the business case for diversity and how our programming can be more authentically reflective of the communities in which we reside and bring in greater audiences as a result

- **Smart and equitable hiring**: using inclusive practices to attract, recruit, and retain the best staff and artists across the full spectrum of talent available

- **Company culture**: onstage and off, in the galleries and in the office; creating high-performing teams, workplaces of belonging, and embracing the evolving nature of hybrid and remote work

- **Organizational structure**: constructing the org chart in a way that more effectively serves the work ahead of us instead of perpetuating departmental silos and an "us versus them" mentality

- **Advocacy**: following Patagonia or Ben & Jerry's examples by demonstrating for our local, state, and national legislators how we use our platform for good in order to secure funding from officials and foster values alignment with consumers

- **Brand relevance**: pursuing the ultimate goal of having an indispensable place in the lives of patrons, donors, and broader society

As management demigod Tom Peters says, "Business is not part of the community—business *is* the community."[18] By the end of this book, my hope is for you to feel empowered and energized to do the necessary work ahead to build vibrant futures for our cultural institutions, in our communities and country.

Last, as we begin this journey together, there's one more concept I want to introduce in this overture: the flywheel. In his book *Good to Great*, Stanford Graduate School of Business professor Jim Collins examined companies that consistently outperformed their peers and evaluated what separated them from the pack. The biggest differentiator was that the best-performing companies worked hard to execute multiple strategies over time. "In building a great company or social sector enterprise," Collins writes, "there is no single defining action, no grand program, no one killer innovation, no solitary lucky break, no miracle moment. Rather, the process resembles relentlessly pushing a giant, heavy flywheel, turn upon turn, building momentum until a point of breakthrough, and beyond." Collins's comparison companies instead sought a quick fix or grand new program, as if to skip the work required and hope for a lone breakthrough.[19]

Southern Methodist University's National Center for Arts Research found the same pattern. "Across the board," their report states, "organizations that outperformed their counterparts financially over time were dedicated to myriad strategies, with a cornerstone commitment to high standards in the creation of work that is meaningful to the local community." Many strategies, diligently executed around a strong artistic product. That's the playbook.

In other words, for anyone wanting a book about a silver bullet solution to save arts and culture in one fell swoop, there is no one-stop-shop solution. #SorryNotSorry.

These pages are devoted to the layers of this multifaceted, flywheel approach—ten strategies to execute over time—as well as to the best news of all: by doing this work, you *can* surmount the challenges facing our cultural institutions. Chances are, you're doing pieces of these strategies already, and hopefully this book brings them all together for you. It's different work than we're used to in some (read: many) cases, but it's not particularly *new* work. That means these concepts are proven. I've seen it, and I believe it—and I believe in our sector. When we run it like a business, the arts can start unleashing their full power to achieve transformational growth in the world ahead—and, thank goodness, with no bathroom meetings required.

1.

It's Not the Product, It's the Packaging

People hate United Airlines. Like, really hate them.[1] **Ask folks to** tell you their worst flight stories, and they'll light up with tales of the not-so-friendly-skies.

Meanwhile, people love Costco. Ask a person why they're obsessed with the wholesale warehouse and you'll hear them rave about rotisserie chickens, affordable clothes, free samples, and the food court (I mean, they're not wrong).[2]

Yet, ask people what they think about an orchestra or museum—or any cultural institution—and . . . it's a mixed bag.

Whereas consumers frequent airlines and wholesale stores out of necessity, that's not the case with arts and culture, and the numbers confirm this in startling ways. Nationwide, 90 percent of first-time orchestra attendees never return (these data come from the biggest orchestras in the US, but it's held largely true for organizations I've worked with at various budget sizes).[3] That means almost everyone who gives the symphony a try decides it's not for them. Ouch. And other artistic disciplines see similar churn in their newcomers.

1

Though the industry cries, "We need new audiences," we have misidentified the problem. Yes, we do want new folks, but every year thousands of new patrons are already giving cultural organizations a try. According to an analysis of nearly four hundred arts databases across North America and the UK, half or more of all ticket buyers are first-time bookers.[4] The issue isn't getting people to come to the arts; it's getting people to come *back*. And the art itself is not what's keeping first-timers from returning. It's everything tangential to the art—the user experience.

But to begin, why does it even matter if new attendees come back? Because arts organizations have what I call the iceberg predicament: the relatively small group of patrons visible above water who drive most of the revenue (e.g., people who have some sort of recent ticket or donation history) and a giant mass of patrons below the surface (people who have gone completely cold with no activity in recent years) who represent a source of all kinds of revenue if we could hook them before they go under. Getting those first-time audiences back matters because they are the entry point from which all other relationships develop. Data from across the performing and visual arts tell us *the number one indicator of subscriber or member potential is attending a second time within twelve months of the first visit*—and the top prospect pool for potential donors is existing subscribers and members. If arts organizations don't have growing numbers of returning buyers—if nine out of ten new patrons are going straight underwater—then we have a serious pipeline problem for potential donors. That iceberg is going to sink our ships.

USER EXPERIENCE RESEARCH: IT'S ALL GREEK TO ME

Duolingo had a similar problem. With more than 500 million total users from every country in the world, Duolingo is the most popular way to learn a language globally and the most downloaded education app.[5] Yet, of those half billion customers, only forty million are active monthly users. That's just 8 percent, aka the tip of our metaphorical iceberg.

Whereas in the arts, we want to get patrons to come back within a year, Duolingo defines a user as inactive—dead in the water—after thirty days off the app, because, as they say, "when learning a language, a month away is a major disruption to your language learning journey."[6] Duolingo knew that on any given day, 5 percent of those inactive users returned to the app. You'd think this would be cause for celebration, as a 5 percent resurrection rate amounts to twenty-five million users coming back every day. But then Duolingo found something surprising. These resurrected users were 20 percent *less likely* to stick with Duolingo seven and fourteen days later compared to brand-new customers.[7] In other words, the resurrected users didn't come back for long. Duolingo found that focusing on the early window of a new user is more fruitful than reviving past users.

Duolingo knew it had to find a way to get those first-time customers coming back again and again, forming a habit before they ever went cold. Duolingo is constantly running experiments to improve the user experience: how a customer feels about the ease of use and pleasure derived from a product.[8] Turns out, how a person feels the first time they do something has a huge bearing on whether they do that thing again.

When I was executive director of the California Symphony, we dug into user experience research with our own focus group project. We knew that, like Duolingo, we needed more first-timers to come back, and we were determined to learn more about what was keeping them away. We put out the call for people who "should" go to the symphony—meaning millennials and Gen Xers who self-identified as smart and educated, had expendable income, and frequented other live entertainment options—but for whatever reason just . . . didn't attend.[9]

The deal we offered was that participants could attend as many concerts as they wanted, with a minimum of one particular required concert so that they'd have a shared experience on which to base a discussion a few weeks later. Our promise to the participants was to listen only and not jump to defense. (This proved to be a tremendously difficult exercise. People are likely to give you an earful if you give them the chance to tell you how they feel about any consumer brand, be that United Airlines or Costco, Duolingo or an arts organization.)

We heard everything from "Your website reads like inside baseball" (burn), to "Can I pluck an oboe?" (that's not quite how an oboe works), to "You go to a place to experience culture, but the lack of diversity made it feel un-cultured" (third-degree burn).[10] Our project was completely unrelated to Duolingo's user research, yet we unearthed some strikingly similar customer frustrations:

FRUSTRATION	DUOLINGO[11]	CALIFORNIA SYMPHONY
Feeling overwhelmed and confused when they opened the app/ website	Colorful and busy design User: "Little did I know I was about to get hit by a rainbow"	Terminology they were never taught in school, such as "concerto" or "instrumentation" User: "Insiders would know these things, but it seems like you might be able to engage people with more layman terms."
Too much upselling	App: "Up your progress score." User: "I'm not ready for that; I just want to practice for now"	Sending too many follow-up solicitations for more tickets, subscriptions, and donations
Shaming	App load screen: "15 minutes a day can teach you a language. What can 15 minutes of social media do?"	Shushing when someone applauds at the "wrong" time
Assuming an overly advanced understanding of the subject matter	Being prompted after a few lessons by a message asking if they wanted to listen to a Spanish podcast. User: "Why would I leave Duolingo to listen to a podcast now? Going from learning the word 'leche' a few moments ago to listening to a full podcast in Spanish?!"	User: "Is this piece going to be more fast paced? Is this one going to be more romantic? We can't tell from the composer name. It's almost like 'is this a romantic comedy or is it a tragedy?'" User: looked up repertoire on Wikipedia to learn what it was about—abandoning their purchase on the symphony's website to do so

Armed with their user research, Duolingo prioritized the pain points they heard based on impact (i.e., which changes, if made, would potentially help users the most). This list became their roadmap, and they started chopping away, taking steps to retain users before they ever left and updating their onboarding experience (we'll talk more about the importance of onboarding in the next chapter).[12] Through their changes, Duolingo saw retention increase significantly, with one change alone to the new user experience driving a 7 percent retention boost.[13]

As for the California Symphony, with pages and pages of feedback, we set out to change the experience online, in person, and in our marketing. The board was nervous. The musicians were skeptical. But by the end of that season, tickets sales had jumped 14 percent, and first-timer retention eventually grew to three times the industry average. I've seen these results repeated with my clients across artistic disciplines by using what I now call the three Fs of the new customer experience: having a newcomer *focus* on the website, being newcomer *friendly* in the venue, and creating newcomer-*facing* marketing.

1. Have a Newcomer Focus on the Website

For every cultural institution, the website is the most public-facing ambassador for the brand. We touch more people via our website than any concert or exhibit we produce, any free outdoor community event, or any education program. Yet too often when arts organizations design websites, they don't account for the majority of people who visit.

At the symphony, then again at a festival I partnered with, and later at a private gallery, we learned that around two-thirds of all website traffic was coming from brand-new people. I don't mean first-time buyers; I mean visitors who'd truly never been to the site before. I almost didn't believe it when I first saw how many new people that was. But it makes sense: when someone wants to learn more about anything, the first thing they do is usually google it and go to the website.

Still, most arts organizations aren't designing for the newcomers the data show are visiting the site. Instead, 62 percent of arts organizations are designing their websites for "internal priorities" and another 24 percent for the board.[14] Internal stakeholders and board members are the opposite of newcomers. Because of their deep knowledge of the institution, their experience, needs, feelings, and motivations as users simply do not represent the majority of visitors.

The good news is we can often improve the online customer experience without an expensive and time-consuming redesign. In fact, it can take as little as zero dollars to make a big impact. Some changes that can be immediately made with no cost include the following:

- **Drop the jargon and technical words** (or *define* those terms when you use them). Very intelligent adults today often don't know words like "arabesque," or the difference between "form" and "shape," because they have never been taught.

- **Cut flowery language**. Instead of subjective descriptors like "beautiful" or "beloved," newcomers want to know what makes each event *interesting*. (Channel Joe Friday on *Dragnet*: "Just the facts, ma'am.") "A high priestess had children from an affair with a Roman soldier" is a lot better than "one of the pinnacles of classic bel canto, with long, melodious lines and vivacious coloratura." Which phrase makes you want to see *Norma*, the opera being described?

- **Lose the paragraphs**. People don't read websites; they skim them. "Some information was in paragraph language," said someone in one of the group discussions, "but when you don't go to these things regularly, that made it harder to [find] what makes going to this one special." Swap paragraphs for bullet points, cutting the copy way down to keep it short and direct.

- **Bring in information**. Smart people want to learn, not feel sold to. During one focus group, a participant's desire to learn led him to look up every work in the season on Wikipedia—and just when I was thinking that was a bit eccentric, others jumped in saying that was a great idea and they wished we included that information without them having to seek it out. At first (with no money) the organization simply linked each piece on every program to its corresponding Wikipedia page. Later, when the team eventually undertook a redesign project, they knew to require a slick Wikipedia integration from the design firm.

- **Have better concert and exhibit titles**. Catchy and specific titles perform best. Remember, is it a romantic comedy or a tragedy? Theaters, opera, and ballet companies get a pass on titling because you're working with what the playwright or composer gave you (although I—and your audience—am begging you to translate all your production names to English or whatever language is most familiar in your country—*L'Orfeo* is a big barrier for many new people when *Orpheus* is more familiar), but ensembles and exhibit-based organizations have work to do here. One music group went from a title like "Season Opener" (too vague) to "Mozart & Beethoven" (snooze fest) to "Peace, Love, & Beethoven," a small but meaningful update nodding to another piece on the program that night: Christopher Theofanidis's *Peace, Love, Light YOUMEONE*. Look at TV guides or Netflix show descriptions for ideas on how to pique interest in a snappy sound bite.

- **Add running times** (e.g., "1 hour, 48 minutes with intermission"). Although almost every program may be near the same length, newcomers don't know that, and it makes it hard for them to make their post-performance plans or know what to anticipate. Even for an exhibit, you can explain how long it takes the average person to complete the audio tour.
- **Swap the images.** Instead of artist photos, headshots, and images of the artwork only, trade some of that real estate for photos of the customer. People bursting into applause, riveted by the play, or stunned by the work of art hanging before them.* When trying to convert a new buyer, it's about them, not us.

The research shows that, ultimately, embracing a newcomer focus with your online experience is not the same as dumbing it down. "Audiences have lower levels of context and knowledge now," said arts management consultant Alan Brown while summarizing his research in a 2010 presentation—six years before my user experience findings began coming to the same conclusion.[15] Making the online experience approachable and consumable can go a long way toward closing that knowledge gap—and opening more minds to attending.

---

* Check to see if consent to be photographed is in the fine print on your website or ticket stock.

2. Be Newcomer Friendly in the Venue

It's on us to welcome our attendees with open, judgment-free arms; they're guests in our homes. And these new guests have almost no idea what to wear, where to find the best place to park, when to applaud, the difference between tempera or acrylic, and how to preorder drinks or reserve a table at the café (#priorities). But why *should* they know these things if they've never attended before? I admit that at first, I wanted to laugh off the question of what to wear—especially here in California where, like, everything's cool, man—but then participants *kept talking about* their anxiety around this topic. They didn't want to dress down, we discovered; they wanted to fit in. Guests were reporting stress and concern around the experience before it even began.

Arts organizations have multiple opportunities to solve these challenges and create a more inviting environment:

- **Set expectations in advance and repeat them often**. If the opera has arias,* applause is not only allowed, it's expected, and the orchestra will usually stop to wait for it . . . yet at the symphony, the applause is often held. At a jazz show, by contrast, you clap after the solo while the band never stops playing; and at the theater, reactions of all kinds (applause, laughter, cheering) occur in the moment and can vary from night to night depending on the crowd—no wonder this stuff can be confusing. So if you don't mind applause between each of three parts in a dance work, tell them that. Same thing across questions of what to wear, where to park, and yes, how to preorder that drink or snag that table. We already have many ways to answer these questions: placing them alongside the event details or in a First Timer's Guide online, sending customer service emails before the event, printing them in the program book itself, and conveying them in pre-performance remarks. A lot of organizations do one or two of these, but you can uplevel for newcomers by sharing the message consistently across *all* these channels.

---

* To practice what I preach for the non-opera folks, an aria is a solo song sung by one artist.

- **Print running times**. Hands down, this was the smallest, easiest change we made that received the most positive feedback. Newcomers don't know, say, the standard length of the first act, or that the concerto typically lasts around twenty-four minutes, or that the story ballet is going to run differently than the Alvin Ailey showcase. First-timers deeply want to be informed and educated attendees, and making this small addition—for instance, on the specific page in the program book or posted where people enter an exhibit—will set their expectations. Moreover, they will feel more comfortable. Guests in our homes, right?

- **Have more and better signage**. So boring, I know. But it makes a big difference when someone needs to find their seats, or the bathroom, or bar, or gift shop, or next part of the museum. For those of us who have been to our venues countless times, this is one of the hardest issues to address because we know these locations like the back of our hand. Bring in some newcomers, have them tell you what's confusing, and then make signage to address it.

- **Tell stories with the program notes and artwork labels**. "They sound like a wine description," said someone in that very first focus group. Everyone nodded in agreement, until one person said, "But wait, Rachmaninoff's Second Symphony should have never happened—"

  "That's right!" interjected someone else, "his first symphony was a disaster, and he waited twenty years before writing his second!"

  "Yeah, that took a lot of gumption," another added, "but boy was it marvelous!"

  "Whoever wrote those program notes should have written them all," someone concluded.

  "The same person *did* write all the program notes . . . ," I said, perplexed, but then found that the other pieces on the program were written in a much more technical way (*listen to the melody as it passes from the flute to the violins*), while the notes on Rachmaninoff's Second Symphony contained a story about his life. The story was so impactful, this group remembered it and repeated it back to me in the discussion group two weeks later.

Other discussion groups I've seen throughout my work played out the same way. How many people really want to know about Shakespeare's comic vision? Not that many. But they were very interested to know that Shakespeare was an investor in the Globe Theatre. And that biographer and historian Clive James claimed that George Balanchine ruled his ballet company like a fiefdom. "He'd be cancelled today," one person observed, leaning in, not judging so much as processing. Another loved that Claude Monet ran a tight household when he wasn't painting water lilies; being late for dinner was unheard of.

This is a neurological fact: humans' brains evolved to respond to, be motivated by, and remember stories. Stories are how our prefrontal cortex processes information; they cause our brains to produce the feel-good chemicals dopamine and oxytocin.[16]

If feelings of stress and concern about the in-person experience are what we don't want, nature's love hormones are what we definitely do. Whether through story, signage, running times, or other information, the way we design the experience in our venues directly affects if newcomers want to come back.

APPLICATION BOX

Concept: Newcomer friendly in the venue

Organization: Ballet Austin

"If we can get them to come three times in eighteen months, we essentially have them for life," Ballet Austin executive director Cookie Ruiz told me about their newcomers. "We work to make them two-timers, then three-timers. At three times, they become donor prospects."

Their process starts when you enter the building. The Ballet Austin team knows all the friction and frustration an attendee experiences before the curtain goes up; if they can convince patrons to arrive early, however, they can mitigate a lot of those pain points. Ruiz explained, "We tell them to come an hour early. They're dealing with traffic, the garage is challenging, they have to pick up their tickets . . . there's lots of stuff before you get a glass a wine in their hand. If we can get them there an hour early, it's our best chance of them saying they had a good experience."

When I arrived, they had a Welcome Center within three steps of the front door. They had bars set up inside and outside on their terrace overlooking the downtown skyline, with piped-in orchestral covers of pop songs: ABBA's "Dancing Queen," Lady Gaga's "Poker Face," and Katy Perry's "Firework" to name a few I heard (and may have been humming along to). It was a whole vibe—a carefully planned one. The volume levels never dipped, there was no dead air between tracks, and the ushers and staff were intentionally helpful—they have a team meeting, less than five minutes long, before the doors open where they debrief on any issues from the previous night's performance and course-correct for the performance ahead. *No maps at the west door*? Let's restock that now. *The elevator got backed up at nine o'clock*? Keep an eye on the traffic flow there tonight and redirect patrons to other options.

To fill that hour between arrival and showtime, in addition to the bars and multiple social media stations (*Yes, please take your photos and tell everyone you know you're here*, they telegraph), patrons were also invited to attend "Ballet-o-mania," a free, self-guided tour in a lobby that is more like a mini-museum, with photos from the production, plot points to know before seeing the ballet, and costumes from upcoming shows. Even though it's free, they scan tickets to see the exhibit because Ballet Austin is tracking the data; they now know that people who do the lobby tour buy future tickets sooner.

And, speaking of selling future tickets, before the performance began, trailer videos ran on an onstage screen—one previewing the remaining ballets in the season and one for their dance academy. During intermission, the screen came back down and ran ads for those of us who stayed in our seats (I overheard the woman next to me saying she wanted to take their adult dance and fitness class). Drinks were allowed back in the theater, where, by the way, the seats of major donors had a fabric sign embroidered with "principal partner" draped over them to identify their support. The signs signaled to them that they're special and Ballet Austin knows who they are, and signaled to the rest of us that supporters help make all this happen.

At the end of the night, I was on cloud nine. I don't know a lot about dance, but they adequately prepared me for what I witnessed onstage, which happened to be a ballet only produced twice before, meaning it was new to me in every way and pretty new to everyone else, too. And, as Ballet Austin's final grande jeté of being newcomer friendly, they turned the music overhead back on as patrons were leaving. Instead of patrons exiting in hushed chatter, coming *down* off the artistic high, their energy remained elevated. It was particularly noticeable because although I felt it, I realized something so seemingly simple as this doesn't often occur in our venues.

The onsite experience was thoughtfully planned from beginning to end, and newbies can't wait to go back—Ballet Austin consistently makes their sales goals. And by goals, I mean they often sell out. "Everyone has a job front of house," Ruiz shared. "Every single person is curating the experience." An experience on pointe.

3. Create Newcomer-Facing Marketing

Before someone visits the website or the venue, chances are they first see an ad. Newcomer-*facing* marketing is the third and final F of the new customer experience. After all, for decades, the prevailing marketing approach was outbound, where brands send their message outward to consumers. Think *Mad Men*: media buys, print advertising, radio ads, cold calling, brochures, billboards, and bus campaigns. In recent years, though, the marketing landscape—in response to consumer behavior—has shifted toward an inbound approach, where customers find you when they need you. Think opt-in emails, internet searches, and online content. Today, most cultural organizations have figured out some form of email strategy. Some also have a handle on paid search placements. Online content—also known as content marketing—is where a massive opportunity lies.

Content marketing has three components:

1. it involves the creation and sharing of digital material (such as blogs, videos, infographics, photos, GIFs, etc.);
2. it does not explicitly promote a brand;
3. instead, it is intended to stimulate interest in the brand's products or services via *information*—not sales.

Earlier I mentioned that people want to learn, not feel sold to. Well, content marketing answers that call with interesting, informative material; offers more opportunity to share stories; and helps to close that knowledge gap between what a newcomer knows versus someone more versed in our art forms.

In one experiment, consumers were divided into two groups: the test group, which was given an educational article, such as "How to Make Almond Milk" or "Backpacking 101," produced by a mock brand; and a control group, which did not receive this material (in both cases, the made-up brand was used so the participants would not have any predisposed opinions). The two groups were surveyed about the fictional brands immediately after reading (or not reading) the content. The people who read the educational articles were more than twice as likely to want to buy from that brand compared to those who did not read the articles.[17]

Additionally, the same study found that this feeling of brand affinity lasts. When surveyed again a week later, participants were even *more* likely to buy from the brand they learned from—and rated the brand as even more trustworthy than when they had first read the content.[18] Plus, another thing people do when they have great trust in and affinity for an organization is donate. In other words, content marketing is not a marketing-only play despite the name; it's a fundraiser's game, too.

The pandemic made our field collectively more competent at the first part of content marketing (creating and sharing digital material). But the second part (not explicitly promoting the brand) is where many institutions can benefit from shifting gears. Ways to do that include the following:

- **Stop cheesy copywriting**. *Fun for all ages! Don't forget to get tickets for this weekend!* No one forgot to get tickets, and "one size fits all" language does not convert buyers. Instead, lead with a story sound bite (*Sergei Rachmaninoff's first symphony was a failure*).

- **Lay off salesy lines**. *Last chance to make your gift!* I don't know about you, but in my book, it's never too late for someone to make a donation. Organizations will always take the money. Deliver interesting information or offer social proof (*128 new donors have joined the matching campaign*), not explicit marketing messages.

- **Drop exclamation points**. *New video out now! So excited to announce this! Follow us on Instagram!* Exclamation points are fine for people, but from a brand they convey forced enthusiasm. Take a look at billboards around you or ads in your feed; probably not a lot of exclamation points there. Calm and clever makes for stronger advertising.

- **Reduce overt calls to action**. *CLICK HERE, BUY NOW, DONATE TODAY.* Those directives are no longer as effective. People scrolling through their feeds know where to click or tap. Trust me. Trust them. Trust the twenty-first century.

So what are organizations to do instead? Follow the final part of the content marketing definition: make sure content is designed *to stimulate interest in the brand's products or services.* When one client asked their very well-known and scholarly program annotator if he could focus on the stories behind the music going forward, he glimmered, "Of course! There are so many salacious stories to tell!" Publish those same stories in a blog post, pull the juiciest bits and post them on social media, and—connecting with the first F of designing newcomer-friendly websites—distill them to bullet points for the program's landing page.

All of this can be applied to our traditional outbound marketing, too. Be more informative, less on-the-nose salesy. We're using our content to invite our newcomer audiences on a learning journey, which makes them not just more likely to buy, but also to return.

REMEMBER: THE ART IS NOT THE PROBLEM

Despite my team and I taking many verbal bruisings from user-experience research participants over the years, one piece of glowing feedback has consistently emerged.

Whenever the discussion gets to the art itself, the emotion expressed by virtually everyone in the room is awe.

> *"The artists were GREAT."*
> *"I liked the splendor of how it all comes together."*
> *"Seeing it live was so different than TikTok."*
> *"It was weirdly cool to not have to focus on other things."*
> *"It was nice to see the passion of the artists and how much they were into what they were doing."*
> *"[The artist] thought of all of this in their head so many years ago . . . that's amazing that we are hearing this now, today."*
> *"Complete awe." [Nodding heads everywhere.]*

Ultimately, the problem isn't the product; it's the packaging. The art is what we do best. If we want to grow our audiences, the customer experience surrounding the art is where we stand to improve the most.

ABOVE ALL ELSE, MAKE IT EASY

Everything in this chapter is about helping our patrons have an easier time at our institutions. Research from Yale, Google, and others says the top predictor of customer purchase behavior is *not* the quality of the product, the price, or even customer desire. It's how easy it is to do what we want them to do.[19] When we fix the experience to make it easier for people to want to come back, we will start to see changes in our sales and our audience.

If cultural institutions boldly embraced prioritizing the customer experience, we'd have an easy, slick online ordering flow on desktop and mobile as beautifully designed as the art it's selling. We'd have rapturous applause bursting out of the audience because it's so good, they can't keep the response bottled up (and they'll know it's okay for them to applaud). We'd have drinks in the galleries and at our seats; friendly and welcoming docents, ushers, and front-of-house (FOH) staff;*

---

* "Front of house" refers to all the public spaces, like the lobbies, restrooms, and concession stands or cafés.

approachable museum object labels and program notes that divulge the most interesting stories about the work on the wall and the stage; patrons posting photos and videos for everyone in their network because they want to document, remember, and share their experience with others; and a collective feeling of complete and utter awe among a growing community. I'm here for it.

"But what will happen to the 'core audience' if we make all these changes?" I'm asked all the time. "Won't they leave?" To be frank, no. They won't. You might have the odd one out, like the patron who approached me in the lobby one day, wagging his finger, saying, "If you tell the audience to have fun and clap when they like what they hear one more time, I'm out of here." But such threats are isolated events: whereas up to 90 percent of new attendees don't come back, up to 90 percent of longtime attendees *do*, barring global pandemics. And as for the subscribers and members that have returned since the shutdown, they're *really* not going anywhere now. They've proven a worldwide contagious disease won't keep them away.

After making changes (and around when I met the finger-wagger), the California Symphony audience nearly doubled over the next four years. Through some of these same efforts to attract and retain first-timers, LA Opera has generated an extra twenty grand a season—all by enticing new patrons to come back again.[20] And changes at Australia's Castlemaine State Festival, a multidisciplinary series of events spanning performance, literature, visual arts, and film, helped new-subscriber renewal rates soar and donor contributions increase 25 percent year over year, defying the trends.[21]

One disgruntled subscriber in exchange for doubling the patronage—I'll take that deal any day of the week.

Prioritizing the customer experience is a big step toward keeping new audiences coming back. But how do we then help them develop a patronage habit? How do we reach that extreme loyalty of longtime subscribers or members? For that, we turn to the world of the binge watch.

2.

If It Works for Netflix

Recurring Revenue and the Subscription Economy

My dog, Molly, loves food so much, it's almost unbelievable. She's a basset hound: long ears, sad eyes—basically a lovable, dense-as-hell, sixty-pound sandbag on stumpy legs—and a breed known for being "food motivated." Off the streets of San Francisco alone, she's gobbled up everything from days-old pizza, bird-ravaged bagels, a decaying chicken bone (that one definitely came back up later), and even a joint (honestly, I think that's happened more than once). She always acts like she's starving (she's not; maybe it's the marijuana). And I spend way too much on the bougie, human-grade dog food that comes to my doorstep every month. I don't cancel it despite the fact that I clearly could be feeding her something of far lesser quality at a much lower price. Yet Molly's food just shows up; it's super easy, the packaging is compostable, and on and on go the reasons to keep subscribing.

It turns out, I'm not the only one spoiling their dog. The Farmer's Dog posted 500 percent year-over-year growth by their fourth year in business.[1] In 2019, they secured the largest second funding round for a pet startup ever at $39 million, and in 2020 they secured over $100 million more in a third investment round. Joining subscription darlings like Spotify, Stitch Fix, Dollar Shave Club, HelloFresh, and

Strava, The Farmer's Dog is one of tens of thousands of subscription-based businesses now in existence. The subscription economy is so huge, so prolific, it captures nearly 20 percent of the $41 trillion in global credit card transactions each year.[2] That's right; almost one-fifth of all our credit card charges go to our monthly pet food supply, replacement toothbrush heads, grocery delivery, daily news consumption, fitness routines, clothing rental—all this automatically recurring as we wait for our new delivery with its two-day transport while eating the twenty-five-minute dinner-in-a-bag we whipped up and bingeing true crime documentaries.

So why, then, if the subscription economy is more prominent today than ever, are memberships and subscriptions at arts organizations on the decline? How come revenue from single-ticket buyers—people who only purchase a few tickets a year—now comprises a greater share of total income than money from season ticket holders?[3]

These trends are a big deal because they indicate attendees are becoming less loyal overall, even when we improve the experience as described in chapter one. But it doesn't have to be that way. This chapter unpacks three reasons why the subscription economy dominates elsewhere but isn't working in the arts, then tackles why we do it the current way (to be fair, there are some good reasons, and these are our barriers to change). Last, we'll conclude with an updated model that addresses these issues in order to build the patron loyalty we need.

REASON ONE SUBSCRIPTIONS ARE WORKING ELSEWHERE BUT NOT IN THE ARTS: THE FIRST-YEAR CLIFF

In chapter one, we looked at the iceberg predicament—how the lack of newcomer retention is choking up our patron growth pipeline. But cultural institutions face another alarming drop-off point: only about half of first-year season-ticket holders renew their subscription or membership.[4] Across the board nationwide, new-donor retention is at an all-time low of 19 percent according to AFP, the Association for Fundraising Professionals.[5]

I call this the First-Year Cliff. We succeed at engaging patrons for a season, and then dramatically lose them. With data showing that only a slight improvement in retention would result in a considerable uptick on our bottom line, reversing the massive drop-off even a little would be huge. How do we know this? NICE Satmetrix is a leading vendor for customer experience management software. They make programs that measure customer engagement, experience, and happiness. If you've ever heard of the Net Promoter Score (those little mini-surveys you get from businesses: *On a scale of 0 to 10, how likely are you to recommend us to a friend?*), NICE Satmetrix does a lot of benchmarking for that. And what they found across all the industries they track (and they track a lot), is that a 2 percent increase in customer retention has the same effect as decreasing costs 10 percent.[6] So what can organizations do specifically to see those impacts—to increase retention and conquer the First-Year Cliff?

I took this question to Robbie Kellman Baxter, the mastermind of subscriptions. She coined the term "membership economy," wrote two books on the subject, and has worked with just about every leading subscription brand you can think of across more than twenty different industries. Here's what she had to say about reversing the First-Year Cliff.

Invest in Onboarding

The biggest drop-off is always after the first period, whether that's a monthly billing cycle, two-week free trial, or yearlong membership. Therefore, Baxter is adamant that most organizations must better invest in onboarding, the time between the sale and when the new customer begins interacting or engaging with the product or service.

A lot of organizations send a welcome letter with the ticket mailing or membership card, maybe a customer service email or two, and then that's about it until we start upselling the patron to the next thing (*make a donation, come to the gala, renew the subscription*). Instead, we need to take a beat to roll out the welcome wagon, which parlays into the second step.

Reinforce the Wisdom of Their Decision

The best thing we can do is remind the patron how smart they are. They did a good thing by purchasing a membership. Tell them that. All those selling points we used to convert them in the first place? Remind them. They saved a lot of money by doing this. We're so glad to offer them first dibs to keep their same seats next year or be first in line to make a change request for different seats next year. They definitely get members-only days because they are so important. Make them feel loved and brilliant. Whatever benefits you offer, double down on highlighting that those exist as a way to reinforce the decision so they feel great about it.

Make Sure They Get as Much of the Value They Are Entitled to as Possible

"You are really choreographing that new subscriber experience," Baxter says. "If somebody misses a performance, follow up. Remind them they get free exchanges—and go ahead and let them exchange into something else so they get the value they are entitled to. That kind of thing in the first month or two can really deepen the relationship."

That means we have to be proactive. After every performance, especially early in the season when most subscriptions tend to start or after that first big exhibit in the fall, run the report of first-year subscriber tickets that weren't scanned. Reach out, tell them the records show we might have missed them, and that we want them to take advantage of all the benefits their subscription offers, so we are going to move them into the next performance of their choice with our compliments. There are probably only a few accounts each week that miss a show, but helping a few accounts maximize their subscription benefits every so often over the course of the season might just make that 2 percent retention increase attainable.

Get Them to a Second Type of Content

"If I sign up for Netflix because I want to watch a rom-com, I might stay for a while," Baxter offers. "I might even watch other rom-coms. But if Netflix can get me to enjoy a documentary, a drama, or crime series, I'm much more likely to stay."

When I worked with a large public media company, we interrogated this idea. A big question was what matters more: if someone goes deep into one product (*I can watch their YouTube videos all day long!* Or, *I never miss the morning broadcast during my commute!*), or if someone consumes multiple products (*I read articles online when I see them in my feed and sometimes listen to the podcast as well).* The debate was hot.

"The YouTube people will binge hours and hours of past content; how is that not a mark of loyalty?!" someone asked.

"But the total time consumed might be the same—or at least close—when someone is engaging in multiple touchpoints over the course of the same week. And they clearly know more about the breadth of our offerings!" said another.

"All right," I chimed in, "let's settle this." I wanted an indicator of extreme devotion. "Can someone here run a report that shows all of your donors last year who engaged across multiple platforms?" Clickety-click-clack went someone's keyboard.

"Got it," their in-house data wizard said. "It's almost everyone." Turns out, around 75 percent of their donors were consuming multiple content types, regardless of if they were a one-time giver, monthly supporter, or major donor. Only a quarter or less were engaging with only a single content type. In other words, consuming a second content type was the bigger indicator of donor behavior, no matter how deep someone went on a single product.

Arts organizations need to get those subscribers to a second type of content, like a pre-show talk, director's talkback session, or artist meet-and-greet. Invite them to a special exhibit opening. Give them killer online content. Help them download the podcast. Make sure they eat at the café or preorder an intermission drink (yes, I know food and beverage sales don't usually go back to the organization; we're after a bigger prize here). Think of anything else you offer, point the way to that content, and make it as easy as possible to consume.

APPLICATION BOX

Concept: Investing in Onboarding

Organization: Ontario Health and Human Services Association

This Canada-based healthcare advocacy group supports organizations that provide programs and clinical services to special-needs youth and families. Carefully stewarding new members over their first year via onboarding has become a significant area of focus for them.

Jonathan Bennett assisted with the creation of this onboarding program for new members as then-CEO of the management consulting and training firm that partnered on the project. He paired the CEO or executive director of each of the association's new member organizations with an existing member for informal networking as needed, plus scheduled quarterly check-ins, with the goal of ensuring the new organization was fully taking advantage of their member benefits. Additionally, the association invited each new member to present at the annual conference on a topic or innovation they wanted to share, spread, or scale. The idea was to further integrate each new organization into the membership as soon as possible, deepen those connections, and reinforce the wisdom of their decision to join via the added exposure and access.

The onboarding concluded with year-end interviews with each new member organization as they approached renewal time. The findings from those meetings were shared with the association's board.

Bennett likens the onboarding strategy to the psychological framework of attachment theory—that humans need to develop relationships with a primary caregiver in order to properly develop. He explained to me that the association is the primary caregiver to their members and helps new members become safe in this new environment, all in service to retention efforts. Having first created connectedness and safety through onboarding, loyalty followed.

REASON TWO SUBSCRIPTIONS ARE WORKING ELSEWHERE BUT NOT IN THE ARTS: BACKWARDS RENEWALS

Of the three ways arts organizations handle subscriptions and memberships differently from other sectors, this one is, to me, the most divergent from standard practice everywhere else. Instead of making customers opt *out* before their next billing cycle à la Hulu or HBO, we wipe the slate clean each season and ask everyone to opt back *in* with an annual renewal. We essentially cancel for them, then have to build our base from scratch every year.

The modern subscription economy is all about *recurring* revenue. So when we don't automatically renew subscriptions and memberships, well, it's not exactly recurring. You could even argue that arts organizations don't really offer subscriptions at all any more by today's definition—they're more of a package deal or bulk discount.

Businesses, including cultural entities, like subscriptions because they help us project income. Whether we charge monthly or yearly (yes, it's fine to continue charging annually, although on the fundraising side, there is mounting evidence that monthly donations can produce more lucrative, enduring results—more on that later in the chapter), auto-renewal is the key to income prediction. "Opt-out is the standard across industries," says Robbie Kellman Baxter. So how do we move toward this model?

Give Customers a Choice When You Move to Opt-Out

When I asked Baxter if there is normally a subscriber drop-off when organizations first switch to an opt-out model, she told me, "If people know that it's happening and why it's happening, they are more likely to stay." And you can message the shift in a way that you yourself would like to be communicated with as a patron of other brands and subscriptions. Send a message with the season brochure mailing saying you are moving to an opt-out system. It's fine to include, "We'll always remind you before we charge your card on file. If you'd prefer us to ask each year, let us know."

Reinforce the message in your email communications as well. Some customers will migrate to the new system, making your renewal period a lot easier going forward. Some may wish to continue receiving the renewal invoice instead. That's fine; you can legacy them in. As for new subscribers? Definitely offer them opt-out only. After all, it's standard.

Incentivize the Desired Behavior

We are going to spend a lot more time on incentivizing desired behavior in the rest of this chapter. For now, though, consider offering a lower price to anyone who chooses the opt-out option as you migrate them. Brands do this all the time. And for everyone, whether a new subscriber or long-timer, if you do offer a mon versus a yearly option, remember to make the annual fee cheaper. Give people a reason this benefits them, not just the organization.

When People Want to Leave, Let Them

If someone wants out after the first period (whether that's a month, year, or some other billing cycle), don't fight it; let them go. Baxter is unwavering about this. "By the time someone's telling you they want to leave, they've already decided," she says. To mitigate this, invest more in the onboarding experience, going right back to point number one about reducing the First-Year Cliff. And keep the good times rollin', which brings us to the last point.

Start on Renewals Earlier

Historically, the data show most institutions don't start working on retention until thirty to sixty days before renewal, and by then it's usually too late to keep anyone who has decided to go. Stop investing so much into repeat renewal solicitations. (How many orgs do a second or sometimes even a third renewal mailing, and then keep the unrenewed accounts on every new subscription offer that goes out for the rest of the season?) Instead, spend that money earlier, on onboarding. Once more: A strong onboarding experience is the first step to a strong renewal rate.

Consultancy Oliver Wyman offered similar recurring revenue advice to arts organizations in their report, *Reimagining the Subscription Model*, where they recommended we allow "subscribers to pay in monthly installments, perhaps through an auto-renewal system. This is how many modern subscriptions models like Amazon Prime, Netflix, and the new Apple Music service work."[7] That was back in 2015. They were onto something.

REASON THREE SUBSCRIPTIONS ARE WORKING ELSEWHERE BUT NOT IN THE ARTS: WE'RE BAD AT BEHAVIORAL REPETITION

Back in 2008, Starbucks used to give morning coffee drinkers a special receipt with language offering a discount on any purchases later that same day after 2

PM. The "treat receipt" program amassed thousands of repeat customers every day for the coffee behemoth while increasing average daily customer spend. Originally designed in response to the financial crisis that began a few months prior, the program was so successful, Starbucks brought it back annually for the next eight years.

What Starbucks did not do was say, "You tried a latte, so here's a discount to prepay for ten more when you buy a coffee membership." Instead, the strategy was successful because they asked patrons to do one simple thing: repeat their previous behavior (walk into the store and buy any drink). In the arts, we are asking patrons too soon to advance-purchase every type of macchiato we offer when they've only just committed to standard drip. *Dear new subscriber, would you like to make a donation? How about a gala table?* Sometimes the upsell comes before the first event in their membership or subscription ever occurs. It's one thing to ask a longtime subscriber for these next steps—they've already demonstrated their loyalty. It's another to call someone for a donation when they've barely left the theater.

Maybe you're wondering how this is different from Netflix asking documentary people to also watch a drama. The former is about upselling too much, too soon, and the latter is about maximizing the value of the existing benefits available. It doesn't cost more to watch *Tiger King* followed by *Squid Game*. In fact, accessing both just adds more bang for every subscription buck.

Back to behavioral repetition: the way for institutions to get patrons to repeat the behaviors we want is through what's called behavioral segmentation.

Generally, cultural organizations lean toward either *psychographic* segmentation ("You liked this so you might like that," but we don't really know our patrons' interests so we tend to put them on every mailing list), or *demographic* segmentation (come to *Harry Potter* in concert if you're a millennial, *Porgy and Bess* if you're Black, and the Frida Kahlo exhibit if you're Latinx* or female). Not that this is unilaterally bad per se—these offerings are popular and box office data show they

---

* Labels for racial and ethnic groups are imperfect and ever changing. Some people who trace their roots to Latin America and Spain prefer "Hispanic" or "Latino/Latina," while some prefer "Latinx" as a more gender-neutral term. And some prefer "Latine" or "Latin@." So, I use various terms throughout the book.

usually do attract their intended demographic—but they're not the most effective ways to retain people.

Research shows the most effective way to segment our customers if we want better results is *behavioral*. Ask patrons to repeat the same behavior until a habit is formed, *before* introducing anything new. Come back and buy another coffee, and we'll make it a good deal for you.

One day I received a call from the British Museum in London asking about behavioral segmentation. They had heard I'd had success with it and they were researching the various ways cultural organizations in the UK and the US segmented their patrons and trying to uncover which type of segmentation might produce the highest returns for them. What they had found from everyone they called was that most organizations were using psychographic and some demographic segmentation. However, when they drilled down, they found that every single organization that was seeing *any kind of growth* in their audience had incorporated some sort of behavioral segmentation into their strategy.

APPLICATION BOX

Concept: Behavioral Segmentation

Organization: Mongoose Education Software

Mongoose works with colleges and universities to better communicate with all the constituents in the admissions pipeline. A particular challenge in higher ed is that "all the constituents" is a lot of different people, including prospective students, their parents, rising seniors applying to college, the admissions office, financial aid staff, current students, alumni, the advancement office, and on and on. Mongoose's most popular product is a texting and chat platform that allows for conversations among all these groups, not just one-way messages like traditional email blasts, or blanket, one-size messages like social media pushes.

Behind the product development, Mongoose is always looking at behavioral segmentation—at what's the next step for each constituent group, says client success partner Mike Kochczynski. For example, "How do we make a pre-college path?" The parent gets a text offering tickets to a basketball game or science day at the school. "We want it to become second nature to come to that campus," Kochczynski explained. "Then it's, 'How do I get you on campus for a tour?' Then, 'How do I get you to start an application?' Then, 'How do we give a great student experience?' Then, 'How do we stay in contact after graduation?'

"But who owns all those communications? Whose job is that to manage that entire journey?" Kochczynski continued. While some higher ed institutions have a "constituent relations" role to address the student or alumni journey, usually it's unclear who owns those communications—it's often multiple people within multiple departments (spoiler: partly because of the trouble this causes, I make the case later in this book for one position overseeing patron loyalty). Mongoose wants their software to be the connector—the driver of the communications that invite the right next behavioral step among each of the different constituent segments.

No matter the person or product guiding this work, using behavioral segmentation to inform the journey is the recipe for success. Within a year of adopting Mongoose's product, their partner schools report increased applications, higher enrollment, higher event attendance rates, reduced "summer melt" (i.e., fewer admitted students dropping out before their freshman year begins), an astounding 98 percent retention rate for students who use the product, and increased fundraising dollars. Mongoose's diligent approach to moving people one behavior at a time is working every step of the way. No matter your corner of culture, whether a school or an arts organization or a vendor or anywhere else, overseeing the customer journey one behavioral step at a time—and allowing the customer to take a *single* step at a time—is key to the journey lasting at all.

A NEWER, BETTER WAY: BUILDING
BEHAVIOR OVER THE LONG HAUL

Our budget and organizational structures incentivize the old methods of unfocused communications and upselling too much, too soon. Marketing and development teams are almost always separate departments with separate goals. Any gaps in the earned-revenue line that remain after the subscription campaign concludes must be plugged by single-ticket sales, and whatever budget hole *those* sales don't make up has to be filled with donations. This budget cocktail means we end up putting almost every patron account on every communication, resulting in a bombardment of messages. I call it the Free for All Model.

In 2014, I sketched out a new approach to audience development. I knew the stats: 90 percent of new attendees weren't ever coming back, 50 percent of first-time subscribers weren't renewing their season tickets, and the new-donor renewal rate was about that bad, too. And all of those national stats largely held true for the orchestra I was running. I also knew that for any artistic discipline, just getting a new patron to come back for a second visit within twelve months of their first made them much more loyal to the organization—and thus, more helpful for our budgets.[8]

I further knew that human behavior could be changed with the right motivation. And last, I knew from my experience leading marketing and fundraising teams that patron segmentation was key, meaning targeted communications produce better results (aka more sales and donations) than one-size-fits-all type messages.

So, I put pen to paper (er, type to screen) on what I wanted to do for each segment of the audience to move them toward ever-increasing engagement with and loyalty to the organization. Instead of a free-for-all, we reconstructed the patron journey so that no matter where the patron was in their relationship with us, there was one—and only one—next step. I call it the Long Haul Model.

Group 1: First-Time Attendee

These are mostly patrons truly new to our files, though this group also included folks who hadn't attended in four years or more. (The thought was that if someone hadn't visited in four years, they definitely weren't a loyal patron, and a lot had changed with the organization in that time. And given how much *anything* changes in four years these days, that statement probably holds true for every organization on the planet.)

AUDIENCE JOURNEY
The Long Haul Model

Major
Donor

Renewing
Donor

New Donor

Renewing Subscriber

Season Ticket Holder

Multi-/Repeat Buyer

First-Time Attendee

The only message this segment received was an invitation to come back again. This came in the form of a welcome letter on their seat saying we noticed this might be their first time, or first time in a while, with a $20 voucher (as an aside, cash vouchers are often more effective than discounts—think Nordstrom Notes over Priceline deals) toward any concert remaining in the season. They got that same message in a follow-up email after the concert. Then again as a postcard in their mailbox a few days later. (Another side note: the image on the email and postcard was the same marketing image from the performance they attended, not an image to promote an upcoming event. The idea was to help foster memory recall, especially given all the work from the last chapter to improve the customer experience.) Last, a second email was sent a few weeks later—before the deadline to use the voucher (deadlines create a sense of urgency).

If you think this is a lot of communications, you're not wrong. But those newcomers were definitely receiving four (or more) messages in the Free for All Model; it's just that now, the message was targeted and consistent. It invited them to do the one behavior we really wanted: come back again. Within the first season of implementing this, we saw a 14 percent uptick in newcomer retention. By year three, the first-timer retention was reliably around 30 percent for any given concert in the season—three times the industry average.

Note for visitor-based institutions like museums and gardens and zoos (oh my!): a lot of times, we're not capturing patron information, so we're missing the critical opportunity to invite them to return. Try selling tickets in advance online so you get names and addresses, or at least names and emails. Give people a reason to buy online, even if they're buying the same day they're coming, by letting them skip the entry line, waiving the order fee, or preselling parking. Whatever it is, do something to incentivize the behavior you want—in this case, giving you their contact info. Even if your admission is free, find a way to at least capture an email, so you can invite them back later. Offer timed admission (I'm seeing more and more visitor-based institutions do this) or a discount at the gift shop. Or move to mobile ticketing so the email becomes necessary.

This extra effort is so important because for every exhibit-based patron that doesn't come back, only .94 people are replacing them.[9] This means more people are exiting and never returning than coming in and staying. Every cultural organization needs first-timer retention.

Group 2: Multi-/Repeat Buyer

Anyone who attends twice in a twelve-month period is a multi-buyer. In our outreach, this group received a card in the mail after their second attendance, but this mailing was different from the newcomer postcard in a few ways. First, it was in an envelope (subtly suggesting we spent a little more money on this nicer communication; the relationship is getting serious now). Second, the photo on the front was now the music director and the orchestra. We used to plaster that type of conductor photo on all kinds of marketing materials, but we had intentionally gotten away from that (see the last chapter about using customer-centric photos in materials). But now these patrons were more likely to recognize that person on the podium, and hopefully the artists in front of the baton, too. Third, we didn't offer a discount with the multi-buyer communications because there are only three occasions I believe in discounting: (1) when someone is new so we can get them to come back again; (2) when someone subscribes, as I noted earlier in this chapter; and (3) when someone has gone dead-in-the-water iceberg cold and it's time to pull out all the stops to reactivate them (more on that one later).

Instead of *money-off*, the strategy for multi-buyers was to move to *value-add*. The back of the card featured a voucher for a free glass of wine at their next performance. While that wine could be sipped whenever they came back next (we usually made it valid for a year), ideally that next visit would be the first performance in their new season ticket package—because these multi-buyers were then our top prospects to offer a subscription when we announced the new season. Everything in Groups 1 and 2 is in service to feeding the subscription pipeline.

Group 3: Season Ticket Holder

Hurrah, this group took the plunge and bought a subscription! We decided to roll out the welcome wagon as best we knew how at the time in order to have a super onboarding experience. For the first performance in members of this group's package, we had a welcome gift on their seats: a CD recording of the orchestra (later we moved to a card with a streaming link), a preprinted welcome note signed by the music director and me telling them we noticed the records say they are a new subscriber and we're excited to have them, plus a list of their subscriber benefits, reminding them of all the perks they get because they are in the cool kids' club now—reinforcing the wisdom of their decision. All of this was tied together, literally, with a bow.

Now, I know from Robbie Baxter's work that it's also important to make sure they take advantage of those benefits, so I'd suggest following up if they miss a performance to ensure they actually use the benefit of free exchanges. But, *for none of these groups so far did we ask for a donation.* The only thing we invited this group to do was renew their package. The renewal rate for these first-year subscribers went from hovering at that national average of under 50 percent to nearly 70 percent—a percentage that held even as the new-subscriber pool continued to grow each year.

Group 4: Renewing Subscriber

This is the crowd that's held their season ticket package for a second year or longer—the group where we really start cooking. And by "cooking" I mean "making money by growing that audience base." Industry-wide retention rates show that about 70 percent of second-year subscribers keep at it.[10] By the time someone has stuck with the organization for three years or longer, at every organization I've worked for, we've seen around 90 percent coming back.[11]

Recognizing that the loyalty payoff had begun with this group, we told these folks we loved them. A lot. It started with an over-the-top email confirming their renewal was received (one time, the email even said we were jumping up and down in the office). We followed it up with a special version of the cover letter sent with their season tickets, this version telling them we see their longtime patronage and are so grateful for it. Then (and a lot of organizations already do a version of this), about halfway through the season, we held subscriber appreciation days (the first-year subscribers were a part of this, too). In our case, every package holder found a card on their seat, signed by members of the orchestra, thanking them for their loyal attendance. As an aside: the number of subscribers who came up to me and other staff at performances to ask us to point out who in the orchestra had signed *their* card was, first, an indicator of how much they think our artists are total stars (about which they are correct), and second, the reason we eventually had to move to "name + instrument" when asking the musicians to sign.

On those appreciation days, we also dedicated a full-page "ad" in the program book saying "Subscribers Give Us a Reason to Play" and that we're so grateful for this growing base. I reiterated this message in my welcome remarks from the stage, and the music director acknowledged the subscribers from onstage as well. We were telegraphing, *You're loved*, and *you're special*, and *you're a part of something that more and more people want to be a part of*, again and again, and broadcasting it to everyone, including guests who weren't season ticket holders so they could join the bandwagon, too.

The timing of this lovefest was important. Subscriber appreciation days were intentionally scheduled for the concert that immediately preceded the renewal period, and we made sure the program was full of blockbuster repertoire. (We'll talk more about programming in chapter five, but for now, right before subscription renewals is not the most strategic time to program the experimental new music showcase.) First, have a programming home run; then, two days later, let that renewal packet hit their mailboxes. Today my advice also would be to make sure the renewal packet lets them know that their card on file is being processed (opt out, not opt in) and we can't wait to see them again soon. And, of course, these renewing subscribers are now (at long last) the top prospects for a first-time donation ask.

Group 5: New Donor

Sometimes new donors don't follow the exact progression laid out so far—but a lot of times they do. Meaning, by the time they become renewing subscribers, if they aren't yet donors, it's time to finally solicit the gift via whatever channels you typically use (mail, email, phone calls, website). This is pretty straightforward, but also, when I consider the journey to get to this point, I'm like, *OMG, this is incredible.* And as with the preceding segments, a great onboarding experience really matters here, too.

For many new donors, they've come all this way with us, leveled up in the best way while exhibiting the behavior we want . . . then after they get here, all we welcome them with is a mere tax receipt. (Cut to image of a balloon deflating.) By the time someone donates, we have done so many things right as an institution that there's a reason (or several) why that person decided to open their wallet. So, just as we do with the other groups, we tell these new donors we're grateful, celebrate them, reinforce the wisdom of their decision—and do this again and again. For the organizations I work with, that tax acknowledgment letter includes a line saying we noticed this is their first gift—*we see you*—and that we're so excited they decided to join the family. At one organization, this group also received a new-donor brochure with the acknowledgment: a pamphlet that included all the various programs their gift supported (performances onstage, musicians in the orchestra, living composers we commissioned, student education programs, etc.).

Today, I would do a few things slightly differently. First, the appeal itself would try to solicit a recurring gift. Getting low-level annual fund donors into a monthly cadence matches everything this chapter is about in terms of leveraging the membership economy for greater returns and greater loyalty, and an increasing amount of case studies across the nonprofit sector back this up (we'll hit a few at the end of the chapter).

Second, think about anything else possible to enhance the onboarding experience while also providing multiple thank-you touchpoints throughout the year. Engage in donor stewardship and plan events, donor newsletters, and receptions—but *also* help supporters take advantage of those donor benefits. After the first period (i.e., during the second credit card charge after the initial gift), maybe that looks like sending a thank-you note from an artist (preprinting these things is fine, by the way, as is a triggered email; I'm all for automation, and we have so many tools available now for sending customized messages and even prerecorded videos that are tailored to the donor). Or maybe if they skipped the wine reception, we write a note telling them we missed them and send a wine voucher for their next performance instead.

Third, shake up the acknowledgment letter (the tax receipt). You can start mailing thank-you cards instead of gift receipts like one organization that I worked with. Their idea was that receipts are for transactions; thank-you cards are for relationships (though, to be fair, the card had a basic receipt inserted to meet legal requirements). Try adding a donor-wide mailing in early January that includes a Happy New Year message along with providing each donor a courtesy summary of all gifts over the past year that they can use for their taxes. So many development staffers get calls in January or February from donors asking for their gift history for taxes anyway, so this mailing gives you a touchpoint while providing a service.

Last, in all this, there's one thing I wouldn't change: if that first gift was a thousand dollars or more, my staff knew to send it straight to my attention as chief executive, so I could get on the phone as soon as possible with that donor. No one gives away their last thousand dollars as a first gift; there's definitely more where that came from.

Group 6: Renewing Donor

The people in this level are not just valuable in terms of the monetary gift they've now opted to repeat at least once; they're also valuable potential advocates for the organization if we play our cards right. This is usually the point at which organizations are already generally more organized with behavioral segmentation and do many things well. For new and returning donors alike, we often have stewardship plans by giving level (the $250 donors get their name in the program book, the $2,500 donors get the meet-and-greet, etc.), and we naturally segment communications (making sure the $20 donors aren't getting the invitation to the dinner with the cast). Organizations also often use segmentation to personalize renewals (they merge fields to renew at the same amount as last time or increase the gift by 10 percent, for example).

Yet, donor renewal rates are frequently lower than we'd like. And the reason isn't because the renewal ask was wrong somehow, or the benefits weren't what they wanted, or the tax write-off wasn't big enough. By far, the top reason donors say they don't renew their gift is because they weren't sufficiently thanked.[12] That's why it's so important to say thank you early and often, at every step of the journey.

Methods for conveying your thanks to donors include the following:

- **Organizing lots of thank-you notes to donors from artists.** We give them a script, stationery, stamps, everything—yes, you can preprint these notes too for larger shops. And maybe at an exhibit-based organization, those notes are from curators or the animal caretakers or anyone else connected to the front lines.
- **Arranging lots of thank-you calls from board members.** They get a script, too, and assign these calls at an appropriate giving threshold for the size of your donor base; you'd be surprised how many board members loved connecting with $1,000-level donors they hadn't previously met.
- **And definitely sending lots of cute crayon thank-you notes from kids in the school programs.** Pick the best ones, color photocopy, and voilà.

Last, in addition to being thanked, donors also want to learn. In the next chapter, we'll talk more about how offering interesting and informative digital content isn't just for marketing teams anymore.

Group 7: Major Donor

We've reached the pinnacle of the patron journey. The people in this category are folks we know by name. They're the lifeblood of a lot of our organizations—albeit too much, sometimes, to the point that cultural institutions tend to overrely on donors at the top of the giving pyramid. This doesn't mean major donors aren't critical—I'll say yes to a big gift any day, as long as the money didn't come from a toxic source, such as an industry, person, or country that may be laundering their reputation. But in order to grow and expand that base of support so that we aren't utterly beholden to the donors at the top, remember that the steps before this one are just as important.

For this group, as well as the lower-level donor segments before it, try to dial back how many donor "benefits" we're giving away and really focus on connecting donors to the art and the mission (starting with that new-donor brochure they receive). As one chief development officer at a major opera company put it, arts organizations try to reward donor behavior with too many things and events. She came to the arts from a background in healthcare fundraising. "How do we get back to cause-based giving?" she said. "When you give in healthcare, it's because you want to cure cancer, not another wine reception."

For major gifts, we need to know what our donors care about, then constantly work to connect those cares to our cause. Bring artists and curators along to the lunches and dinners, have the board members' thank-you call script say they'll look for the donor at the next performance or exhibit opening, and keep on thanking them. Organizations usually have gratitude nailed down pretty well with major donors. Bringing that same love and fondness in a scalable way, at every point in this pipeline, is what helps us grow first-time attendees to major gift givers—and to appreciate and retain them even if they never become "major donors." It's *all* major because it all adds up.

Final Behavioral Thoughts

This pipeline takes time. Even though organizations I work with on plans developed from these behavioral steps start seeing results in year one, the big gains come later. We're not here for a quick fix; we're here to build relationships to sustain our organization for years to come. We're in it for the Long Haul.

One more note: In a perfect world, people behave the way we want and climb right up that pyramid. But meanwhile, here on planet Earth, we also have to plan for a few other segments: people not on the pyramid because they came to us in a way other than a ticket purchase, or those who fell off the pyramid along the journey. This includes attendees of special events (fundraising galas, opening-night parties, private viewings of special exhibitions, etc.), lapsed buyers and subscribers (after all, even as renewal rates improve, they're never 100 percent), lapsed donors (we have a fair amount of them over the years), and inactive accounts (they've gone stone-cold underwater iceberg on us). But no matter why they're not currently climbing the pyramid, our goal is to get them right back on it.

When it comes to special event attendees, we miss the next behavioral step for them because a lot of times we think the finish line is the event. Which, believe me, I understand—those big events are tons of work. But that's just the beginning of the journey for some guests. So, have a follow-up plan for them. It could even mimic the steps just described: for the event attendees who are new to the organization, send them an email or postcard like the first-time ticket buyers, saying we noticed this was their first event with us. Or for guests who joined the donor family at the event via the auction or raise-the-paddle, send them the donor-welcome brochure detailing all the ways their gift supports the organization.

For the lapsed ticket buyers and subscribers, a reactivation campaign launched every few years with a big discount to come back for a performance often works. Usually those folks have been receiving single-ticket mailings and subscription communications, respectively, for at least three years. By the fourth year of not responding to those communications, though, they're the definition of inactive. Stop mailing them—and the people who have been inactive for even longer—and wasting money. Instead, every few years, think about sending a steep incentive (read: steal of a deal) to reactivate those ice-cold folks. Don't do this kind of offer every year because the chances of that singular mailing to an unengaged audience turning a profit are low, but it *can* reactivate a few accounts each time. And, once you reactivate, folks who haven't been on the pyramid for four years or more are treated as first-timers, so into the machine (because at this point, it is definitely a machine) they go.

And for inactive donor accounts—the ice-cold, no-recent-activity-but-donated-in-the-past, this-is-our-last-ditch-effort people—one time we ran a One & Done campaign based on research from the University of Chicago.[13] The envelope and the appeal letter inside it said the recipient could check a box on the response card if they never want to hear from us ever again. Only five people out of several thousand checked the box to never be contacted again. But beyond them, the mailing garnered *seventeen* times the response rate of our previous lapsed-donor solicitations and generated nearly *fifteen* times more revenue as people rejoined the donor family. Back on that pyramid, baby.

If you want a calendar and a step-by-step checklist to help you track when to take these various actions and send each segmented communication, visit www.aubreybergauer.com/RunItLikeABusiness.

WHEN CHANGE FEELS HARD

For anyone reading this and thinking their organization could never embrace the membership economy or develop discipline around behavioral repetition, whether you're feeling the ship is too big to turn, or the board and staff too entrenched, or that patrons just won't go for it, you're not alone. In 2012, tech giant Adobe knew they needed to evolve to keep up, but were hesitant at first. For decades, they had sold software like other first-wave tech companies—as a onetime license at upwards of $2,500 each—but they had started losing market share. So, they decided to jettison the one-off model and introduce Creative Cloud at a monthly $50 subscription, a gargantuan shift for the software company.[14] (Seriously, can you imagine tossing a $2,500 sure thing for a maximum of $600 a year from the same customer? Actually, sounds a lot like what I hear from some organizations when they argue against moving to monthly giving.)

Adobe's entrenched customers didn't like it at first either. Thousands of disgruntled complainers emerged, including a Change.org petition protesting the new model. But Adobe knew the data showed they should continue . . . and could read the writing on the wall if they didn't make the shift. One year later, the naysayers had subsided, and Adobe was making so much money under the new model, they largely discontinued onetime license sales altogether. By 2013 the subscription service accounted for 86 percent of their total revenue, and it continues to rise.[15]

In the nonprofit space, charity: water went all in on the membership economy, making moving away from one-off gifts to a recurring opt-out monthly gift their top priority. In three and a half years, they saw 40 percent growth in revenue, year over year.[16] Muhlenberg College followed suit and was one of the first (if not *the* first) higher ed institutions to transform their development operation to make monthly giving their main focus rather than a side project or secondary giving option. I spoke with Louis Diez, who led the charge as executive director of Muhlenberg's Annual Fund. "Monthly giving—thumbs up or thumbs down?" I asked. Two thumbs shot up through the air. "Up like a rocket ship," he said as he gestured. The school had gone from around sixty monthly donor households before the change to more than six hundred within one year.[17] "But here's the thing. You can't do it halfway. It's a shift. It takes time, but it works."

In the arts, developing lasting revenue takes time. One study even concluded that a cultural donor's first gift usually lags behind their first attendance by ten years.[18] The Long Haul Model aims to get patrons to become donors in three to four years. But whether it takes three years or ten, building recurring, sustainable relationships is achievable.

It all starts with getting first-timers to come back again. And then again. Behavioral repetition builds loyalty. Loyalty equals recurring revenue. Recurring revenue requires organizational muscle. The membership economy helps the lift.

bad lover

3.

Don't Fear the Machine

So, we've embraced the membership economy. Now, how do we price it? For some artistic disciplines, prices have risen at nearly double the rate of the Consumer Price Index over the last decade, making a mostly unchanged experience substantially more expensive than in years past.[1] Because of this, I used to be very worried about the steep increases in arts prices keeping buyers away. I've since learned it's not so simple; there's more to it than higher prices bad, lower prices good.

There are three nuanced reasons price alone isn't the driver of attendance decline. First, the arts aren't subject to elastic demand, the way Doritos fly off grocery store shelves when they go on sale. On the whole, cultural experiences—particularly subscriptions, the part that intersects the membership economy—generally have somewhat *in*elastic demand. The arts have fewer direct product substitutes, which makes our mental calculus a bit fuzzy. (Doritos vs. Fritos is pretty clear to most people, but the symphony versus [insert other entertainment option] isn't a direct dollar-for-dollar replacement.) This means price alone isn't quite the barrier I suspected, and prices within a *reasonable range* (operative words) aren't dramatically impacting purchase decisions. (I mean, I did shell out three hundred bucks to see Gwen Stefani perform in Las Vegas. Would I have *preferred* for tickets to be $5? Yes. But I wanted to see her over other shows available, so there wasn't a direct, cheaper substitute.)

What's more important for subscriber or member drop-off—in any sector—is when prices *change*. This is the second nuance to arts pricing: any time there is a subscription price change (usually an increase), people leave. And experts say that raising prices because you don't have enough customers is a doom loop.[2] That's where arts and culture have gotten into a bit of trouble. As audiences have diminished, prices have swelled to keep revenue stable, which is a fast track to stifling attendance. So we need to slow down on raising our prices. We do not, though, have to walk prices back; just stop increasing them so often going forward. Side note: Single tickets are a little different from subscriptions in that the price range is usually larger to begin with. In those cases, we absolutely should employ dynamic pricing just like the airlines when the demand warrants it, while keeping the lower end intact to offer an accessible entry point.

The third reason prices are not the harbinger of attendance decline but still a very complicated subject is because growing loyal members and subscribers is more about perceived value than dollars and cents alone. "Your customers have to feel like they're getting great value for the amount that they're paying," Robbie Baxter emphasized again and again in our conversation. NYU's Scott Galloway agrees, saying that across all sectors, subscriptions that thrive offer incredible value to the customer.[3]

Cultural institutions and organizations know their product is excellent and that every ticket they sell comes at a fraction of the cost to the customer compared to how much it takes to actually produce the art. But how do we help patrons and prospective patrons understand the magnitude of what we do? That's where technology and digital content can help us elevate our brand.

———

Before Airbnb was a household name, it was flailing. After multiple pitiful launches over four years (air mattresses on a stranger's floor? Hard pass.), the startup only picked up speed upon winning the breakout mobile app award at South by Southwest in 2011. Airbnb didn't offer a better hospitality experience than its hotel competitors. What set them apart was their technology powering the back end and beautiful digital design on the front end, which the SXSW judges noticed. With Airbnb having grown to a 2023 market cap of more than $76 billion, its computer engineers and designers are driven by their customers' basic need: a place to stay while traveling.

Like Airbnb, almost every company "disrupting" an industry today isn't creating a brand-new product. Rather, these unicorns are using technology, digital content, and design to better meet an existing human need. Examples include Uber (digitally enhanced ride hailing), Insurify (shopping for insurance), Redfin (real estate), One Medical (healthcare), and Ellevest (investing).

This is great news for arts organizations. We meet—or at least have every potential to meet—fundamental human needs for belonging, connection, and entertainment, to name a few. And when we double down on virtual content, strong design, and technological proficiency, we stand apart from other services meeting those same needs, adding value and driving consumers to our bread and butter: an analog, in-person product.

The rest of this chapter breaks down this topic into some basics on content creation and planning, and explains the role of streaming.

ENTER: DIGITAL CONTENT CREATION
AND PLANNING, STAGE RIGHT

In chapter one, we talked about the definition of content marketing: providing digital material to stimulate interest in a brand or service, without being overtly salesy. The purpose is not necessarily to be product specific (come see these artists or that show on this date) or to directly make the sale or ask for a donation ("your gift will be matched dollar for dollar"). The purpose is to build brand awareness and affinity (here's something interesting that makes you stop scrolling).

The general rule with content creation is that the vast majority of what you produce needs to be informative, engaging, and "thumb-stopping." Remember, people want to learn, and they always want stories. Cultural institutions possess both these assets—lots of educational topics around what we do and lots of stories behind every artist and artisan—so dole them out generously. This establishes brand trust, and as you build that trust, that then allows for a few moments within your content to ask for something in return, like visiting the website or buying a ticket.

The thing is, establishing that trust takes time—a lot more than many of us probably imagine. Google conducted a massive study of ticket buyers and found across all forms of entertainment, including arts and culture, people they dubbed "casual fans" (as opposed to subscribers or frequent attenders) ponder a ticket purchase for thirty-one days on average before actually buying.[4] Even people buying at the last minute, the data show, have contemplated that purchase for much longer. Yet, all too often, organizations' social media posts are filled with events happening *this weekend*, which is (1) way too directly salesy and (2) way too late when the average consumer needs to think about the event for a month first.

One way to help those casual fans get and stay curious about our offerings until their brain is ready to seal the deal with a ticket is to create content cycles—lots of content developed around a central theme posted over a predetermined period (in this case, thirty-one days). For example, one organization I worked with planned a monthlong content cycle for every upcoming production:

- Just over four weeks out, they'd publish a blog post about the show and its creation or some other interesting story behind it. Then they'd push that out on the various social channels and email.
- Three weeks out, they shared a behind-the-scenes video across platforms.
- Two weeks out, the content featured an interview with an artist.
- One week before opening, they posted the program notes (which they'd filled with stories and made easy to consume), along with additional quippy commentary (e.g., *That feeling when your first symphony is a disaster and you wait twenty years to write your second*).

Along the way, they supplemented these posts with repurposed nuggets like sound bites, interesting stats, and the OG social media content—pretty pictures. Ticket sales marched up steadily over those four weeks (some people weren't waiting until the last minute—hurrah!) and sure enough, really took off leading up to every opening night. As the fable goes, the tortoise beats the hare every time. With their sales more predictable, they were able to stop biting their nails after frantically pushing sales two days out with last-minute BUY NOW and *don't-miss-this* messages. All because their diligent digital content plan assiduously drove in-person attendance.

Even if you have lots of productions, exhibits, or different things to sell, and feel like you can't dedicate a month of content to each because there's just way too much, you still have options. One is to pick the shows/exhibits that need the most help and build your content plan around those. Another is to go the opposite way and pick the blockbusters to optimize for a sellout with dynamic pricing along the way (raising the prices in tandem with demand), which in turn generates overflow demand for other offerings when people feel the scarcity. You can also try some combination of all of the above. Your social channels don't have to be dedicated to one product at a time; you can run multiple content cycle plans concurrently. Seven days in a week means you could be posting seven times or more if you're really loading up your channels . . . so long as you're only doing this with quality content. Otherwise the whole exercise is moot.

Or try my personal favorite: creating content that's not product specific but keeps your organization top of mind without directly pushing *any* specific event. Talk about what your artists are growing in their garden at home, post photos of your venue's interesting architectural features, latch on to other events or memes in the broader cultural zeitgeist, make a how-to for preordering intermission drinks, or share the recipe for a dish in the café. With so many options for evergreen content, you can have some fun with it—because if you do, chances are your followers will enjoy it, too. And here's the best part: because we've established that affinity and therefore trust, when we do this well, we're building fans of our brand, not of specific programming. And when people are fans of your brand, your specific offerings matter a lot less.

One more digital content planning strategy I'm loving more and more is to activate the influencer army, aka our artists. Whether these influencers are dancers, singers, instrumentalists, or visual artists, people trust people more than they trust brands. Plus, living artists have an extra-fast track to this trust because of their inherent ability to establish a connection with audiences. That's what they do with their art every day, so to leverage this in the form of digital content is a huge opportunity in today's influencer world. I'll share more about this strategy later in the chapter from a brand going all in on it. For now, just know that utilizing social accounts beyond the organization's account is one more tool available in your content-planning tool chest.

APPLICATION BOX

Concept: Using digital content to draw people to in-person experiences

Organization: Museum of the Shenandoah Valley

Virginia's Museum of the Shenandoah Valley covers a lot of ground, physically and digitally. The museum inhabits 214 acres—more than twice the size of Disneyland—of which 7 acres are maintained gardens and 90 acres are trails. A 50,000-square-foot building, built to share an art collection along with history of the valley, ties it all together.

Online, Shenandoah pairs objects and stories of the museum in an especially mouthwatering series called "History in the Kitchen." The series is a bunch of short Facebook videos in the style of those cooking "tutorials" that always get tons of shares: an overhead camera rolls a time lapse of the lightning-fast recipe (crack the eggs, add the flour, etc., and, poof! A really cool and beautifully decorated cake arises . . . or, in Shenandoah's case, waffles from a 1960 recipe). The accompanying post talks about how the recipe was one of the museum benefactor's favorite recipes and links to a full class the museum offers on the same topic.

Shenandoah also produces longer virtual programs within the series, where people register online and pay what they can (we'll talk more about monetizing education programs in the next chapter). One episode is called "History in the Kitchen: Fall Flavors," where the Curator of Collections Nick Powers discusses teakettles and teapots in their collection followed by Horticulturist Chantal Ludder sharing how herbal tea is made. Another episode showcases a historic restaurant on the property led in the 1900s by Black chef Susan Tokes, honoring her contributions to soul food, and finishing with how to make her yeast puffs from the menu. The Museum also offers events like "Meet the Bees & Beekeepers," where the garden beekeepers teach you how to keep your own garden bees happy.

With every video, from a sixty-second baking hot take to information that helps improve my own backyard, I become more interested in their on-site offerings. I'd find myself wanting to get a closer look at that teakettle, or eat in that restaurant, or get some garden inspo so I learn how to not kill everything in mine (I have a pretty brown thumb). And it turns out I'm not the only one. Since the museum started offering this type of accessible, interesting, virtual content, they've seen major gains. "We have evidence from evaluations that virtual program participants have deepened their connection with the museum and are more engaged with the organization, including on-site visits and participating in other programs," Director of Education Mary Ladrick shared with me. "We have no plans to drop or scale back."

LIGHTS, CAMERA, ACTION: THE ROLE OF STREAMING IN CONTENT PLANNING

When the pandemic hit, cultural institutions quickly pivoted to a fully virtual world. We had to, as it was the only way to deliver any kind of product during lockdown. That inadvertently framed digital content as a product substitute (which, to be fair, it was for a while) while quickly forcing us to consider the question of *How do we pay for this?*

As we know, streaming is costly. Equipment, camera operators, postproduction (if not a live stream), artist fees for the capture, and music rights. It's everything we do normally and then some. So it makes sense that many organizations wanted to charge for their streams, only to be disappointed when people weren't flocking to pay for it. Other organizations blasted their streams out for free far and wide to get as many eyes on them as possible, just hoping people would then come in person when venues opened up again. Either way, pretty much no one was making a profit, and many organizations have since swung back to not including streaming in their digital content plans.

First and foremost, the reason to offer streaming video is *not* primarily to drive profit; it's to drive brand engagement. The profit comes later in the form of more ticket sales, subscriptions, and donations. It's not "step one: stream; step two: people pay for it." Instead, think "step one: stream as part of the larger digital content plan just discussed; step two: stimulate interest and trust in and engagement with the brand; and step three: consumers want more of that content in the form of an analog, in-person experience."

This is true of basically all non-broadcast-television streaming services except for Netflix. There, streaming is actually part of the core mission and vision, but just about every other major streaming provider is using digital content to move consumers toward their analog, physical product. Disney has the parks and the box office,* Apple has the iPhone and MacBook and AirPods and more, Amazon has everything in the universe they want to send to your doorstep. And all of these companies use streaming to keep their respective tangible products top of mind and add value for their customers. While you wait for Uncle Bezos's delivery or drool over your next big tech gadget purchase, or think about where to take the kids on spring break, you're devouring these companies' latest binge-worthy series. Streaming is an entry point to the organization for people not yet connected, and a driver of brand affinity and loyalty for everyone else. These tech companies aren't guessing at this strategy; they are investing billions of dollars because the data support it.

In May 2021, Amazon announced one such investment: their acquisition of MGM. *Wired* magazine covered the sale, citing this exact value-add strategy, "Streaming is not [Amazon's] only source of revenue, or even the main focus of its subscription offering. Prime Video remains a nice bonus when you pay

---

* As I write this, Disney is publicly grappling with how their streaming isn't making them a profit either. (Source: Ryan Faughnder, "Disney+ Keeps Growing Fast. But Streaming Loses $1.5 billion," *Los Angeles Times*, November 8, 2022, https://www.latimes.com/entertainment-arts/business/story/2022-11-08/disney-earnings-fourth-quarter-streaming-loses-1-5-billion-hulu-espn-chapek.)

for a year of two-day shipping. Amazon doesn't need to have the best library of prestige movies and television; it just needs to give customers one more reason to not cancel Prime."[5] Amazon's move is not the same as HBO Max (or I guess just Max now) licensing *Friends* or even Disney buying Star Wars or Marvel. Instead, Amazon bought the whole studio, meaning they got the back catalog of hits like the James Bond and Rocky series *and* a built-in house that allows them to produce original content. This parallels the production capabilities of most cultural organizations: we have a trove of past streams, archival footage and recordings, and other digital content we've created over the years. We're also constantly producing new, original work (new concerts, productions, exhibits, and brand-new commissioned pieces are all ripe for streaming). And again, like Amazon, none of that digital content is our top priority; it's in service to the greater goal of not losing people, giving them one more reason not to cancel. The digital experience doesn't replace or detract from our bread and butter; it makes people want it.

This entire strategy is also true for audio streaming in terms of releasing recordings via platforms like Spotify and Pandora. Studies show that nearly a third of all Americans enjoy listening to classical music—a lot more than attend live—and it's the fourth most preferred music genre.[6] Organizations have an opportunity to more effectively convert those listeners to audiences by putting their performances online, especially now that these audio platforms don't require a label to broker the content. Meanwhile, zoos, aquariums, and the like have something even more people like: animals. Wow, have I ever spent a lot of time ogling over the National Audubon Society's puffin cam—or one of their many other active animal cams, which they have lined up next to each other online to stream simultaneously so I can see all the action at once. Cultural organizations all have assets to stream that help connect people to what you do each day.

We don't have to go broke or even stream a lot for streaming to be useful. Stream only a few performances a year or even part of them. Stream just the opera overture; stream the first ten minutes of the play or ballet; stream a bit of rehearsal; stream a quick tour of the new exhibit; stream the animal cam. Leave folks wanting more. And to more successfully convert streaming interactions to in-person buyers without breaking the bank, our administrative teams and our artists need to play a role.

First, to our administrative teams, who make this strategy possible: this is not digital spray and pray. We're not trying to give all the streams away for free and just hope the viewers choose to attend in person. It's on us to make sure we are tracking the viewers we have within the parameters of consumer privacy laws. Set up that Google remarketing for YouTube views, put that tracking cookie on the website so you can show them ads later, and build that viewership list on Instagram and Facebook to start inviting those who engage to attend in person. These are not sophisticated marketing steps; they are baseline fundamental. No matter which platform you use to deliver your streams, be proactive in converting those viewers to buyers. Take everything from the previous chapter on inviting patrons to the next desired action and apply it here, too. At the very least, put up an email gate to collect viewers' addresses in exchange for watching the stream, then automate those follow-up communications after the stream to invite viewers to engage again. The marketing funnel is alive and well, but the funnel does not run itself.

Next, to the incredible artists who make this strategy possible: this isn't something the administrators can do alone. Our union agreements often nearly prohibit this strategy due to the compensation structures, specifically the need to pay additional fees up front for the capture. I want every artist to make more money, so by no means is this strategy endorsing the idea that you shouldn't charge for your work or shouldn't participate in revenue share—but I am saying consider altering *when* the payment occurs. We're this deep into this book because we know arts organizations need to combat the declining trends the industry is facing, and we don't have the type of sustainable audiences we need. So perhaps we can consider new pay structures that incentivize and reward movement toward that goal of growing our base of fans, as opposed to disincentivizing capturing content to drive brand awareness and sales in the first place. I don't know at what point an audience has grown "enough" to make payouts, but I do know that that figuring out what to do with the money we're making from an expanding audience is a nice problem to solve together, and that artists are essential partners if more organizations are to execute this strategy.

APPLICATION BOX

Concept: Streaming to make money without charging consumers directly

Organization: Dallas Black Dance Theatre

Zenetta Drew is a Texan in all the good ways (I say this as a fellow native Texan). She is a Dallas Cowboys mega-fan. She has big ideas. She cites data from inside and outside the arts, is bullish about the decline in audiences and how now is the time to redefine how we operate, and, in her words, "loves the money" as an accountant by training. She has led Dallas Black Dance Theatre (DBDT) since 1987 and has grown the company from a tiny, baby organization to a sizable, multimillion-dollar institution serving hundreds of thousands of people annually and touring to thirty-one states and fifteen countries.

When I first spoke with Drew, she said streaming is just like sports in the early days of broadcast television. "Nobody understood why the Dallas Cowboys played football on Thanksgiving in the '60s. Twenty years later, every team was building a new stadium. Why? Because the broad transmission created all these new entrants. They used the digital format to be able to grow exponentially the number of people who had access to the game, who understood the game, and then had interest to go to the stadium. We have the opportunity to create the same thing in the arts."

During the pandemic, Drew was dogmatic that opportunity existed amid the crisis to keep growing our brands and use the disruption to our advantage—and that is exactly what she did. Today, DBDT continues to use streaming as a strategy to offer access to arts education and drive in-person attendance. Streaming also offers them a way to "tour" virtually, bring remote students to their academy, and get corporate sponsorship. Streaming has proven incredibly lucrative for the institution without them ever needing to ask individual consumers to pay directly for the streams.

Access to Arts Education. DBDT uses their virtual content to serve every student in the Dallas School District—all students in all grades, at all schools. And the district reached out and offered to pay for it, which is the opposite of how community education efforts normally work. Usually the organization gives their education programming away to a school for free (and hunts for grantors and donors to fund it) in hopes those kids grow up and eventually become ticket buyers. "The default for education has been outreach," Drew said. "That outreach has not turned into paid attendees." Plus, if DBDT had offered their education programming in person, busing in kids for performances as is so often the practice, they only would have been able to serve 5,000 students. Now they serve upwards of 150,000 annually and get paid to do so.

Driving Analog, In-Person Attendance. DBDT usually streams only thirty minutes or so of a performance, Drew said, because "what we are trying to do at Dallas Black Dance Theatre is to create desire so people want our product. You see individuals from all economic backgrounds invest in sports gear and all other types of entertainment because they desire to have it." And people do want what arts organizations have to offer. For example, someone who wanted to provide programming to children's hospitals across the nation bought matinee *Nutcracker* performances to stream for children who were patients.

Now, new people are showing up all the time because they saw DBDT virtually. In fact, Drew told me she's wondering when they'll need to construct a new theater to hold their growing audience.

Touring Physically and Virtually. Early in the pandemic, DBDT realized that performing arts centers did not have products to present onstage, so they offered their virtual product for sale to the presenters, who then offered the stream to their respective audience bases. Today DBDT is touring physically and virtually at the same time with two touring companies (one on the road and the other filming content). "Dancers may be in Maryland, but the streaming may be in Montana," said Drew. "We're visiting cities we'd otherwise never travel to."

Dance Academy Streaming. Like many dance companies, DBDT also operates a training academy, which they now offer in person and virtually in parallel. They've found older students (ten years and above) want a virtual option, as do parents who want to save time, gas money, and the effort of travel if they aren't local. Many of their academy students now reside in places far from Dallas; young dancers have enrolled from Philadelphia to Los Angeles.

Consumers Don't Pay for It; Corporate Sponsorship Does. Broadly, corporate support for the arts has been declining for years, yet this is one more area where DBDT is bucking the trend. First came the corporation who underwrote the streaming to children in hospitals. Then another corporate client paid for online dance classes for one hundred employees and clients. Another bought virtual products to send to their international customers. Then came Verizon. The telecom conglomerate, which had not sponsored DBDT since 2001, got wind of all that was happening via streaming, and reached out to them (seriously, when was the last time a corporation initiated contact to offer funding?). Verizon created an app to send performance content to their customers, and paid for it all and then some.

And my favorite: The American Association of Retired Persons (more commonly known by their acronym, AARP), bought some virtual content in multiple states to share with their thirty-eight million members. The exclusively *older demographic organization* bought *digital* content. For anyone thinking older audiences aren't online, can we please put that to rest once and for all?

"Who are the folks that are most likely to be susceptible to marketing for virtual events?" Drew asked in our conversation. She didn't say millennials or Gen Z. "Seniors. Mature audiences. The people who are now challenged to go into the theaters have a provider who they trust bringing them content. Folks who also love *Great Performances* on PBS have been enjoying the arts in this digital format for years."

All of this points to another script for arts organizations having the streaming conversation. While this entire chapter, up until this case study, has focused on the business-to-consumer streaming strategy (brands offering digital content directly to customers or potential customers), what Zenetta Drew and Dallas Black Dance Theatre have done so brilliantly is captured the business-to-*business* market (securing other brands as third-party brokers of the content). Drew is adamant there is a way to make money doing this after all. If the direct-to-consumer model isn't where the revenue potential lies, selling to other entities—the school district, hospitals, and corporations—absolutely is.

"We don't believe this is a short-term fix," Drew concluded as we wrapped up our conversation. "This is to help us grow our audience over the next twenty years." Just like the Dallas Cowboys, I can't wait for her vision to lead to a bigger stadium.

DON'T SAY "M*CBETH." INSTEAD, SAY "WE'RE A MEDIA COMPANY"

During the pandemic, many arts organizations embraced their overnight pivot to becoming self-described "media companies," and we can all learn a lot by looking at one more business who still calls themself that. A company that, like arts organizations, has incredible talent and a pricey physical product—but that leverages this talent via savvy social media, offers tremendously high-quality production, and sells digital subscriptions consumed by a ridiculously rabid fan base. It's the company I believe is the foremost digital-drives-analog company the arts can and should emulate: Peloton.

If you've followed their pandemic surge to home fitness stardom or some of the reality-bites headlines since, you know Peloton has seen, well, a bumpy ride at times. Nonetheless, the cycling unicorn still ended 2022 with somewhere around $3.8 billion in revenue.[7] Its subscriptions continue to surge, and the bikes are now in every Hilton hotel in the US.[8]

It's true that at-home fitness has been around for a long time. Cue the VHS tape with Jane Fonda and legwarmers, followed by Suzanne Somers's Thighmaster, ripped sweaty men with their Bowflexes, and obsessively counting your daily steps with Fitbit. But when Peloton entered the scene in 2012, they set out to brand themselves in a different product category entirely. Sure they sold fitness equipment, but they said they weren't here to market exercise. They were there to build community as a media company.

They haven't always gotten it right—Peloton ran into trouble in 2019 with music rights, getting sued by Lady Gaga and others.[9] Then they made headlines again with a product recall in May 2021 after a child death was linked to their treadmills.[10] Despite these setbacks, the company doubled down on their wellness ecosystem/digital media strategy along the way, and the numbers don't lie: their subscriber rate has grown every year. Even after their pandemic-induced boom, today the company still boasts a holy grail 95 percent customer retention rate.[11]

Beyond both arts organizations and Peloton calling themselves media companies, both also say they want to build community, offer outstanding talent, and sell an expensive product. There's a lot cultural institutions and the bike behemoth have in common, and therefore some things we can pattern ourselves after.

High-Quality Production Value

Peloton has their studio game down: moving cameras, lighting, curated music timed to the second, and meticulously scripted classes.[12] Every moment is planned, both for the in-person riders and those watching the stream. The instructor knows which camera to look at and when, brings their thoughtfully yet authentically branded personality, and takes great care to do their own hair, makeup, and wardrobe (presumably, there is quite the Spandex selection).

Arts organizations have come so far in terms of video production quality, yet still have room to uplevel to match this type of detailed sophistication and better appeal to consumers.

Accessible Digital Content

You don't have to own an expensive Peloton bike or treadmill to take advantage of their virtual offerings. With the app, you can access all kinds of workouts that don't require hardware, such as yoga, core, free weights, and stretching. They even offer outdoor running, which at first blew my mind—it's so counterintuitive, given that part of their core business function is selling treadmills. But they care more that you're in their ecosystem, subscribing to their content, because they know chances will be high that you'll eventually splurge on the hardware.

Cultural institutions can adopt this strategy—it's the point of the whole chapter. Lavish digital on people so they get sucked into the ecosystem.

Additional Digital Options

Peloton wants their digital content to permeate your life so much that all their classes are available live and on demand, with benefits to each (live classes give you a real-time leaderboard; on demand is of course on your own schedule). They also make their playlists available on Spotify, allow you to "like" songs during your workout that automatically populate your own personalized Spotify playlist, publish YouTube videos (ranging from celebrity users like Ashton Kutcher marathon-training on their treadmills to studio tours to Earth Day yoga), and deliver new podcast episodes every week—all so they're top of mind even when you're not working out.

Think about what other content your organization can offer as a way to stay front of mind for consumers.

Activating Talent as Influencers on Social Media

At the end of every class, instructors aren't saying, "Follow Peloton on social media." Instead, they are giving their own personal handles, which has amassed incredible free marketing for both the company and the talent: as of June 2022, Peloton instructors had a combined 9.62 million Instagram followers across fifty-one accounts; the Peloton brand account, by comparison, has less than one-fifth the following.[13] They're talking about their classes, their favorite wellness tips, and all kinds of other topics, too (Tunde's fashion, Cody's gay pride, Robin's baby, even their makeup routine before going on camera). Their personal content is driving engagement and sales.

Arts organizations have a mega-bench of talent that could do the same thing. Some institutions like London's Philharmonia Orchestra have already instituted training for their artists who were interested in building a stronger social media presence. Our marketing teams can work with such artist ambassadors, and we could offer instruction and media assets for staff, too, from curators to administrative personnel, given that we're in the day and age of C-suite celebrities. We can reach more people collectively than a brand account alone ever could.

Content Motivates a Desire for Analog Experience

The analog experience here isn't just a hardware purchase, but a trip to Peloton's studio. A few years ago, I was on a work trip to New York, and I carved out time to go to Chelsea and take a spin class in the flesh. There I was, in one of the greatest cities in the world with endless things to do, and I factored into my schedule multiple hours to travel across town for *a workout*. (And then also ate a billion cupcakes afterward at Magnolia Bakery.)

The funny thing is, every time I tell this story, someone else inevitably says "Same!" or "I wanna visit the studio, too!" These aren't just anecdotes and I'm not generally a workout freak like that, I can assure you; they're indicators of a growing body of people driven to consume the in-person entrée because of the great online appetizer. Arts organizations can create that kind of passion—where residents and tourists alike carve out time to come see *us*.

Partnerships That Aren't One-Offs

In the arts we tend to partner for one-off events or community activities, but Peloton has unlocked the benefits of longer relationships. When the company expanded operations to serve Germany, they promptly became the two-year "fitness innovation partner" of the German Football Academy, providing subscribers the opportunity to train virtually with the national players. They've launched similar partnerships with celebrities from Usain Bolt to members of Queen, plus apparel collaborations with Adidas and Lululemon. Peloton's Artist Series classes highlight the musical catalog of pop, rock, and indie darlings—most famously Beyoncé, in a multiyear partnership that's since grown to include gifted Peloton memberships to students at historically Black colleges and universities. Peloton constantly reaches across product categories and genres for multifaceted relationships that keep the spotlight on the brand.

Arts organizations often form amazing partnerships with celebrities and influencers (Metallica rocked with the San Francisco Symphony, Benedict Cumberbatch played Hamlet at London's Barbican, film director Julian Schnabel guest-curated an exhibit at Musée d'Orsay), but they're usually one and done. Yet, these partnerships can be extended to create a bigger splash, like New York's Museum of Modern Art podcast hosted by actress Abbi Jacobson (*Broad City*, *A League of Their Own*), a comedian who also knows art history from having earned a degree in fine arts before moving to New York to pursue acting. Each episode brings on other famous voices like Questlove and RuPaul, who together with Abbi visit a work at the museum and unpack its significance.

Data Informing Service

Last, Peloton isn't guessing what customers want. Users rate each class, and Peloton analyzes those data to further inform how their instructors deliver content. Remember all those liked songs that form your own playlist? They use that intel to create more classes around the most popular songs each year (when they partnered with Beyoncé, they knew Beyoncé was the artist most requested by their then 3.6-million-plus members before they shelled out the money for her contract).

Then there's the white glove delivery of the product, a master class in partnering with third-party vendors (shout-out to everyone who knows the difficulties of working with outside venues, caterers, parking attendants, and so on). By the time someone's taken the plunge to invest in their pricey hardware, Peloton has ensured their onboarding experience is top notch with a slick online portal to schedule delivery, plus drivers who are on time, friendly, make sure your bike or tread is connected to your home Wi-Fi, and give you a tutorial on adjusting the equipment to your body specifications (i.e., seat height, armrest adjustment, heart rate monitor if you want). They go the extra mile because the digital data tell them if you aren't using the new gear within the first twenty-four hours or so of delivery, you're less likely to renew. It goes back to making that onboarding experience effortless to ensure your customer journey kicks into high gear as quickly as possible.

To bring all of this home, everything that Peloton is doing on the digital side comprises only a quarter of their revenue, but the company makes the investment because they understand it is all working to feed the pipeline for the other 75 percent. Peloton has about three times as many no-equipment digital members as the number of people who own physical products.[14] Once people purchase the analog hardware, though, more than 90 percent keep their subscription for twelve months or longer. That's especially impressive when you think back to the last chapter: the subscriber renewal rate in the first year for cultural organizations is around 50 percent, depending on the discipline. The king of at-home fitness hasn't gotten it right every time, but there's a reason why, beyond the 2020 lockdown, the brand has seen meteoric growth. As they mentioned in their S-1 filing to go public, "usage drives value and loyalty."[15]

Or, as Kamal Sinclair, senior adviser of digital innovation at the Music Center in Los Angeles, which operates venues such as the Dorothy Chandler Pavilion, Walt Disney Concert Hall, and Ahmanson Theatre, puts it, "For the sector to remain relevant, the 'brick-and-mortar experience' needs to join a larger creative conversation involving new technologies and multiple platforms."[16] On the whole, digital content is about adding value and therefore funneling people to our core product—not about creating a new revenue stream in itself. Sometimes people are disappointed when I say that. Don't get me wrong, though; that doesn't mean there aren't new revenue streams to be had—which brings us to the next chapter.

4.

We Have a Lot to Offer
Besides the Art

The Case for Vertical Integration

One day in 1859, a twenty-four-year-old man named Andrew was promoted to superintendent of the Pennsylvania Railroad. He was precocious: after immigrating to the United States as a boy with no formal education, he taught himself by reading books he borrowed from a neighbor. As a teenager, he memorized all the various pitches of incoming telegraph signals so that he could translate by ear, skills he then brought to the burgeoning railroad as a telegraph operator.

Trains in the mid-1800s were used primarily to transport goods. People traveled mostly by stagecoach or boat, but Andrew saw that passengers were viable cargo, too. While still at his job at the railroad, Andrew decided to invest his own personal savings in the Pullman Company, manufacturer of one of the first luxury sleeping cars. The gamble paid off. Using trains for overnight transportation took the country by storm, and his investment returned more than $5,000 (about $176,000 today) each year—more than three times his salary at the railroad.

Why doesn't the railroad company develop their own passenger cars? Andrew wondered. He applied this school of thought to a new business venture, but took it even further. What if one company brought under one roof not just transporting multiple product categories (goods and people), but also using the raw materials they transported to manufacture their own products? This concept, now called vertical integration, combines multiple stages of production or operation normally overseen by separate companies into one. The strategy not only accelerated the Industrial Revolution but made Andrew one of the richest people in all of modern history when he put the idea into practice. He called his new company the Carnegie Steel Corporation.[1]

Andrew Carnegie went on to own and operate the mines where iron ore was extracted as well as the mills that produced steel. He secured contracts to produce the iron rails for the trains. He then acquired steamboats to transport those raw materials from mines to mills, as well as to ship the finished product back out. Along the way, he created the Keystone Bridge Company to demonstrate proof of concept for steel bridges—infrastructure that previously had only been constructed of wood or concrete—that would allow the trains to travel farther (and therefore need more steel for tracks and to construct the bridge itself). Carnegie's wealth grew to $309 billion in today's dollars, more than the peak wealth of Bill Gates, Sam Walton, and Warren Buffett combined.[2]

Some say vertical integration is owning as much of the supply chain as possible. Others say it's about a firm's ability to control product creation from A to Z—we make the steel, lay the tracks made from it, build the cars that run on those tracks, and transport goods or people in those cars to their destinations. Today they'd also be selling those passenger tickets on the website they built. This chapter is about identifying opportunities for vertical integration in our cultural work.

────────

Modern examples of vertical integration abound. Amazon is the king of this. Just like Andrew Carnegie, they took ownership of shipping and distribution (first distributing just books, then other goods, which later became known as Amazon Prime). Then they started creating their *own* products (Amazon Basics) and letting others sell directly on their platform (Amazon Marketplace). Along the way they decided to stop outsourcing their web hosting and integrate that—and then when *that* became a core competency, they started offering their hosting service to others. Called Amazon Web Services, it's now the largest web-hosting platform in the world.[3]

Another example is Apple. They control the hardware (laptops, tablets, phones), the software powering those devices (iOS and countless apps), the entertainment on them (Apple Music, Apple TV+, podcasts), and the accessories/wearables that accompany them (Apple Watch, AirPods, Beats). Plus they sell all these products online and in stores they own and expressly designed to fully control the branded customer experience. And now they are making the silicon chips that go in the hardware, thus owning even more of the product supply chain.[4] A. To. Z.

One more: Our friends at Peloton from the last chapter. We know Peloton produces hardware (equipment), software (their customized operating system and app), and content (streaming classes and social media). But what came after that? The upped their vertical integration game with apparel. It started as only 1 to 2 percent of their revenue in 2014 but has since grown from $2 million of their business in 2017 to topping $100 million in 2021—demonstrating that we have to start somewhere, even with small returns at first. In 2018 their next vertical integration move was to acquire a company to help with their music licensing. Remember how they got into rights trouble with Lady Gaga? Yeah, Peloton brought that in house to fix it.[5]

I said in the last chapter that streaming is not the way to develop significant new revenue—but vertical integration is. In some ways, it's like investing: don't put all your eggs in one basket. Often in the arts we diversify our portfolio within the same product line: pops versus classical, comedy versus tragedy, bel canto versus Wagnerian, touring exhibits versus the collection, contemporary dance versus ballet, Dixieland versus swing, and on and on. None of that is bad (we'll dive deep into programming in the next chapter), but there's more on the table for enterprising organizations that want to expand their revenue streams.

Think about what aspects of your artistic discipline—what parts of the experience, product, or supply chain—are normally not available through your organization. Things you already might have integrated include recording and distribution (many organizations have brought that in house over going with a label), the gift shop (an often small but important revenue vertical), and sometimes owning and operating the venue itself.

There are other components (verticals) of the industry cultural institutions normally don't touch but could. We'll explore three of them related to education: studying with artists, art appreciation programs, and arts management training.

STUDYING WITH ARTISTS

Usually only children growing up or students enrolled at a conservatory, art institute, or collegiate degree program receive individual instruction. But cultural organizations could offer people the opportunity to study with artists. If you're an adult who wants to continue learning or pursue instruction for personal enjoyment (vs. landing a job as a working professional artist) but want a top professional to be your teacher, you're largely out of luck. And for our artists, only some are fortunate enough to have an academic or conservatory job flowing pupils their way each year.

Some entrepreneurial artists are filling this void already, and they are making bank. One such impresario is Nathan Cole, the first associate concertmaster at the Los Angeles Philharmonic. Cole has created online offerings that are now a six-figure annual income for him in addition to his symphony salary. A few years ago, he began offering a six-month program that afforded participants one lesson each month, some group classes, and some prerecorded content. His first iteration of the program resulted in twenty people registering at $5K each. That's $100K in just half a year out of the gate.

"The work I do online has since eclipsed the money I get from my day job," Cole said. "I'm able to spend time teaching the people I want to work with and focus on the material that's important to me. I really look forward to seeing my students. It leaves me more time for my life. I get to spend more time with my family and worry about money a lot less!"

Other orchestral musicians are doing this, too. Elizabeth Rowe, principal flute at the Boston Symphony, started a coaching practice (in fact, she is leaving the coveted chair at the BSO in August 2024 to take the coaching practice full time); percussionist Rob Knopper of the Metropolitan Opera Orchestra offers an audition training institute for preprofessional musicians wanting to land the big gig (his website says the best part is it works for any instrument, not just percussionists . . . brilliant); and back at the LA Phil, cellist Gloria Lum, violist Mick Wetzel, principal trumpet Thomas Hooten, and second trumpet Christopher Still are also offering their own adult education courses. "My business has grown to over $330,000 the past few years, as my momentum and experience grows. It's pretty unbelievable," Still told me. These musicians and many others have developed sizable income streams outside of their orchestra jobs. (There's probably some sort of joke in here about multiple brass players doing this at the same orchestra, but as a fellow former brass player myself, I choose to stand in awe instead.)

Dance companies have been better at this for a long time, offering instructional classes like Pilates, yoga, and barre. Even New York City Ballet principal dancer Tiler Peck has embraced vertical integration with her own brand: she teaches classes on Instagram Live, authors a children's-book series about Katarina Ballerina, and designs her own studio-wear fashion line available for purchase on her website. Who needs the Sugar Plum Fairy when you have the Vertical Integration Queen?

For artists concerned about the quality or level of ability of their students, or for anyone thinking performing artists have to teach performance or be employed by a big, well-known ensemble, take a cue from the jazz world. Bassist Danny Ziemann has had incredible success *not* teaching lessons on how to play the double bass better. By the age of thirty he'd already self-published several jazz textbooks and is as dedicated an educator as he is a player.

APPLICATION BOX

Concept: Monetizing studying with artists

Organization: You(th) Can Compose!

Whereas the examples just listed focus on adult education, most cultural institutions already have some type of childhood education program. The trouble is those programs are often not a revenue stream aside from grant funding and donor underwriting. Composer Sakari Dixon Vanderveer flipped the script on that dated model when she launched an online training academy for young aspiring composers aged 10 to 18 called the "You(th) Can Compose!" summer workshop.

Like many artists, Dixon used to have a day job in addition to composing on the side and orchestra ringer gigs (subbing in for other players). She herself had been taking composition lessons online years before the pandemic, which informed her decision to try building a virtual course for young composers with little to no experience composing. Dixon teaches the basics of musical notation, helps the kids workshop pieces in the class, gives lots of hands-on feedback, and gets them from have-never-composed to writing and performing their first solo within a few weeks. Their final pieces are usually a minute or two each, which they all perform in a class recital at the end of the program.

What's great about this format, says Dixon, is that the program doesn't have to be long. She intentionally runs the workshop three to four weeks during the summer when ensembles are mostly off but parents are hunting for activities for their kids. The same theory can apply to arts organizations whose stages are dark and want to offer their artists work and simultaneously realize an extra revenue stream. For exhibit-based institutions, you've got summer in your pocket, too: your doors open, and parents get an outlet for their kids.

Dixon says the best part is this work opened up avenues for her she didn't see coming. Offers to teach composition other places, as well as new commissions, started coming in because other people and institutions saw her online presence. Now music activities are her full-time job.

Almost all organizations have an online presence and education infrastructure already, and therefore have a leg up in launching this type of content. Whether an individual or institution follows this route, vertical integration through educational programming is a path to increasing revenue through activities artists are often most qualified to do.

Not everyone is as entrepreneurial as these artists, and that's okay. For artists who are interested in this type of additional income stream but aren't wanting to solopreneur it, or who could do it alone but simply prefer the administrative support, our institutions could help broker these opportunities and share the revenue. What if we agreed on something like a 50/50 split for the division of labor? A few Nathan Coles or Sakari Dixons, and that is some serious money, even when profit sharing. Imagine what our artists could achieve if they had the weight of the organization behind them. Again, some don't need the help, and some don't want to take on any ancillary work (both fine). But some artists are enterprising, love to share their expertise, and interested in additional income. Bingo.

Last, there are secondary benefits for organizations who embrace an artist study program. As more students begin to study with our artists outside a traditional studio setting because technology allows this type of instruction to scale, the artist grows their online brand—and as the last chapter showed, artists are built-in potential influencers. In turn, more people connect with the artist and the organization, which in turn sells more tickets, as followers want to see that artist perform. What a virtuous cycle.

ART APPRECIATION PROGRAMS

Another area where cultural institutions can monetize education is via art appreciation programs—classes for adults who want entry-level, beginner content to better understand the art form. Most organizations provide little adult education, and when they do, it's often limited in two ways. First, it comes *after* the ticket purchase (pre-performance talk, guided tour, program book), not before. Second, it's generally designed for aficionados (community lectures by academics, program notes by specialists, audio tours written by scholars). Think back to chapter one on how foreign and therefore off-putting this content feels to a big portion of our patron base.

Because of the decline in public arts education over the last several decades as public funding for music and art education was cut from school districts across the nation, increasing numbers of now-grown, intelligent adults are willing to pay for this type of learning. Back in 2010, arts research firm WolfBrown realized this educational opportunity. They found only 3 percent of arts audiences across theater, dance, opera, and music want a deep dive before attending a performance, while most everyone else wants something more 101 level. Their report encouraged organizations to engage this "big middle" of our patron base, as they called it, with this type of introductory education.[6]

WolfBrown concluded that we need to give people options for how deep to go, which means we need a wider range of educational products. For the people who want a little, that's our digital content from the last chapter. For those who want more—the big middle—vertical integration will allow us to make money serving that market. And today we have tools and competencies that weren't available to us when that report came out in 2010: namely, the ability to provide this education virtually, live or on demand, and serve more people because of it.

Sometime around 2017, my education director at the California Symphony approached me with the idea for what turned out to be proof of concept for this type of paid beginner education. We were brainstorming how to engage a greater subset of the audience with an easy, fun, adult music-appreciation class designed to teach new or new-ish attendees more about the art form. The original class structure contained four weeks of classes over the summer at the local library, one hour each, for the basement low price of $25, which you'd get back at the end as a voucher to put toward any ticket purchase in the upcoming season (we were first thinking of this as a gateway to ticket sales; the more profitable part comes in a bit).

That first class sold out at seventy-five participants (room capacity), and most had been to the California Symphony only once or never before. Mission to target non-aficionados achieved. The next year, we rented the library's largest room, which held one hundred people, and sold that out, too. Both those iterations ended up making the orchestra money—but summer of 2020 is where it gets much more interesting. I had left the organization by then, so what they did next was completely without me.

As we know, summer of 2020 was on lockdown, so the symphony moved the course to a virtual event . . . and three hundred people registered. That's $7,500 for one class at a dirt-cheap price with no venue rental fees, no costs for printed materials, and no significant time spent on curriculum development, as it had all been created three years earlier. In other words, they generated that revenue with relatively little effort or investment. That went so well and was easy enough, they then rolled out the virtual offering again in early 2021, this time using the pre-recorded content they captured the previous summer (read: even less effort). They were getting $25 a person for pushing PLAY. *That* is high profit margin. They still offer the class today both in person (which is still selling out) and on-demand (now they make $30 a pop for the customer pushing PLAY themself).[7]

The Richmond Symphony similarly offers a suite of virtual education via their online Symphony School of Music. It ranges from academic classes (music theory, history) at $85 to $120 for about seven weeks, to chamber music instruction at $250 for eight weeks, to an in-person conducting seminar with the music director where you can even conduct the orchestra.[8] Dallas Black Dance Theatre, whose digital programming we learned about in the last chapter, now offers a full online slate of 101-style, beginner-level appreciation classes with information typically only available through an outside continuing education program.

If you're an exhibit-based institution, there's a lot to learn from the Smithsonian. They've monetized their way to become the largest museum-based education program in the world. Most classes are a cool $25 ($20 for members, which is a whole lesson in tying these types of programs to a rewards system for our most loyal patrons) and include topics ranging from "Elvis and the Monkees," to "Privatization of Space Exploration," and Food Network's Delicious Miss Brown hosting "Kardea Brown: Celebrating Gullah Geechee Culinary Traditions."

Their programs are mostly online via Zoom, meaning even organizations with massive budgets are fine with no fancy platforms. Plus, they now offer in-person experiences as well. Think *Night at the Museum* with "Smithsonian Nighttime Adventures" at the Natural History Museum, or curating your at-home collection with your favorite fine art prints and poster art via their "Art Collectors" program, or exploring Japanese rice wine in "Sake 101," along with Michelin-starred bites to pair. And lest you think the Smithsonian can do all this because of their government subsidies, these programs receive no federal funding.

All of these courses surrounding introductory appreciation dovetail with using early-stage educational content for marketing (from chapter one), no matter how much ancillary revenue they provide. People pay us to get some of that content, and then pay us some more to come see the art in person.

ARTS MANAGEMENT TRAINING

A third area where vertical integration can benefit cultural organizations is in arts management training. Generally, there's very little training for professional administrative roles, especially compared to the years-long rigorous and systematic training professional artists undergo. There are no art administration institutes, only a handful of undergrad and graduate level programs in arts management (vs. the larger number of performance programs), and a few one- or two-week professional development seminars. And that's about it. In terms of the supply chain for the business side of the arts, there's not much. But with a desperate need for administrative talent, there's space for cultural organizations to train the highly skilled staff this work requires—and, of course, monetize it. Thousands of dollars are to be made here, as some institutions have already figured out.

Beth Morrison Projects, an organization known for commissioning new opera and vocal theater work, launched their Producer Academy to teach others to bring new work to the stage. The academy includes modules on fundraising, budgeting, and other necessary administrative functions. In their debut offering, they had thirty participants and netted around $80,000—nothing to sneeze at for organizations of any size.[9] They ran the program again the following year with similar results, but with a higher ROI since all the curriculum development work had already been done.

They later expanded the academy with one-week intensives on fundraising, budgeting, and touring—all topics Beth Morrison Projects has built proficiency around in their twenty-year history of developing new work. In 2021, the Producer Academy leaped to the next level when the Mellon Foundation awarded the organization a nearly half-million-dollar grant to fund the next three years of the program. As of 2023 they've served over a thousand students.[10]

Lisa Bellamore, a publicist who's represented artists and organizations including the L.A. Philharmonic, YouTube, UCLA, and the GRAMMY Museum, now teaches the skills necessary for successful public relations through her firm, Crescent Communications. Courses include workshops that teach how to pitch a journalist, write and distribute press releases, and integrate key messages into talking points for media interviews.

The job functions that Beth Morrison Projects and Crescent Communications teach are vitally necessary in terms of skill development for our field, but they're normally only taught in one of two ways: if you get a masters in arts administration or arts management, or if you learn on the job over the years. The latter is not delivering the results this demanding work requires in a timely manner, and the former can be cost prohibitive.

In fact, since such training programs are where entry-level staff usually come from, they can be doubly useful in fueling the administrative talent pipeline. Companies could build an offering that teaches a core capability needed in arts administration and offer an internship as part of that. Or we could let the program participants get first crack at applying to summer jobs or entry-level roles we need to fill. If we invite participation from unrepresented groups, we could also use this training to directly address not just skills we want to build, but the lack of variety in administrators' backgrounds. We would open up the pipeline so rising talent is paying to learn from us (or receiving scholarships when financial need warrants), train people to have exactly the skills we need, and then invite those who have demonstrated learning those skills to work with us—this time, for a career.

As a related aside, I believe in paying interns (we'll talk more about how the industry underpays staff labor in chapter seven), so please only pursue this idea if you can commit to paying folks. Beth Morrison Projects is doing this: anyone who completes their course is eligible to apply for a one-year, salaried fellowship.

If you're looking for more proof that this works, look no further than good old Andrew Carnegie. He owned all the steel sourcing, production, and transportation that forged the vertical integration backbone of his company, and then he created a training program to develop talent he wanted working in these various roles. This program grew into a technical school, and eventually into an established institute of higher learning to teach the steel processes to the next generation—one that we know today as Carnegie Mellon University.[11]

Why Online Education Works—and Why Now

All of these vertical integration examples work because of the culmination of four factors the pandemic accelerated:

1. Arts organizations are now very good at producing online events.
2. Consumer trends are gravitating toward online education.
3. Online education is easy to scale, which means easy to monetize.
4. Higher education as the primary vehicle for adult education has been disrupted.

None of these conditions were at the fore for arts organizations prior to 2020, but they all existed—and have since exploded into the cultural mainstream.

Take the first two—the proliferation of online events for organizations and consumer trends. Anyone working in or anywhere near arts and culture knows firsthand how our collective competency at producing virtual programming skyrocketed. It had to. Long before lockdown forced this pivot for us, though, online education was already rising. It was an established $107 *billion* industry back in 2015, had reached nearly $200 billion before the pandemic, and was expected to triple over the next ten years to $350 billion by 2025—a projection blown away by a global emergency lockdown. Now the market for e-learning is expected to hit $1.72 *trillion* in the next few years.[12]

The third reason online education works—it's easy and lucrative to scale, especially compared to streaming performances, which are very much *not*—is, well . . . math. Streaming eighty or ninety people onstage and in the pit is expensive. Staffing up a gallery or garden or animal exhibit is costly, too. Streaming one instructor is much cheaper.*

As for the fourth factor, a top signal that an industry is ripe for disruption is increasing prices without increasing value or innovation. We talked about how this is a death spiral for arts orgs in the last chapter, but we're not the only ones facing this. Other industries primed by this definition include healthcare, insurance, and higher education.[13] Higher ed used to be the primary vehicle for adult education, including non-degree continuing education programs. But as anyone who's still paying off student loans or has sent a kid off to college knows, the college

---

* Jennifer Rosenfeld is the mastermind behind this strategy. A former board member of the L.A. Philharmonic and L.A. Master Chorale who has worked with many of the artists and organizations I spoke about in this chapter, Rosenfeld says that when we put on a performance onstage, we lose money (that's why we're nonprofits and have to fundraise to make up the rest of the budget). Online education, by contrast, is about creating high profit margins.

experience is *expensive*. It's also largely unchanged over the past several decades despite the astronomical increases in tuition. To be clear, I'm not suggesting cultural organizations need to roll out four-year degree programs. What I am suggesting is that there are a lot of adults who want to continue learning, whether for professional training or personal enjoyment, who aren't willing to shell out twenty grand a semester, because the market has shown cheaper options are now available.

Enter opportunity for us. Programs like MasterClass, Skillshare, and Coursera have already figured this out, as have Nathan Cole, Beth Morrison Projects, the Smithsonian, and others. Google is getting into adult education, too, having rolled out online certificate programs in data analytics, project management, and user experience for under $300 a program.[14] And Amazon launched their Technical Academy to train and fill one hundred thousand engineering roles by 2025.[15] It's completely feasible for our education departments to become revenue generating—and not in a way dependent on grants, where we sometimes make the program fit the funder, but as a vehicle to funnel cash back to our missions.

Andrew Carnegie put the cash back toward the mission, too. As his wealth grew, he was dogmatic that his profit should be reinvested into what we call today mission-driven work. For him, that infusion back into society established over 1,600 free public libraries, paid for thousands of church organs, built Carnegie Hall, funded the development of insulin, and launched the charitable foundation that lives on today, among other philanthropic endeavors.

Now organizations have the ability to offer products besides the art—verticals that help support the art—with higher returns than ever before.

5.
Who's on First

Raise your hand if you watched *Bridgerton*. **If that's you, you're** one of eighty-two million people worldwide who binged the racy love story of the Duke of Hastings and his co-conspirator, Daphne Bridgerton. What started as a ruse to pretend to court each other to get everyone off their backs about getting married went awry when they actually fell in love and had tons of sex on-screen. Like, tons (if you know you know).

The thing is, even though *Bridgerton* set a record for the most-watched original series on Netflix, nothing about its plot or steamy love scenes is new.[1] That story of fake-it-till-oops-you-made-it love has been told a million times (*Pretty Woman*, *To All the Boys I've Loved Before*); a lot of other shows have been set as British period dramas (*Downton Abbey*, *The Crown*); plenty of titles have been racy (*Fifty Shades of Grey*, *Gossip Girl*); and just about everything Hollywood makes has smokin'-hot actors (shout-out to *People* magazine's twice-named sexiest man George Clooney, or one of *Forbes*'s top-paid actors and personal favorite Chris Evans . . . although seriously, *Bridgerton*'s Regé-Jean Page is gorgeous too . . . okay, focus, Aubrey). The point is, what *Bridgerton* producer and showrunner Shonda Rhimes did differently from all the others was cast people who looked more like the show's potential audience—that is, the world.

A beautiful interracial leading couple, a Black queen of England, a mixed-race seamstress, and other BIPOC* actors cast as high society broke the mold for an otherwise typical Regency melodrama. And it worked. The show ranked number one not just in America, but overall in eighty-three separate countries, including the UK, Brazil, France, South Africa, Singapore, India, and Thailand. Netflix knew this was coming (although admittedly viewership stats exceeded even their own bullish projections). Bela Bajaria, head of global TV for the platform, told *Vanity Fair* that the viewership trends of their local-language originals across Europe, the Middle East, Africa, India, Asia, and Latin America "foreshadowed how something like *Bridgerton* might pop all over the world."[2] They even hired Shonda Rhimes away from ABC in the first place because of how the winning formula of diverse casting, nuanced characters, and female-fronted storylines delivered mega-hits there (*Grey's Anatomy*, *Scandal*).

Cultural institutions can find that same sort of success. Historically, however, arts organizations, especially legacy institutions who almost always receive the lion's share of public and private funding, are generally made by White people for White people—at the exclusion of others who don't match that profile.† If that sounds harsh, yeah, but also, the facts don't lie. The National Endowment for the Arts reports that 76 to 83 percent of traditional arts audiences identify as White despite America becoming more diverse as a nation.[3]

---

* Labels for racial and ethnic groups are imperfect and ever-changing. Here I use BIPOC (Black, Indigenous, people of color) to be more specific than the umbrella term "people of color."

† A note to say I'm capitalizing all races, ethnicities, and population groups, as I've learned not doing so, specifically not uppercasing "White," frames Whiteness as the standard.

DEMOGRAPHIC BREAKDOWN:

US POPULATION VS. ARTS AUDIENCES

Race/Ethnicity	White	Hispanic	African American	Asian + Other
US Population (2020 Census)[4]	60.1%	18.2%	12.2%	9.5%
Classical Music	83.2%	5.5%	5.1%	6.2%
Theater (Non-Musical Plays)	80.7%	6.4%	8.5%	4.4%
Opera	78.0%	7.8%	6.2%	8.0%
Ballet	79.4%	9.2%	6.9%	4.5%
Places Visited for Design or Historic Value	78.6%	8.5%	6.2%	6.6%
Art Museums or Galleries	76.0%	10.1%	6.50%	7.4%

Source: NEA Survey of Public Participation in the Arts. Note: The data for "Other" are aggregated by the NEA, and contains populations including Asian, Pacific Islander, Native American, and any other race or ethnicity that doesn't fall in the categories for Hispanic, African American, or White.

The artists creating the art we produce also underrepresent the breadth of outstanding talent available. According to the Actors' Equity Association, the labor union representing American actors and stage managers in the theater, the racial and ethnic breakdown of all acting and stage management contracts comes in at 64 percent White, 10 percent Black or African American, 3.6 percent Latino or Hispanic, and 3 percent Asian (and the balance either chose "other" or declined to identify their ethnicity).[5] Of traditional visual art institutions, 85 percent of the works in the collections of all major US museums were created by White artists, and 87 percent were made by men.[6]

The ten most frequently performed operas are by dead White Europeans, and the vast majority of singers cast in leading roles are White—a figure all too obvious when we see repeated occurrences of blackface and yellowface still happening today.[7] The Metropolitan Opera, our nation's largest performing arts organization, didn't produce a single opera by a Black composer until 2021 with Terence Blanchard's *Fire Shut Up in My Bones*—which was a massive hit. Then there's ballet. We'll talk more about Misty Copeland being *allowed* to break through in the next chapter, but the lack of representation has long been widely reported.[8] And the League of American Orchestras found that only 2 or 3 percent of professional orchestral musicians are Black or Latinx, respectively, while until 2022, only 4.5 percent of all symphonic repertoire performed was composed by a person of color or a woman.[9] This is shifting for the better in real time, but there's still a long way to go toward full representation.

To be clear, this is not a pipeline problem. There are far more exceptional, truly talented artists out there—exceedingly worthy of the biggest stages and exhibits—than are being given opportunity. Just as America is a country built on systemic injustice, sexism, and racism, this is also true for the history of Western art. There is absolutely a *moral* case for diversity, equity, and inclusion—dismantling and rewriting the patterns of structural racism is the right thing to do, and the next few chapters talk more about some steps we can take as we look internally at our institutions. But with a whopping eight out of ten of our patrons identifying as White, expanding the arts to a wider, more diverse audience is not just a moral imperative. There's also money on the table.[10] That's why I am also a fan of the *business* case for diversity. This chapter therefore looks at the external-facing aspects of this work, especially the results we can achieve.

THE BUSINESS CASE FOR DIVERSITY

Diverse teams make better decisions, produce higher financial returns, vet more options as they bring more and varied perspectives to the table, and, according to *Harvard Business Review*, are just downright smarter.[11]

In the UK, the government is increasingly requiring that grant recipients meet diversity standards in order to continue receiving public funds.[12] Foundations in the US are looking at this too, now often requiring potential recipients to demonstrate EDI statements and action plans before they even qualify to apply for funding. Poor diversity costs more than just grant money, though: a 2021 McKinsey study reported that lack of Black representation is costing Hollywood $10 billion every year.[13] Regardless of casting decisions or genre, films with two or more Black people in creative roles such as producer, director, and writer make 10 percent more at the box office for every marketing dollar spent, compared to films with only one or no Black creative professionals.[14]

A big reason for this is audience demand. When the artists employed reflect the world around us, the world shows up and buys a ticket, whether that's at the multiplex box office, on the TV screen at home, or at our own venues. We don't have to be in the movie business to know that our audiences often don't look like the communities in which we reside—but the chart on page 80 shows the ticket sales potential if our patron demographics did expand to match our communities' demographics.

The first row shows NEA data for the breakdown of audience demographics for a hypothetical city's art museum. The second and third rows show the actual demographic breakdown per the US Census for that given market or city, first as a percentage, then actual population, respectively. The fourth row shows the current actual audiences served, in this case by a regional organization that sees 15,000 visitors a year. The final two rows do a little math: first the current conversion rate (e.g., if 11,400 White attendees are coming, out of a total White population of 366,840, that's about a 3 percent conversion rate). And the final row shows what would happen if that conversion rate held true for the second-largest ethnicity as well (e.g., in this city, if the population of "Asian + Other" also converted around 3 percent). In other words, how would attendance change if the organization were converting the second-largest demographic population at the same rate as the White population? In this example, if the museum diversified its audience and brought in more Asian Americans and other groups at near the rate that we're bringing in White audience members, its attendance *would increase by 7,757 attendees* each year.

REPRESENTATION

The Business Case—Art Museum in City A*[15]

	White	Hispanic	Black	Asian + Other	Total
Audience Breakdown (Art Museum)	76%	10.1%	6.5%	7.4%	
City Demographic Breakdown (Actual US Major Market)	45%	15%	5%	35%	
City Population (Actual)	366,840	122,280	40,760	285,320	815,201
Audiences Served Annually (Regional Org)	11,400	1,515	975	1,110	**15,000**
Conversion Rate (% of Population Attending)	3.1%	1.2%	2.4%	0.4%	
Audience if Reflective (i.e., If 2nd-Largest Demo Converted at Same Rate)	11,400	1,515	975	8,867	**22,757**

Increase in tickets sold: 7,757

To see what increasing the diversity of your audience could mean for your specific organization, swap out the NEA audience breakdown for your actual

---

* Note on the demographic data: This breakdown of arts patronage demographics comes from the National Endowment for the Arts, which reported Asians and "other" ethnicities together as one number, used here. This rollup is not meant to further diminish or erase underrepresented groups, but instead reflect that further breakdown of the data was not available. Values have been rounded to the nearest tenth of a percentage.

audience breakdown. Then plug in the demographics for your city, and use your own annual visitation/admissions/tickets sold to calculate your current conversion rates. From there, you can extrapolate what it would look like if you converted other demographics at the same rate as your dominant (usually White) audiences.

Here's a second example with a different artistic discipline in a different city. If this midsize opera company's patron base reflected the demographics of their city, they'd sell another twenty thousand tickets a year.

REPRESENTATION

The Business Case—Opera Company in City B[16]

	White	Hispanic	Black	Asian + Other	Total
Audience Breakdown (Opera)	78%	7.8%	6.2%	8%	
City Demographic Breakdown (Actual US Major Market)	53.2%	14.0%	24.3%	8.5%	
City Population (Actual)	366,786	96,523	167,536	58,603	689,447
Audiences Served Annually (Midsize Org)	58,500	5,850	4,650	6,000	**75,000**
Conversion Rate (% of Population Attending)	15.9%	6.0%	2.7%	10.2%	
Audience if Reflective (i.e., If 2nd-Largest Demo Converted at Same Rate)	58,500	5,850	26,721	6,000	**97,071**

Increase in tickets sold: **22,071**

Even if your organization realized just a fraction of these gains, the upside potential of greater representation in your patron base is no joke. And, lest anyone think "they won't come" or "they can't afford it," let me stop you right there. Those comments are a self-fulfilling prophecy at best, and grossly generalizing based on race at worst—to assume different races possess distinct characteristics, abilities, or qualities, like whether they can afford a ticket or like a certain art form, is a dictionary definition of racism, even if unintentional or well meaning. Plus, most organizations have pretty affordable base prices, so truly, economics isn't the biggest barrier keeping people away. What *is* keeping people away, research shows, is our mostly homogenous programming. To be clear, this section does not offer a full and complete solution to the systemic racism in our field. But getting people in the door is a good start. By the way, if you're wondering if City A and City B are real places or made-up examples, City A is my home base of San Francisco, and City B is Nashville, Tennessee.

"Stop Serving Mexican Food to Mexican People"

I used to think the best way to bring in more diverse audiences was through culturally specific programming—the Lunar New Year event or the Black History Month concert or the Día de los Muertos celebration. But that approach oversimplifies the representation solution to one-off programming, which limits our organizations' potential. While there's nothing inherently wrong with those programs (when thoughtfully and authentically curated), and they do sell, they have the same retention issue we've been talking about since chapter one. There's no incentive for the audience to come back.

There's more to building an audience reflective of the community than one-and-done programming or simply casting more diverse performers. Building a more reflective audience requires intersectionality—a true blend of people and cultures and backgrounds. Not in the sense of erasing unique identity, but the kind of blend that we see in things like food.

"Think about L.A.'s Grand Central Market," said Salvador Acevedo, managing partner at Scansion, gesturing to the food hall just steps away from where we were speaking. "There you see Korean people eating Ecuadorian pupusas,

Mexican multigenerational families eating sticky rice, and Latino and Black construction workers eating chow mein—even Sushirrito is a blending of cultures in the food itself."[17]

I had always sort of laughed at the kitschiness of Sushirrito (if you're new to this food, no worries; they make handheld sushi burritos) rather than stopping to realize that it's a popular merging of two different cultures. And a very delicious one. But the fusion is significant: Sushirrito shows that people regularly love things that are not only not solely "their" culture, and that we enjoy and appreciate the mixture of cultures, flavors, health, convenience—you name it.

Those humans-have-multifaceted-taste findings hold true for music, too, as the pop world has had figured out for a while now. Acevedo pointed next to "Despacito," specifically the remix performed by two Puerto Rican singers, Luis Fonsi and Daddy Yankee, and one Canadian named Justin Bieber. A song that, while admittedly at the top of the charts upon its release in 2017, felt like music about as far possible from the genre I usually serve. But, as Salvador reminded me, regardless of what I think of the song, or Justin Bieber, or pop music, "Despacito" was not only the most-streamed song in the US *ever* at the time—it was just as popular in several other countries as well. It was a worldwide phenomenon, one that took over the record for most-streamed song from another globally known intersection of cultures: "Gangnam Style" by Psy. Fast-forward to the song that took the throne from "Despacito," and we get "Old Town Road," the rap-meets-country mega-hit by Lil Nas X and Billy Ray Cyrus that went on to be the first song in history to reach fifteen times platinum status (as of 2023).[18]

Whether genre-bending hits, food, or *Bridgerton*, Acevedo challenged me to think about how the intersection of cultures in art is proving time and again it can appeal to a greater share of the population than one dominant culture can alone.

Of course, sometimes people want to take pride in their culture, explained Acevedo, who also helped a major institution develop a fantastic Día de los Muertos program. But often all we're serving is "Mexican food for Mexican people," he said. Just as we're missing out on the vast richness of our world when we don't taste other food, we're also missing out on the vast richness of our communities when we silo our programming. We can weave other cultures, races, and ethnicities not just into but throughout what we do, without appropriation.* And appropriation, to Acevedo, is unacknowledged and blatant stealing of cultural ideas and elements. That's different from appreciating other cultures. As he said, "We are usually misguided when we say 'cultural appropriation.' Those words really mean 'exploitation,' 'oppression,' 'taking advantage of people with less access and privilege.'" He pushes back on the idea that culture can belong to someone. "My view is that no one can claim, 'I am the depository of the culture.' That's why creating relationships and partnerships is the best way to bring visibility and a place at the table for people who traditionally have not had that access. And we should always be mindful of power dynamics and approach every partnership with cultural humility."

To Acevedo, that's the beauty of weaving together cultures—it lets us make relationships and partnerships, which help us to speak authentically to multiple points of view, learn, and create something appreciative rather than appropriative. A lot of people, as he relayed, "want intercultural experiences. [They] want to learn new things. [They] want to uncover new connections through the arts." In all, "the best tool for programming is not based on demographics; it's based on the experiences people are looking for."

Scansion's research backs this up. They've found that organizations often try to attract the Latinx demographic by appealing to one's ethnic identity, but they note this approach is limited because our identities comprise far more than our ethnicity. For example, Acevedo says he's also a dad, a husband, and a professional researcher.[19] Organizations are missing out on so much of the potential audience because they—we—are missing out on so many pieces of audience members' identities. All this is to say, culturally specific programming alone is not enough to build a lasting, more diverse audience.

This rest of this chapter is about how we can change what the audience sees so they better see themselves. (Then, in the next chapter, we'll look inward at who is

---

* I am not an expert on this topic. I know cultural appropriation is sensitive, that talking about it requires treading difficult waters, and that these words have nuance and complexity—but I believe I have a responsibility to honor this topic as best I know how rather than not include it at all.

making the decisions that affect those areas.) From the artists onstage and on the walls, to the front-of-house staff we employ (e.g., ushers, docents, food and beverage servers, coat check attendants, audio guide assistants, and anyone else patrons interact with), to the language we use in our public-facing materials, and how the website supports this work, we need to examine each aspect to make sure we're better reflecting our communities.

Diversify the Artists

Diversifying artists means we are enriching and better serving the artistic mission by representing the full spectrum of top talent available. To be crystal clear, in no way does this jeopardize any kind of artistic quality. As Afa Dworkin, president of Sphinx Organization, a nonprofit social justice organization supporting diversity in the arts, says, "This is not a pipeline problem. The talent is there." Diversification across multiple cultures, races, ethnicities, and genders enhances all our offerings, in turn allowing them to appeal to a broader, more representative audience consistently, not just at one-off events. (And for visual arts organizations, maybe the question is not so much around pipeline, but more examining—and changing—why is art "primitive" or "folk art" when it's by Indigenous or Black or Brown people, but elevated to "fine art" when it's European?) Whether in our galleries or onstage or in the pit or in the outdoor sculpture garden, the blending of artists from various backgrounds can happen in intentional, thought-provoking ways.

In this work, it helps to develop a policy that sets targets for composers performed, visual artists displayed, actors contracted, and the like. Rather than thinking of setting quotas as bad or poor form somehow (I know I used to), Dworkin emphasizes that if we don't set goals in this area, we simply will not diversify. It's just not going to happen. Nothing will really change. And she's beyond right. I set targets for so many other things because what gets measured gets managed. Targets hold us accountable. This metric is vital in pursuit of more fully serving our communities, so we ought to track it like any other kind of important goal. One ensemble I worked with made the following commitments, which you can use to brainstorm the types of objectives to measure and track each year at your organization:

- **Repertoire.** We commit that 80 percent of programming honors core masterworks repertoire of the European tradition and 20 percent focuses on underrepresented talented constituencies. For every fifteen programming slots, we commit to program at least one female composer, at least one composer of color, and at least one living composer.

    We acknowledge that often, but not always, a female composer or composer of color will also be living. In these circumstances, we still commit to filling all three slots, meaning an additional living, female, or POC composer will be programmed on the season.

- **Guest artists.** For every guest artist opportunity (i.e., soloists performing, narrators for pieces with spoken word, conductors, stage directors, etc.), consider 50 percent women and persons of color for every solo opportunity. For every White man offered a guest artist appearance with our orchestra, strive to offer a guest-artist invitation to a woman or person of color. And for guest conductors, make every effort to offer the guest conducting role to a woman or person of color for every White man who is made the offer.

    [As anyone who has programmed a season knows, there are a lot of moving pieces, like who's available when, which repertoire the artist is performing, and who is traveling in your region when you need them. Having this list ended up really helping with the jigsaw puzzle of filling all the guest artist slots in the season.]

- **Composer-in-residence.** Move the application process to an anonymous review, intentionally emulating blind auditions. Applicants will submit resumes, scores, and work samples with all identifying information redacted. The staff member administering logistics for the program will assign numbers in place of names for the review panel. In addition to typical marketing efforts for this program, special recruitment will focus on women and people of color. This may be achieved through digital ads targeting these groups or any other such method specifically inviting minority applicants.

APPLICATION BOX

Concept: Diversifying the repertoire

Organization: Gleeson Library at the University of San Francisco

"We're an academic library. We're about old books and dusty old stuff," mused Shawn P. Calhoun, dean of the library at the University of San Francisco. "We didn't have a Stephen King book until recently." Well, it turns out Stephen King represented not a path to academic demise, but a gateway for the library to become the heart of campus as they doubled down on a multicultural, multigenre approach to everything in the building.

Carrying a few pop-culture titles was just the beginning for the USF Library, which is home to 1.5 million books. Calhoun described how they then opened the Black Student Union Resource Center, where they didn't just name a room or put some posters on the wall, but bought a whole new collection of books and housed Union documents like a 1969 list of demands to the university administration.

This diversification strategy went beyond books. Calhoun's team established a food bank in the library; now any student or faculty who is food insecure can come and get food when needed. They followed this by instituting a Seed Library in partnership with the school's Urban Agriculture program to offer seeds, so anyone in the university community could grow their own food. The connections between people, the food we eat, the land where it grows, and the labor that goes into it is now integrated into the curriculum for Urban Agriculture and Environmental Studies classes.

The library also maintains an art gallery, which then led Calhoun to introduce live music in the library, featuring student chamber-music groups. "Why don't libraries offer music?" he asked me. "We think of people getting shushed. We're turning old tropes about libraries into something positive. We're engaging a changing demographic—it attracts people who maybe wouldn't come otherwise."

Perhaps the most striking thing about all these things isn't the breadth of who the library now regularly attracts, but how these initiatives are featured front and center. None of these items is a side project or one-off event—no one-and-done programming here. Instead, these initiatives are on the library website homepage. The seed garden is on the first floor. The food pantry is in the atrium. All of this is a priority, and it shows.

"There isn't one thing we've done," said Calhoun. "If you double down on one thing, you're going to miss the boat. Librarians are often 85 percent White women; that's reflected in the material chosen. We want people to feel welcome, feel valued, and see themselves."

Brb—I'm headed to the library.

Diversify Front-of-House Staff

There's a group called We See You W.A.T. (White American Theater), a cohort of BIPOC theatremakers, who in 2020 published a resource and testimonial letter in response to civil unrest in our country. In the letter and accompanying demands for change, they talk about the importance of our FOH staff in making more diverse and inclusive audience spaces. Their document shows that we can diversify programming all we want, but before any visitor sees their first piece of art or hears the beginning chord or opening line of the play, they have to enter the building. And according to We See You W.A.T., there's a lot we can do there to ensure those spaces evoke an inviting place of belonging:

- *"Abolish the policing of BIPOC audience members inside of lobbies, rehearsal studios, and other theatre-related spaces."* Let's train our ushers and staff to start every patron interaction from a place of warmth and welcome, not with a purpose to bust anyone who's not adhering to some unspoken rules. This not only matches so much covered in chapter one for all audiences; it also goes a long way toward creating a safe and antiracist environment for BIPOC audiences.
- *"Provide theatre personnel (including ushers, front of house, concessions, etc.) with Anti-Racist, Implicit Bias, Anti-Oppression and Bystander Training."*[20] In my experience, cultural organizations only tend to train their administrative staff with this in mind. That's fine and useful, but our ushers and lobby personnel have far more contact with patrons than any single person in the office.

You may be thinking that your FOH staff is generally not struggling with these issues, or that their training is sufficient, but I'm not so sure. While I was working on this chapter, I was at a major institution's performance, and the ushers were literally pacing up and down the aisle with signs in big block letters that said YOU MUST WEAR A MASK. This was a time when almost every space in this particular city was no longer requiring masks, let alone paying people to patrol for it with signs in hand, so it was striking. To make matters worse, my partner's mask accidentally broke as we were finding our seats (the elastic popped off), and he began flagging down one of these ushers to ask if they had any extras. The usher made eye contact with him, then promptly looked away and wouldn't take his question. It felt rude and unhelpful. Later another sign-wielding usher passed by and snapped at him to fix his still falling-off mask. And it's not so much about the masks themselves (I doubt that, by the time you read this, anywhere is still *requiring* masks), but this vibe of *we're here to bust you, not help you and welcome you* is problematic for your patrons and your organization. And the data show that this type of excessive regulating happens a lot more to people of color.[21]

Incorporate Other Languages

The third way to begin diversifying the audience is to have a presence in other languages prominent in your community. This isn't because those residents don't speak English. In fact, as an example, over three-quarters of Spanish-speaking adults read both English and Spanish, and most bilingual Hispanic workers are more likely to choose conversing in English when given the option.[22] Rather, this is about making a concerted effort to help a group feel invited and seen.

- **Translate digital ads**. It's relatively easy and cheap to take the same ad and update the copy. One organization I worked with doubled its Latinx audience after a simple pilot test running their Facebook ads in Spanish with Hispanic and Latino users within a twenty-mile radius of their venue.
- **Be ready to respond**. The pilot test at the organization above went so well, they continued the practice for a full season. They got pretty good at it, which then resulted in people messaging them on Facebook in Spanish, asking how to buy tickets and other common questions we often field on social media. The organization worked with their translator to have basic

responses on hand, but it was a bit of a shock to the system at first. So be prepared when a few baby steps catapult you forward.

An important note: We learned in our follow-up efforts that, just like the national data, most of these attendees were fluent in English, but they felt an openness toward the organization for attempting to market to them in their native language. Arts and culture research firm Slover Linett discovered this as well. In a project with Chicago's Morton Arboretum, where they conducted interviews with bilingual Spanish/English speakers, led by a bilingual research manager, they found the participants consistently chose to proceed in English, but also that offering the option was "important to establishing a comfortable environment."[23]

Update the Website

Last, to begin diversifying the audience, update the website to support this work. When someone hears about repertoire or artists that look like them and googles it, or clicks on that ad in their native language, they land on the website.

- **Feature your efforts prominently**. For the USF Library, that meant including information about their initiatives on the homepage. And the advice from the first chapter applies here: use photos of artists and audiences that reflect the community. People want to see themselves in any brand or experience they patronize.

- **Add multi-language toggles**. If our preceding tips have been at the 101 level, this one might be for when you're ready to graduate to 201. I know it takes a lot of time and effort to translate full web pages (Google Translate gets you only so far, and at some point, the human element is necessary for a truly user-friendly translation). But it's work that's worth it, and you can start small. Try translating just the top-visited pages on the site, like the homepage and the purchase path, or even just the landing page for the digital ad. If you see results (visitor demographic breakdown is easily trackable in Google Analytics), you can then tackle some other key pages the next go-round.

At the organization that experimented with multilingual digital ads, Spanish-speaker traffic to the website grew by 34 percent during that same period. And ticket sales to Latinx audiences increased by 50 percent, meaning that those households had a higher conversion rate disproportionate to the increase in website traffic.

The LatinXperience research study gives a reason for this increase in Hispanic and Latinx participation: "Latinos reported that being exposed to the arts is an important part of being 'educated' and a 'well-rounded' person," the paper summarized, going on to say that many feel the arts are an integral part of society, about which they feel an obligation to be informed.[24] That sounds like just about every one of our ideal audience members, no matter their background, and it gives me hope that our core product, with these updates, can indeed appeal to all kinds of people.

Think of how much more effective this engine will be when people in our communities click on the ad in their native tongue or because they see people who look like them, then are directed to a webpage in that same language, and end up coming to a performance or exhibit where a share of the artists look like them, too. Oh, and then at the venue, they would be greeted by warm and welcoming personnel, spot a line or two in the program book in their language, and maybe hear some welcome remarks from the stage in that language as well. It's not about Mexican food for Mexican people—it's about inviting more people in to witness the broad appeal that our art can and does have. When we start making these intentional choices, we will start to see a change in our audience as well.

FINAL FOOD FOR THOUGHT (YES, THAT IS AN INTENTIONAL PUN)

"Food, like language, music, and culture, is constantly evolving," said Peter Yen, founder of none other than Sushirrito. "To deem something as merely traditional is to shortchange continuous human creativity and innovation."[25]

If you've read this far, you're now at the halfway point of this book. Combine everything here on representation with the preceding chapters on user experience, audience retention, digital strategy, and vertical integration, and now we are starting to spin up a flywheel with some real momentum. We're welcoming more people, we're offering more of them a thumb-stopping digital taste of what we provide, they're feeling more seen and like they belong—*and* we're feeding a pipeline to keep them coming back again and again, and eventually to donate. Plus, we have some additional revenue streams to help.

Again, the steps in this chapter are not an exhaustive list of things you can do. All of this, though, is about knowing that our organizations are more whole when we serve a larger swath of our community, and that we'll be making more money when that happens, which means we'll be better executing and better funding our mission. As promised, the next chapter examines who on staff is making these decisions.

6.

Heidi vs. Howard

Hire Fairly, Compensate Radically

Once upon a time, there was an Amazon hiring manager who weeded out engineering candidates with college degrees from all-female schools. This asinine decision maker cared less about specific job skills such as coding or debugging, and more about highly ranked male engineering candidates who said they "delivered results" without much proof as to what those results were. Unqualified applicants advanced regularly because of this, at the expense of prematurely eliminated qualified women. Excuse me while I go barf.

Eventually, this egregious behavior was identified and exposed. It turns out this grossly biased employee wasn't a human; it was a machine. The tech giant had built an artificial intelligence tool to evaluate resumes, and the software developers who created the program taught it to observe patterns in previously submitted resumes that actually advanced through the hiring process over the prior ten years. The problem was the machine-learning software reflected what was already there in the samples it was fed.[1]

Hiring, whether in big tech or any other industry, is so often fraught with unintentional bias and inequity that we don't always see it until a machine spits out a hundred homogenous resumes at once.

This chapter is about how to uncover some of that bias and inequity in how we humans hire at cultural organizations, both for staff and artists. Maybe you've heard of the Heidi vs. Howard study after which this chapter is named. In the infamous experiment, reviewers in two groups were given identical resumes to evaluate, except for one difference: the name at the top. Heidi and Howard were rated equally competent—after all, their resumes were identical—but Heidi was consistently labeled "too assertive," "not likable," "self-involved," and overall not a good fit for the job. All because of a typically female name on a sheet of paper.

We may not have a bad AI machine in the arts to make it so painfully obvious, but we do have people who have shed light on the issue. "In twenty years, I've never been hired by a Black person," GRAMMY award–winning bass Morris Robinson, who has sung at the world's leading opera houses, told the *New York Times*. "I've never been directed by a Black person; I've never had a Black C.E.O. of a company; I've never had a Black president of the board; I've never had a Black conductor. I don't even have Black stage managers. None, not ever, for twenty years."[2] Of course, most people don't want to be biased—and I'd bet everyone reading this right now actively wants to be *un*biased. But if we don't intentionally examine the prevailing practices that led to the experiences that Robinson described, those approaches and decisions will continue—along with the same results. And those current results include nearly forty obstacles that Black professionals in entertainment regularly encounter—"dozens of hidden barriers and other pain points reinforc[ing] the racial status quo in the industry."[3]

Our institutions benefit from reducing such barriers and pain points for professional staff, artists, and frontline employees. This chapter is about implementing research-based best practices on how to identify superstar talent across the full talent spectrum. Because without changes to our hiring practices, we won't see changes in the people we employ. And without changes in who we employ, we won't see substantive change in the art we produce, the experience we're trying to create surrounding that art, or the audiences we serve.

We'll look at equitable best practices for hiring staff, followed by tips on hiring artists and working with collective bargaining agreements (i.e., unions). Last, we'll examine compensation in the arts. Unlike Amazon's hiring machine, the arts' decisions are made by humans who have the power to choose better—all to attract and retain the most effective talent possible.

MAKE A LIST AND CHECK IT TWICE: HIRING STAFF

Most traditional cultural institutions have staffs who are fairly homogenous, largely White, and male dominated in senior leadership roles. OPERA America reports that while women hold more administrative roles than men overall, they're not being advanced into *senior* leadership and only "one-fifth of opera administrators identify as BIPOC, as compared to two-fifths of the U.S. population."[4] The Mellon Foundation found that in curatorial roles at museums, management positions are about 15 percentage points more male than nonmanagement roles, curatorial staff with no direct reports are significantly more female than any other gender identity, and the vast majority of staff (at all levels) is White.[5] At orchestras, about equal numbers of men and women hold CEO roles; however, when you break it down by budget size, the smaller the budget, the more likely the organization is run by a woman. Among the very largest orchestras, only two have CEOs of color—and a disturbing zero have female CEOs of color.[6]

This unbalanced top level exists despite women accounting for 73 percent of the entire nonprofit labor force and people of color accounting for 18 percent of staff and 14 percent of board members across the sector.[7] The good news is that traditionally underrepresented leadership talent is here. It's just that, long before that talent reaches the C-suite, the disparity starts. Beginning with entry-level roles, women and minorities are not being promoted at the same rates as White men. So, when it's time to hire for more senior positions, there aren't as many experienced diverse options, which perpetuates the problem.[8]

Our plight, though, is solvable, with recommendations that come from multiple sources across the nonprofit and for-profit sectors alike. While these steps and best practices are not a comprehensive list of every single thing we should be doing in our hiring (entire books cover this subject alone), this content is meant to be a solid starting guide of the top takeaways I've gleaned. And you, like a lot of organizations, probably already do some of these things—so you're likely well on your way. I hope you decide to do them all.

New Best Practices on Job Descriptions

Whenever a role opens, instead of immediately digging up the old job description and seeing what needs to be tweaked to get it posted right away, do this first: make a list of qualifications you need. What skills and abilities are necessary to do the job well? Make a checklist of those skills and abilities; you will come back to it again and again. If you want, you can further break your list into nonnegotiables versus preferences (nice to haves). For example, if the new hire will

- **oversee a budget**, they need to know how to make highly accurate budget forecasts (not just have "budget experience");
- **hold an operations role**, they need to know how to negotiate an artist contract (not just have "previously worked with contracts and artist managers"); or
- **occupy a major gifts fundraising role**, they need to be able to solicit and secure a gift (not just have been assigned a portfolio; they must actually have delivered donations).

The key is to list literally and specifically what this person needs to be able to do. One time, someone on my team was developing the job description for an entry-level candidate and going through this process. Their list said "proficient with Microsoft Office" (we've all seen this before on job postings, right?), so I probed them to be more specific. "What do you actually need them to do?" I asked.

"They need to be able to do mail merge in Word so they can print out donor tax receipts for donations that come in each week," replied the team member who would be supervising this role.

"Okay, then say that. We don't need someone good at PowerPoint; we need *that*."

Literal and specific. Don't merely say "strong communication skills" if you need them to make presentations to the board. Don't only say "excellent writing skills" if you need them to create quippy social media posts. Describe the elements of the job you're talking about.

Then use that list to flow into the job description. Keep the intro paragraph or two at the top, make it sing, and then do the following:

- **Check for and remove unnecessary standards.** Is seven years of experience in a supervisory role actually necessary? Doing something for a while doesn't prove anyone is good at that thing. It just proves they've done it before. Do they really need a master's degree to be able to do X? (What job in the arts absolutely requires a master's degree? I've worked with great people with and without those credentials and not-so-great people with and without them, too.) In my experience, the qualifications and skills needed, when clearly listed and articulated, separate the people who can do the job from those who can't (and later in this chapter, we're going to generate interview questions that make sure we can spot the difference).

- **Remove gendered or appropriative language (e.g., "rock star" or "ninja").** I used to think I was very clever saying things in job descriptions like, "We're looking for a rock star copy writer" or "a ninja data analyst," but then I learned these words are gendered for some people, meaning, according to linguists, they skew male.[9] This subconsciously signals to the reader that the job is meant for men (and "ninja" is additionally troublesome from an appropriation standpoint). This is true even if words like that are not problematic for me *personally*. Now I look for *superstars* all the way; problem solved.

- **Include the salary range.** This does three things: First, it eliminates people who don't want that salary. It wastes everyone's time to go down the path if the expectations are a mismatch (and if you're thinking you want to woo them first and then convince them to take the job later with a salary you're embarrassed by or think isn't very competitive, just don't).

  Second, publishing the salary range prevents us from lowballing. I've been there, thinking I might be able to shave a few thousand dollars from the offer, which would go really far in helping with the budget. Then I learned the data show this happens more often to underrepresented groups, so let the range be the range, period.[10]

  Third, having a range actually helps when making the offer. When interviewing (which we'll talk about how to do next) for the specific skills and qualifications listed in step one, it becomes clear in the process to both the hiring manager and the candidate where they have chops and where they don't. Maybe they're great and absolutely the right person, but you know they'll need a little more training or mentoring in one particular area. You can say that when making the offer: "We're going to focus on this area as you ramp up, and that's why we're coming in at the middle or lower end of the range." Or maybe they're amazing in every way, and you get to come in at the very top of the range. You can tell them that, too: "You are the one who has it all, and we're so glad to make this offer at the very top of the range for this position." How great is it as a candidate to hear that?!

- **Be transparent.** A great example of this is from OF/BY/FOR ALL, a nonprofit that helps fellow cultural nonprofits make inclusive and equitable action plans. A few years ago, founder Nina Simon decided to step down, and the CEO job description was the most transparent I've ever seen. It talked openly about the CEO transition (mentioning reasons both personal and based in social justice), included the salary range, linked to the employee handbook (it may be dry, but wow, you can learn a lot about what an org prioritizes by their handbook), and even gave specific questions they wanted candidates to answer in their materials so there was no guessing game for the applicants trying to figure out what to include or highlight in their past experience.

  And they nailed the work of including literal and specific criteria. Instead of "strong communications skills," they said, "Clear, powerful, and persuasive communication skills, both written and oral. You can write a compelling grant proposal, give an inspiring keynote address, and lead an interactive workshop." Everything about the job description was crystal clear in terms of what they wanted and needed from the candidates, and what the organization was all about in return.

- **Don't just say you're an "equal opportunity employer."** It's another one we've all seen tons of times, but multiple studies have revealed we can update that statement to attract more candidates. One experiment found saying "equal opportunity employer" actually resulted in fewer applications from minority job seekers than saying nothing at all.[11] Another discovered that when organizations called themselves an "inclusive employer" instead of an "equal opportunity employer," more people applied. Their original hypothesis was that the language would entice greater numbers of women and minorities, which proved true, but it turns out the language brought in more of everyone, no matter their background or identity.[12]

And speaking of inclusivity and attracting more applicants, be sure to also list benefits like remote or flexible work options. LinkedIn found that job listings that promote remote work see 2.5 times the number of applicants.[13]

- **Have some personality in the description**. Clinical and sterile is not fun, not interesting, and not the most effective at attracting candidates. This is our chance as employers to persuade and entice, especially in a crowded market. Why is this organization different from other cultural orgs? We want people to read it and think, "Wow, I gotta apply for this. This company is going somewhere." Also, it helps when reviewing applications—it's so clear when someone has actually read the description and is responding to that in their cover letter. It's harder to suss that out when a pedestrian posting returns uninspiring applications.

Again, most organizations are doing some of these things. Yet *all* of them matter—this isn't a drive-thru menu where you just order your favorites. This matters in recruiting good people fairly and equitably, and in helping ourselves as employers have a robust candidate pool.

New Best Practices on Reviewing Resumes

Now the job description is up, and it's so compelling that applications are pouring in. And then it's time to start appraisal. When reviewing resumes, let's start with what *not* to look for:

- **Which organizations they previously worked for.** Working at a big-name or well-known institution doesn't mean the candidate is any good at the job. It just means they worked at that place. The biggest cultural organizations are facing all the same challenges as everyone else (it's the whole reason this book exists in the first place), so working at that brand-name company isn't a guarantee that a person is necessarily any better for the job. In fact, in some cases I've found it means they're less well suited for a more flexible and forward-thinking position. Trust me, it comes out in the interview questions if they can hack it, no matter the previous employer.

- **If they have a degree in music, theater, dance, art, horticulture, etc.** A degree in your specific artistic discipline really doesn't tell us that much, because these are administrative jobs we're talking about here, not artistic work. Look for evidence of the skills you're seeking, and again, rely on the interview questions to elicit if they truly have the chops.

- **If they've held that exact role before.** At this point, you know what I'm going to say: just because they've had that title before doesn't ensure they're good at the job. I can't tell you how many board members and search consultants at small and mid-size organizations ask me to recommend candidates who have prior executive director experience, for example. Yet there are tons of people who are eager and qualified—they can raise money, develop relationships with key constituents, lead a team, and on and on—well beyond candidates who have happened to hold the title before. I see this in all levels of seniority. It's gatekeeping (even if unintentional), and we miss out on incredibly skilled candidates because of it.

- **Their name.** We infer so much from someone's name whether we want to or not. So much so, this chapter is called "Heidi vs. Howard." For now, I try not to pay much attention to the top of the page (where the resume and cover letter usually have the candidate's name) when I'm first going through the application stack (whether physical or electronic). More and more companies are adopting software that can strip out the names for you, so that's an option, too.

So, while you're not looking for any of *those* things on your first pass through the resume, try instead, to look for *these*:

- **A polished application.** Don't get too fussy with the layout or design, but if it's nicely organized and easy to read, it gets a mental checkmark.

- **Quantifiable impact.** This is a big one. If this whole process is about who has the needed skills and who doesn't, this is a big indicator—*have they* *delivered results?* It's not sufficient to have "overseen this" or been "responsi-ble for that." Instead, ask for the deliverables. (Note for candidates: Struc-ture your resumes to highlight the deliverables—things like "increased [something you did] by X percent," or "managed portfolio of Y donors/artists, which included [all the things you actually did] and resulted in [increased gifts or higher renewal rates or something else great]"—and it'll help you shine, no matter if the reviewer on the other end is consciously looking for this impact or not.)

- **Reasonable employment history timeline.** To be clear, employment gaps should be okay for raising a family, or caregiving for a relative, or taking a self-induced sabbatical (lucky duck if you've done that), or some other this-is-life type event. It's when the gaps aren't clear, or are way too frequent, or every previous role lasted only a few months that maybe we have cause to raise an eyebrow. The operative word is "reasonable," which is hard to quantify, so show some grace and understanding and give peo-ple the benefit of the doubt here.

- **Minimum qualifications.** This is the most important one, and where that original list of skills comes back. Pull up that checklist and see who's got the goods and who doesn't. If you have a wealth of candidates, make a benchmark: only people who have at least eight out of eleven of the skills get advanced, for instance (or some other number that thins the candidate pool to your desired first-round size).

Last, once you've whittled that stack down to what you think is your first-round pool, go back and look at diversity indicators. If there is any category with only a single person who is "other" in some way (e.g., one woman when the rest are men, or one person of color when the rest are White), go back to the stack and add at least one more person who was on the bubble and fits the category you're lacking. To have only one person with a certain identifying characteristic is not just the definition of tokenism; it also measurably cuts the odds of that person advancing through the hiring process. In fact, one researcher found any woman or minority who is an "only" in candidate pools has statistically *no chance* of get-ting the job. If there's at least one other similar person (multiple women, multiple Black women, multiple Latinx people) in any interview round, the likelihood of one of them advancing all the way improves considerably, because mentally the norm has shifted.[14]

We See You W.A.T. (White American Theater), the collective of theatremakers mentioned in the last chapter, says to be mindful that grouping or replacing BIPOC candidates with LGBTQ+ candidates and White women candidates is not enough. They put it this way: "While we recognize their struggle, we are not interchangeable."[15]

One more point on this. People sometimes ask me how they're supposed to know if someone comes from an underrepresented group. The truth is, we don't always know. Here's what you do have available to you, though: the ability to do some outreach. Invite people to apply who meet the criteria and also match the representation you're seeking. There's no shame in openly wanting various identities and lived experiences at the table; these are assets folks bring. Honestly, I don't know all the answers here, and I know I've made mistakes and will continue to make them. But I also know it's on us as employers to be intentional, to make our best effort to get that first-round group as representative and diverse as possible, otherwise nothing changes in our candidate pools and ultimately in our staff.

New Best Practices on Interviewing

Laszlo Bock, former head of people at Google, writes in his book, *Work Rules!*, that mounds of data show most interviewers make decisions about a candidate within the first few minutes of the meeting, and are almost always subconsciously drawn to people similar to themselves. He says we then spend the rest of the time confirming that bias with mostly "worthless" interview techniques. So if we've done all this work so far, what do we do to make sure the interview process itself is helpful and worthwhile?

- **Write questions that directly address the needed qualifications.** Here we are with that skills list again, and now it's finally time to write a question directly corresponding to each needed qualification. There are two main types of recommended questions: behavioral ("Tell me about a time when . . .") and situational/hypothetical ("What would you do if . . .").

Behavioral questions (*Tell me about a time when you had to make a budget forecast. What went into that process and how did you make your projections?*) are best to use as much as you can, because hands down, the research shows past behavior is the best predictor of future behavior.

Organizational psychologists call this *predictive validity*. Go right back to the initial skills list again and map every one of those criteria onto a behavioral question if you can. However the candidate approached the skill/function/requirement in the past is very likely how they will do it again, and these types of questions strongly elicit whether someone knows what they're talking about or is just blowing smoke.

If you have novel situations you need to introduce, that's the only point when using situational questions is a better option. As an example, one time I was hiring a marketing role where part of the job was to focus on search engine optimization (SEO). The trouble was, this turned out to be very challenging, as most arts organizations are not prioritizing SEO, so the candidate pool was really lacking in this particular skill. While for most everything else I was able to ask behavioral questions, for this one, I had to make it hypothetical: *What would you do to ramp up on this skill to become an SEO expert if you came here?*

I used to overrely on hypothetical or situational questions, but now that I've seen how effective behavioral questions are at revealing whether the candidate has the necessary knowledge and qualifications, I'm never going back.

■ **Use the same process for everyone.** This is called structured interviewing: every candidate gets asked the same questions, in the same order. I usually take all my questions from the preceding step and then divide them up into which ones I want to ask in the first-round phone screen, second round, and final round.

■ **Go back to the qualifications list after every round, especially at the finish line.** By the end of the search process, we often feel so far past that initial list, like we know the candidates so well by that point—and in many ways we do. This is both great and exactly why it's important to go back to that list of criteria. Because it's not about who *feels* like the best fit (hello, bias creeping in); it's about who has the chops to do the work. See how the candidates stack up against the skills you originally articulated after *every* round and before deciding who to advance.

- **Use a committee and don't discuss until the very end.** When bringing people in, usually for a final round of interviews, use a committee—around three to five members who understand the hiring criteria, if possible. Committee members with a variety of backgrounds (e.g., expertise, skills, education, tenure) can improve the quality of discussion and lead to better decision making.[16] And don't confer until after all candidates have come through. Each interviewer should take notes and then share their thoughts all at once in a post-interview discussion where you deliberate on each candidate. (If you're at a smaller organization, see if even one other person can meet with the candidate.)

- **Use a rubric.** I have had to really work on this one myself and develop the discipline for it. If you're like me, don't worry; it can be simple. Take the skills list and add a column where each attribute gets a rating from 1 to 5. Throughout the process, evaluate as you go, and at the end, tally each candidate's scores. It's called "behaviorally anchored rating scales," and decades of research show this is fairer and more equitable.[17] And the practice has been particularly helpful in reminding me how each person stacked up on every single criterion.

I know this might sound like a lot of work. But even if it's a little slower at first, it's actually statistically proven to save time while providing more thorough evaluations.[18] And you can use those questions again and again for future open roles that require some of the same skills.

Finally, there's one last thing *not* to do: don't always trust your gut. Going with an instinct or gut feeling is a fast-track way to open ourselves to unconscious bias. We're all human, and we all form first impressions, almost always based on our own predispositions. And then we often unintentionally move to confirmation bias in the next steps whether we mean to or not (*OMG, I* also *actually like the Patriots!*). Challenge that. Because to end with one more quote from Laszlo Bock, "the alternative is to waste everyone's time with a typical interview that is either highly subjective, or discriminatory, or both."[19]

APPLICATION BOX

Concept: Equitable Hiring Practices

Organization: American Alliance of Museums

For many years, the American Alliance of Museums (AAM), the service organization representing the entire museum field—from art and history museums to science centers and zoos—thought they had a pretty good hiring process. But Director of Human Resources Katherine McNamee kept wondering why their staff of about forty full-time employees was so female and White dominated. *It's a reflection of the field*, some people told her, but McNamee didn't accept that. She chose to further explore their recruitment philosophy and underlying assumptions.

By 2017, AAM's job descriptions focused on skills over credentials—and McNamee is clear that "skills" includes not just technical skills, but what we tend to label as "soft" skills like communication abilities and approaches to managing others. She and AAM used a free trial of Textio software to spot words in job descriptions that may be considered feminine or masculine. They found that words like "collaborates" may be more attractive to female candidates and phrases like "drives results" may appeal more to male candidates, then tried to replace them with more gender-neutral terms. From there, they added salary ranges to their postings, provided a list of topics to include in cover letters, and even went so far as to implement identity-blind screening by asking candidates to omit names, addresses, schools, and graduation dates in their materials.

"For most of my career, I was usually looking for ways to screen people out rather than in," McNamee said. "I was trained to seek out the gaps in employment history, typos, and grammar issues and treat them as red flags even though these criteria alone are rarely the most relevant to the job." The interview process has also shifted to create opportunities for candidates to demonstrate skills, such as work samples or asking for a short presentation in later rounds (another method of behavioral questioning) instead of over-indexing on past employers, former titles, or number of years in the workforce.

Fast-forward to today, and job applicants have reported they've had positive experiences and felt seen during recruitment. Thirty percent of the AAM staff now identifies as BIPOC.

McNamee and AAM didn't stop there. They're still challenging past practices like overly focusing on which candidate needs the least amount of training because they had that exact role before versus who brings transferrable skills from another industry, or not seeking "perfection" or "best fit" and instead reminding themselves that candidates may be qualified in different ways for a position. As McNamee tells her colleagues and team members, "This may be harder or longer at first because it's different, but I'm going to walk you through it."

Last, AAM began tackling compensation and level bands (both of which we'll talk more about later in this chapter). Together, the senior leadership team mapped out what they wanted their compensation program to do for them, which McNamee admits was the first time the discussion was with *all* of leadership together, not just one-on-one conversations. That vulnerable beginning was a unifying springboard, though, from which they established pay ranges targeting the fiftieth percentile of the external labor market. Then they came up with career level definitions, outlining the qualities, characteristics, and traits that you would find at each step of seniority—seven levels total from entry level to senior staff. Each of those level bands now has defined knowledge requirements, complexity of work attached to or expected from it, impact deliverables, benchmarks for ability to communicate with and influence others, relationship management (such as working with a lot of stakeholders or groups that may have different views), financial accountability, and any basic minimum qualifications. Each level band also has a corresponding pay range.

"There is a lot you can do. I've been there when it feels overwhelming," McNamee says. And she encourages all of us to ask, like she did, *What are tiny steps we can take when we don't have a lot of resources?* At AAM, many small changes amounted to big outcomes, a journey we all can emulate.

ASKING FOR A FRIEND: HIRING ARTISTS AND COLLECTIVE BARGAINING AGREEMENTS

In 2015, Misty Copeland became the first African American prima ballerina of a major international company. Despite her undeniable talent, she didn't make history by herself; she was allowed to do so. Similarly, predominantly White decision makers allowed opera singer Morris Robinson, who we heard from earlier, to flourish. No slight to Misty and Morris, but they're not the first talented Black artists in their respective disciplines. Doors were opened for them that historically have not been for people of color. Yet, there is so much additional incredible talent that we might be missing out on because, as Robinson concluded, "We have companies now trying to address an issue that don't have the personnel [who] make decisions that are in my best interest."[20]

All of the preceding hiring steps help us combat this. When we have a more fair and equitable hiring process, we're more likely to land the most qualified management talent across the full breadth of talent available—and in turn, that more diverse, representative management talent will be making decisions at all levels that impact the work onstage and in our venues, making that work more representative as well.

Some of our artist hiring, however, is governed not by staff decision making, but by collective bargaining agreements. And that means we need buy-in to these processes from artists as well as the labor unions who broker their contracts. While I don't know the ins and outs of contracts for the American Guild of Musical Artists (AGMA), the labor union representing singers, chorus members, and dancers, or Actors' Equity Association, I've led multiple collective bargaining negotiations with the American Federation of Musicians (AFM) and the International Alliance of Theatrical Stage Employees (IATSE). I know firsthand how these agreements can be slow to change. This means that evolving our hiring processes for artists can sometimes feel like an uphill battle.

So many books, white papers, and case studies across all kinds of industries and outlets use blind auditions as the banner example of equity. I think we should be so proud of that—in a book taking inspiration from outside the arts, this is one area where everyone else consistently looks to emulate us. And yet, the process is simultaneously flawed: we allow bias to creep in at all kinds of points in the process. Still, we can take pride in how blind auditions have helped achieve greater gender parity while also striving to improve them to achieve greater racial equity.

To understand the ways management and artists can work together to address these issues, a few years ago I went to the source and assembled a round-table of top orchestral musicians from various backgrounds across the country who I knew had deep familiarity with the collective bargaining agreement, as well as with the process of hiring players.* These musicians shared their wisdom, leadership, and suggestions for more equitable artist hiring. My hope is their recommendations are helpful to further discussion for all artist labor agreements, not just those at orchestras:

- **Recruit for auditions**. We regularly invite people to auditions, and yet those invitations largely exclude Black and Latinx people. Diversifying the candidate pool by intentionally recruiting Black and Brown talent is imperative—experienced artists are definitely out there. The group was unwavering on this point.

- **Extend invitations for substitute player lists, too.** Orchestras often invite people to join the substitute list, which frequently becomes a source of players who are then invited to audition for permanent spots. There are enough Black and Latinx artists with years under their belts at good ensembles that are ready to be added to the regular sub list. The same goes for cover singers in opera and understudies in theater and ballet. We can feed the pipeline.

---

* All of the recommendations here came from that discussion with those amazing musicians: Jessica Phillips, clarinetist at the Metropolitan Opera who chaired the Players Committee during the 2014 and 2018 negotiations; Jennifer Arnold, former violist with the Oregon Symphony and later their personnel manager, and then at the time director of artistic planning and orchestral operations at the Richmond Symphony; Kale Cummings, president of Musicians Union Local 6 (representing musicians in labor negotiations in Northern California); Joy Payton-Stevens, cellist with Seattle Symphony 2014–2021 who now works at a global consultancy since receiving her MBA from Columbia University; and Igor Yuzefovich, concertmaster at the BBC Orchestra who previously held the role at the Singapore Symphony and as assistant concertmaster at the Baltimore Symphony.

- **Make the process consistent.** As we do this with staff hiring, we should do this for auditions as well, because the audition process can be remarkably inconsistent. Some of the variance is necessary—who is on the committee understandably changes greatly based on what instrument chair is being filled—but we can still have a consistent process despite each instrument's particular nuance. Even if we listen to the violin audition this week and the trombone audition next month, we can still have an intentional, unified approach.

  Questions that the roundtable raised questions around what matters on the resume include the following: Can we look at indicators of talent besides training at top conservatories only, as fine players also come from other places? Could we start with an audio sample instead of a resume? How many people are being invited for the first round? Who is allowed to bypass the first round? Could we consider doing away with the resume altogether and inviting everyone to audition? The answers to these questions can be wildly subjective and inconsistent, and will change in other artistic disciplines, so work to standardize a set of criteria that works across instruments, or across your organization, as much as possible.

- **Have the screen up all the way through the finals.*** Some orchestras do this, including the largest American performing arts organization, the Metropolitan Opera orchestra. Many ensembles, however, take down the curtain for the final round of auditions.

  Here's the deal: Not one Black or Brown person I've spoken with on this topic, including and beyond this roundtable cohort, thinks blind auditions should go away. Yes, they all think the process can be improved to truly be more fair and equitable, and part of that involves keeping the screen up to the end. An even bigger part is all the steps that come before and after that point.

- **Ask the historically marginalized and underrepresented artists what to do.** Bring those important voices into the conversation at your organization. Not every musician of color will want to do the labor to contribute

---

* For folks in other disciplines who may not be as familiar with blind auditions, the identity of the performer is concealed from the judges by performing behind a curtain or screen.

here (consider if it's possible to pay a fair wage or consulting fee for that labor), but many do, as evidenced by the creation of the musician-led Black Orchestral Network, which is bringing awareness to these topics. Artists are well equipped to lead each other in improving these processes—and I'll take that over a contentious management-versus-labor collective bargaining session any day.

Our conversation also covered some ideas for improving the tenure process (usually a whole other ball of wax after someone wins the audition), and more and more headway is being made. Shortly after this roundtable, the National Alliance for Audition Support, a joint venture of the League of American Orchestras, the Sphinx Organization, and the New World Symphony, released formal recommendations for auditions, much of which matched the guidance from this group. Some of the recommendations don't even require union membership to vote on a change to the collective bargaining agreement (like being more intentional on who to invite to audition or establishing consistent criteria around what you're looking for on the resume)—fantastic news for organizations wanting to advance these improvements quickly.

While diversifying the artists onstage is slow (dancers only exit for retirement or injury, operas and theaters can cast only a few roles at a time, hardly any orchestra chairs open up each year, museum exhibits rotate slowly as do curatorial roles), updating the process by which hiring decisions are made doesn't have to be. So much material is out there about blind auditions as the gold standard for smart, fair, and equitable hiring; we have an opportunity before us to really make that true.

IT STARTS AND ENDS HERE: "HIRING" THE BOARD

One more incredibly important group to discuss regarding our hiring practices is the board. Obviously we don't hire trustees like we hire employees, but consider that (1) they're still doing a job serving the institution even if their labor is volunteered; (2) they're definitely still making decisions to advance the institution; therefore, (3) those decisions also must have more diverse and varied perspectives. Here are a few things to consider as you seek to diversify your board:

- **Recruitment matters.** Being intentional with who we are prospecting, cultivating, and ultimately inviting to join the board absolutely applies here, too. One organization I worked with made a commitment that for every White man they brought on to the board, they would also bring on a woman and a person of color (three people total—more on the strength in numbers in the third bullet point). Our choices for board invitations have enduring effects on the organization.

- **Specific criteria matter here, too.** Susan Howlett, author of *Boards on Fire*, says that when recruiting board members, the more specific we can be, the more likely we are to find that person. It may seem counterintuitive at first, but it works. Think about it: Have you ever been in the boardroom when someone says something like, "Okay, everyone submit three names of potential board members"? Crickets. Instead, per Howlett's advice, when we instead say something to the effect of, "We are looking for a financial expert with audit experience who is also from an underrepresented group as we seek to diversify," chances are so much higher that someone will say, "Oh, you know what? I know someone who fits that." Being specific actually helps our minds sort through the mental Rolodex.

- **Bring on a new class.** I try to avoid onboarding one new board member at a time because, no matter who they are, they are a bit of an outsider when they join, by nature of being new. But when two or three do orientation together, attend their first meeting together, and have their first meeting debrief together afterward (with food or drink in hand, if you ask me), they immediately aren't the only newbie. I've seen greater and faster engagement from board members brought on this way.

- **Remind yourself what matters**. We See You W.A.T. adds in their demands that antiracism statements should be read at all board meetings, first rehearsals, and quarterly staff meetings to continue to hold theaters (or truly any organization) accountable.* While this is obviously not a full solution to systemic racism in our institutions, regularly reading a statement is a relatively easy step to take to reinforce the new milieu you want to create.

---

* To see the full list of demands from We See You W.A.T., visit https://www.weseeyouwat.com/demands.

COMPENSATE RADICALLY

The last piece of the hiring equation is compensation. Patty McCord, who for years was the chief talent officer at Netflix and responsible for establishing HR operations from when the service was a tiny startup mailing DVDs all the way through its monster growth to streaming powerhouse, says to hire fairly and pay "unfairly": make sure you pay everyone well, and your superstars exceptionally well. Laszlo Bock echoes this sentiment, saying that when 90 percent of output comes from the top 10 percent of performers, you need to make sure to pay those high achievers disproportionately well.[21]

Personally, while I don't disagree with this philosophy—great talent is hard to find, I want to keep those high performers on my team, level bands should have salary ranges for this very purpose, and we do pay some of our artists this way—I think we really can't talk about the top of the pay scale until we address the bottom. They say pay unfairly; I say pay *radically*. By that I mean we need to pay our administrative talent living wages. Like, actual competitive salaries, not earnings that only cover the bills when folks have supplemental income.

It shouldn't be radical to pay appropriate living wages, but it is, as this pay-disparity disease is rampant in the arts. A 2021 survey of entry-level arts administrators in Los Angeles County found their annual average salary was $36,847 compared to a needed living wage of nearly $41,000 in that market. For BIPOC respondents, the average salary was $32,027, barely above minimum wage.[22] In a separate survey of gallerists, gallery directors were making six figures up to near seven figures (which is fantastic—again, I believe in making money!) while, by comparison, gallery assistants' salaries at the same organizations almost never exceeded $35,000—despite many of these respondents being employed in New York City, one of the country's most expensive regions.[23] That part's not fantastic; it's downright horrific. We're talking about L.A. and New York here: a $35K–$40K salary for a forty-hour a week job (and let's be honest, arts organization jobs often require many more hours) is unequivocally unlivable.

The problem doesn't only lie in major coastal metros either. In recent years, employees have moved to unionize at the Wexner Center for the Arts in Ohio,[24] the St. Louis Zoo, the Columbus Aquarium, and the Hawaii Public

Library—joining staff at more than two dozen other cultural organizations to fight for better, more equal, livable compensation.[25] Crowd-sourced Google docs disclosing staff wages of various artistic disciplines across the country have also thrown light on the issue. These shared documents have garnered hundreds if not thousands of entries within days of going public—all showing abhorrent salaries for very educated workers (seriously, sometimes these are the same institutions saying "Master's degree and seven years supervisory experience required" in their job postings and then paying these paltry wages . . . insert mind-exploding emoji here). In response, the hashtag #ShowTheSalary has become a rallying cry for pay transparency in job descriptions, which we've discussed throughout this chapter in the form of best practices.[26]

Among the reasons behind this problematic compensation paradigm is the pressure to balance the budget. Running an arts organization and generating needed revenue is hard, no question, but doing it off the backs of poorly paid employees is negligent. Something is egregiously wrong when junior staff are so undercompensated, they qualify for the programs our social service counterparts provide. I confess: I've been there before when I was filling an empty role and part of me was just hoping I could land someone for less than what the last person cost. But then at some point I realized this was a scarcity-mindset starvation cycle.

Also, many foundations drive this compensation problem via their grant application process. Calling staff compensation unfundable "overhead" is one of the most backwards practices in all of philanthropy. In contrast, artists are often considered central to the mission, and therefore a portion of their costs are allowable in most grant application budgets. The thing is, the administrative roles are just as necessary as the artistic roles—we need both to run a cultural institution. This trend prevents capital from reaching the lives of important people who further our organizations, communities, and local and national economies. Not every foundation adheres to these backwards guidelines, but many still do, and it's directly contributing to wage suppression for essential staff.

Given all this, paying people a competitive living wage feels radical. But when we as employers do offer more decent and even bold compensation, we get to require more in return. Both Netflix's Patty McCord and Google's Laszlo Bock are clear that gainful, "unfair" salaries come with an expectation for delivering results, such as securing and retaining more donors and audience members, demonstrating the innovative thinking required, and bringing those ideas to execution. So please be a little radical in your compensation. Pay people more and expect excellent work, which in turn brings more revenue to fund the budget.

Lucky for us, however, research in our field and others shows that compensation is not the number one factor in employee satisfaction. Yes, compensate radically, but also, as we head to the next chapter, keep in mind we need to act on the top thing employees want even more than money: a stronger company culture.[27]

7.

We're Not a Family, We're a Team

Company Culture

Online shoe retailer Zappos famously pays people to quit after one month on the job. If you do the onboarding training and then think you don't want to commit to working there, no problem. Here's two grand, thank you and goodbye, no questions asked.

This incentive has grown from its original offer twenty-plus years ago of $100 to quit, then to $500, to today's $2,000. Over that time, the footwear powerhouse in many ways revolutionized retail. When Zappos was founded in 1999, more people believed Y2K was going to destroy the world as we know it than believed that buying shoes over the internet could be easy.[1]

Today, the retailer grosses over a billion dollars in revenue each year and is known for its strong company culture. And the illustrious pay-to-quit deal, while now widely known, is just one small part of that culture. From prioritizing customer service above all else to offering employees a free library of self-help and business books that reinforce its culture,[2] to blogging stories and insights to "share their unique perspective on culture, people, and customer service," Zappos's late founder Tony Hsieh insisted its relentless focus on strengthening culture was the foundation for its growth and success.

Hsieh was right, and the data support him. Having a strong culture directly relates to increased performance, greater job satisfaction, and lower turnover.[3] In a survey of Deloitte clients, 82 percent of respondents believe "culture is a potential competitive advantage."[4] In the cultural sector, a 2022 survey by the Advisory Board for the Arts (ABA) found that the number one thing our workforce wants is a stronger culture, specifically in the areas of organizational transparency, commitment to EDI work, inclusive decision making, and job accountability. The last chapter ended by examining compensation in the industry. Well, having a stronger culture helps the equation: the ABA found that getting those four elements of company culture right is worth nearly $6,000 per staff member per year in salary.[5] In other words, employees in the field are telling us a stronger company culture is valuable, and the ABA was able to put a dollar figure to it.

Maybe you've heard the saying from management guru Peter Drucker: "Culture eats strategy for breakfast," meaning no matter how good the strategies in the plan, they will fall flat without strong culture. I say take this one step further: developing a strong culture *is* a strategy. And that's what this chapter is about.

While a lot of culture setting must come from the top executive, we all have areas of scope that we can control or influence, no matter our role or level of seniority. It's a choice we consciously make as leaders, and this chapter examines six areas of focus for us to do the strategic work of building and fortifying our teams and institutions: determining core values and behaviors that support those values, establishing psychological safety, decolonizing power, having fewer policies, modeling courage and vulnerability, and creating infrastructure for culture.

DETERMINE CORE VALUES (AND BEHAVIORS THAT SUPPORT THEM)

Painting altruistic values on the walls isn't enough, as both for- and nonprofit brands have exemplified over the last few years with botched PR statements and ensuing public backlash.[6] Employees and consumers alike expect and deserve more. That said, the most important piece of advice I've seen on this topic is that effective company values are not meant to be aspirational. Rather, they need to be nonnegotiable—and also as measurable as anything else we care about as an organization. Management consultants, research firms, and organizational psychologists alike are clear on how to ensure our values are nonnegotiable and measurable: define behaviors that exemplify those values.

Patrick Lencioni, author of the best-selling book *The Advantage* (which is about improving organizational health), says the question of "How do we behave?" is one of the most defining aspects of any organization, of any size, in any sector. And he says that confusing core and aspirational values is a frequent mistake that companies make. To give clarity to employees, organizations should establish what he calls "behavioral values that are completely inviolable." Meaning, *"We'll never hire someone who doesn't [demonstrate] those [behaviors] and we'll never make a decision that violates those."*[7] This becomes a company's personality. Here are a few examples of how this could play out.

If we say as an organization we value all genders and abilities, we need to offer flexible and hybrid work options and not penalize employees who use those benefits. Long before the pandemic, at one organization I served, we were set up for remote work in addition to having an office. Employees could leave to pick their kid up from school and get back online at home; younger staff could duck out to look at an apartment they were trying to land and finish their work that evening. And maybe I took the cake when I broke my femur in a bad ski accident and was out of the office for four weeks unable to walk or drive, but able to fully work from bed (I call it my practice quarantine). I've since learned one in four adults in the United States has some type of disability, such as impaired mobility, cognition, hearing, or vision. Policies like these can make their lives so much easier while helping them maximize their contribution to the organization.[8]

To be fair, not everyone likes or wants remote work. In June 2020, McKinsey demonstrated a severe disparity between the satisfaction of women and men working remotely: 79 percent of men reported having a positive experience working from home, more than double the percentage of women who reported enjoying remote work.[9] Most people value *flexible* work options, though, and obviously not everyone feels the same, or even the same all the time, so the key is if we set an inviolable value of inclusion, we have to allow for a range of behaviors in how that plays out.

Valuing all genders also means we need to look at our insurance options and what's covered for all genders, including for people transitioning genders. It means we need to think about our restrooms at work and at the venue. Offering binary options only directly conflicts with that stated value.

Likewise, if we say we value diversity and equity, we need to change hiring practices (the point of the entire previous chapter). If we say we value ingenuity or innovation—statements I see more and more from cultural organizations—then we need to support new ideas from our staff and allow them to figure out how to test those ideas.

Organizational psychologist and Wharton Business School professor Adam Grant says the best framing is to emphasize values over rules. Rules set parameters that offer a fixed view of the world, but values allow people to internalize principles for themselves.[10] In addition to the social and racial justice values I've listed, here are a few examples of values I try to instill company wide and the behaviors that support them:

- **Having a customer focus**. This should be no surprise; you know me well at this point. When this value is part of the organization-wide culture, it permeates the work across multiple teams. It informs artistic choices, affects what the editorial team puts in the program book, determines what signage is in our venue, and explains why we're not putting a giant DONATE button on the homepage of the website (because we all know the data around the newcomers visiting that page). We're focusing on the customer in everything we do.

- **Prioritizing patron loyalty**. Harkening back to chapter two, this means the operations and production staff know *why* the marketing folks want performers to sign subscriber appreciation cards, so they help schedule the time to make it happen; the artists know taking the time to sign those cards translates to more dollars in renewals; and the accounting folks understand why we're spending so much on postcards. This isn't just "marketing stuff"; it's a value that affects everyone in the company. And treating it like that means altering our behaviors organization wide.

- **Representation**. When this value is held company wide, it not only impacts what composers are on the season but also means we examine how we hire people more equitably. And while valuing representation does not address all the systems of oppression and discrimination in our organizations and industry, as discussed in the last chapter, it means we have real conversations about our selection process. We interrogate why, for instance, Black and Brown artists aren't historically being invited to audition (to act, play, dance, or sing), regardless of if that audition is blind or not—*and* state what we're going to do to address that. It means our board begins to prioritize recruiting people from historically underrepresented groups because we value those voices at the table (*voices* plural, not just a single token/other voice). Our behaviors reflect the value.

- **Data are our guide**. This value says that we'll use data and research to inform what we do—not a gut feeling, or the way it's always been done, or what other organizations are doing just because they're doing it. And when we don't have the data, we'll run a pilot test or experiment to get some data.

- **Iteration**. Behaviors that support this value include pursuing progress, not perfection. We celebrate taking good steps, and then assess, evaluate, and do it again—hopefully slightly better next time. This pertains to everything from upleveling our brand Instagram content to our EDI work. We don't criticize when we don't get it fully right out of the gate. We establish processes when a high standard of excellence is necessary (like having a routing protocol so the email blast to thirty thousand people doesn't have misspelled words). And we don't let perfect be the enemy of the good.

- **Go slow when we can, fast when we must**. As a value, this means that all of us plan, as far in advance as possible, for every function—not just the artistic decisions that often get made the farthest out. We double down on putting pen to paper (or type to screen, project to project management software, etc.), and we give ourselves appropriate lead times for our deliverables. Maybe this one sounds basic, but I've seen a chronic lack of this type of planning across all kinds of teams, and at all sizes of organizations. And when we value the behavior of more deliberate and diligent planning, it gives us the slightest bit of bandwidth when something inevitably does come up that requires us to move quickly.

Again, these are some of my behavioral values I hold with teams I lead; they don't have to be yours. Zappos has ten core values that are part of its "Oath of Employment."[11] It polled employees, distilled responses to thirty-seven themes that emerged, and narrowed them down to the final ten in 2006. Maybe you, like Zappos, value passion and determination. Maybe you value problem solvers over problem finders, or you consider conflict to be okay ("we talk it out and work through it; we don't deflect or bury it"), or hold a top value of "don't be an ass" (hat tip to Stanford professor Robert Sutton, who writes about this in his book *The No Asshole Rule*). Maybe we should paint that last one on the wall after all (that was a joke, but now I'm picturing it and I don't hate it).

Whatever values you instill, the point is to make sure they are demonstrated consistently across people, teams, and time. Because "the signature of mediocrity is not an unwillingness to change," says Jim Collins in his book, *Great by Choice*; "the signature of mediocrity is chronic inconsistency."[12]

This concept is reinforced by intriguing research within our own field. A study of more than one hundred professional theaters asked leaders to rate the importance of five values: artistic expression, entertainment, giving to the community, achievement, and financial sustainability. The study found that which value was first or second or last had no bearing on the organization's financial results. Instead, what mattered was everyone's consistent alignment *around* the values. The more strongly leaders within a single organization disagreed about the relative importance of each value, the lower their ticket revenues and net income.[13] Establishing values alone is not enough to influence performance. It's establishing consistent behaviors in service to those values that makes the difference.

ESTABLISH PSYCHOLOGICAL SAFETY

In 2008, Google sought to uncover the differences between their top-performing teams and other teams who exhibited only satisfactory or subpar performance. The tech titan conducted an internal research study among their massive data set of tens of thousands of employees, years of performance evaluations, and meticulously measured deliverables, and what they found surprised them. The number one predictor of a high-performing team was not where the employees went to school, their years of collective experience, IQ levels, or their past well-known employers. It was how psychologically safe the team members felt.[14]

Psychological safety is when you feel okay taking an interpersonal risk, knowing you won't be judged, embarrassed, or punished for asking a question, speaking up, or making a mistake. Google's findings on psychological safety match research from the UK that found by far the best indicator of worker engagement is if they trust their team leader.[15] That trust isn't established overnight, but here are some traits your organization can adopt to build the safety muscle:

- **Transparency**. Human capital research firm i4cp (originally known as the Institute for Corporate Productivity) has consistently found that transparency is a top hallmark of high-performance companies and effective leaders. The more transparent, generally the better. Yet it's often surprising how many companies systematically and consciously avoid sharing information across various levels of staff. In Microsoft's culture overhaul, which i4cp assisted with, CEO Satya Nadella said that knowledge isn't power; *sharing* knowledge is power.[16]

- **Praise**. Positive feedback is proven to be *thirty times* more powerful than negative feedback in creating high performance on a team.[17] And the more specific the praise, the better. Instead of "Good job," or "Nice work," capture exactly what the team member did well in your eyes, so they know to do it that way again and again. The best thing about this is we don't have to be a supervisor to have this quality about us. It matters so much to get in the habit of praising the people we work with, regardless of our role.

- **Clarity around expectations**. In one study on fully engaged employees, the strongest indicator of a worker's feeling of trust and safety with their team leader was how they answered the question, "Do I know clearly what is expected of me at work?"[18] Think like a coach, not a boss, and make sure deliverables and deadlines are clear. Along with transparent information flow and specific praise, clarity will give team members a much better understanding of expectations.

- **Encourage safe behavior and shut down unsafe behavior**. Here's another one that doesn't require you to manage others (but if you do supervise others, you should definitely do this). When someone takes a personal risk, such as asking a question in a meeting, thank them for the question (encourage the safe behavior). Or when one colleague interrupts another, step in and kindly say you'd like to hear the first person finish (shut down the unsafe behavior)—especially if you're observing this among colleagues with the same or lower power or status.

Establishing psychological safety is hard work, especially when it hasn't been an intentional part of the workplace atmosphere. It's a muscle we can build as individuals, though, one that collectively produces big cultural changes.

DECOLONIZE POWER

I don't know if decolonizing power sounds scary to you or not, or new or foreign, or comfortable or uncomfortable. Maybe you've been waiting for this, or maybe you're scratching your head. The truth is, I'm still learning a lot about this topic, too. But it's vital that I—that we all—do the work even while we're still learning and not let chasing perfection kill progress.

Often I have wondered if and how power should be redistributed as part of dismantling old systems. Does this mean everyone should have equal say? How do decisions get made, then? Does hierarchy need to go away completely? What happens when we disagree if there's no senior person to break the tie? Is the organization completely flat? Who's responsible when things go wrong in that case? I had more questions than answers and really struggled to figure out a recommended way forward.

On my personal journey to understand more about the historical systems of power in this industry and parse out what parts of our tradition I want to preserve versus what parts aren't serving us, someone recommended I read *Decolonizing Wealth* by Edgar Villanueva. Villanueva, who identifies as someone with Indigenous heritage as a member of the Lumbee Tribe and works in the field of White-dominated philanthropy, has life experience as both a member of a historically marginalized group and as an insider within traditional nonprofit structures and wealth distribution via major foundations. He talks a lot about how much of philanthropy boils down to the haves and the have-nots, the power dynamics that result from that, and how, in nonprofit spaces, even our well-intentioned community work can take on a White-saviorism approach. He also offers compelling alternatives.

"I am frequently asked," Villanueva writes, "'What does decolonized leadership look like?' But instead of thinking, 'How can everyone have equal power?' What if the question became 'How can everyone be powerful?'" He goes on to quote Frederic Laloux, author of the influential management book *Reinventing Organizations*. According to Laloux, "People can hold different levels of power, and yet everyone can be powerful . . . the point is not to make everyone equal; it is to allow all employees to grow into the strongest, healthiest version of themselves."[19]

This Villanueva–Laloux combo is the most comprehensive, resonant description of decolonizing power I've personally heard. Said differently, decolonizing power is to empower everyone to do their best work. People can hold different levels of power and yet everyone can be powerful.

Ballet Austin is a great example of this. We heard about their customer experience wins in chapter one. When I spoke with Executive Director Cookie Ruiz about that work, she went right to this topic of decolonizing power. She doesn't want to be the originator of ideas and decisions, but instead, to green-light the ideas and decisions of others. "How can you push decision making down as much as possible?" she asked. Laszlo Bock implemented the same ideology at Google, arguing in favor of giving decision-making authority to the lowest levels feasible.

At Zappos, "everybody is expected to lead and be an entrepreneur in their own roles," says John Bunch, who, along with Alexis Gonzales-Black, led Zappos's transition to Holacracy (a method of decentralizing management hierarchy and distributing authority and decisionmaking).[20] Authority comes with answerability, though, he notes. "One of the core principles [of Holacracy] is people taking personal accountability for their work. It's not leaderless. There are certainly people who hold a bigger scope of purpose for the organization than others. What it does do is distribute leadership into each role. Everybody is expected to lead and be an entrepreneur in their own roles."

I now subscribe to what I call the Spider-Man principle of management: with great power comes great responsibility. In other words, give people guide rails and let them make their own decisions accordingly—and have accountability structures in place, which we'll talk about in a moment. But first, the next tenet of strong company culture offers one way to give more of that responsibility and empowerment to our teams.

HAVE FEWER POLICIES

I spoke with Kevin Oakes at i4cp, the human capital research firm mentioned earlier, about how research on renovating culture applies to arts organizations. When I asked what policies are needed to help build stronger culture, he was adamant: "Any time you put a blanket policy across a whole group, you're immediately creating exceptions and creating situations where that doesn't work for everyone."[21] That's because policies are overgeneralized rules that limit people instead of freeing them to govern their own work.

When thinking of examples of this, I went straight to flexible and remote work policies. For some roles in the arts, folks have to be on-site to do the job (performing, maintaining the gardens, setting the stage, opening the doors, etc.); determining a blanket policy would be riddled with challenges. Instead, Oakes advised, "the manager and employee need to look at what's best for the company and best for the individual." This feels somewhat fuzzy. But as I'm learning, sometimes oversimplifying is not the best approach to leading a group of people, and definitely not the most human-centered solution. The answer: Have fewer policies.

Patty McCord, the former Netflix exec we met in the last chapter, concurs. Having developed the now legendary (seriously—it has over twenty million hits online) Netflix Culture Deck, which focused on behaviors and skills over policies as the firm grew over its first decade or so from baby startup to two thousand employees, McCord remains adamant that policies aren't the way to set culture, no matter how many people in the organization.[22] "You should operate with the leanest possible set of policies, procedures, rules, and approvals," McCord writes, "because most of these top-down mandates hamper speed and agility."[23]

As the Alameda Health System Foundation works to strengthen company culture, Lobo Soriano also introduced new onboarding procedures, professional development opportunities, and performance evaluation based on behaviors, where the employee can also explain and evaluate themselves. "Culture change takes time," she concluded. "There's no going back to 'normal'; it's only now and how we respond to that."

MODEL VULNERABILITY AND COURAGE

I'm not going to lie. This one is the hardest for me personally, and I'm working on it continually. I used to think being vulnerable in a professional setting was weak. And by "weak" I mean unpolished and therefore hard-lined as not okay for Aubrey (the thesaurus literally lists "weak" as a synonym for "vulnerable," so that didn't help).

Then I came across Brené Brown's work on this subject, and for the first time ever, I saw that the data support bringing vulnerability to the workplace. Insert brakes screeching to a halt. As a bonus, of all six areas to strengthen company culture in this chapter, this is the one that anyone can contribute to the most regardless of level of authority in the organization. So basically there's no excuse not to be a little more, well, unpolished—and by "unpolished," I now mean "real."

Showing up this way is not easy; that's why it goes hand in hand with courage, according to Brown. Here are some research-based guidelines and advice Brown offers to help us do this:

- **Rumble with vulnerability.** I hear a word like "rumble" and can't help but think about the Sharks and the Jets in *West Side Story*. The rumble scene is uncomfortable and awkward (they're snapping and dancing even though there are strong emotions and serious subject matter)—but it's not an all-out Martin Scorsese bloodbath. Sometimes being vulnerable is a little odd and raw like that.
- **Avoid the cheap-seats feedback.** The best example of cheap-seats feedback in my mind is Twitter. That type of Monday morning quarterback

In her book *Powerful*, McCord offers the following questions to evaluate which policies are truly necessary at our institutions:

- What is the purpose of this policy or procedure? Sometimes it's old and no longer serving us; maybe it made sense at one point, but not now.
- Is your decision-making system clear and communicated widely? The great thing about this one is, once you've established values and behaviors that support those values, a big foundation for decision-making framework is already in place—you don't even need to double the work.
- Are there any approval processes we can eliminate? Could we replace approvals and permissions with analysis of spending patterns and a focus on accuracy and predictability? I love this one. This gives autonomy but also holds people accountable.

I cut my teeth in big organizations with lots of approvals and spending policies, but now I can't stand when people who report to me ask if they can make a purchase (usually folks who are newer tend to do this because that's how they were trained in the past). What I prefer is to try to create a culture that lets employees spend within their budget and empowers them to present their supervisor with a recommendation only when they aren't sure and need a sounding board. An entry-level employee might say something like, "I'd like to purchase this tool because I'll be using it weekly for XYZ." If it sounds reasonable to the supervisor, they should green-light it (and to be fair, "reasonable" might include an expectation of weekly reporting with information gleaned from said tool). At the manager level and higher, they have an annual budget to oversee—one they ideally were a part of developing. Then, they're measured by whether they remained within budget and delivered on the goals of the role. I'm not nickeling and diming along the way when there's a mechanism in place for accountability.

I brought McCord to speak at a conference I was co-chairing one year, and she noted that these same principles apply to arts orgs of all sizes. "Sometimes we make it so damn complicated, we just can't make it any better," she told a roomful of arts administrators. "You either manage the exceptions, or you manage people being responsible."[24] If companies like Netflix can institute this less-is-more tenet of company culture, a big arts organization can, too. Because no matter how large your institution, it's not Netflix big. Plus, they first implemented these principles when they were the same size as some of our organizations, and if yours is on the smaller side, you likely don't have the people or structure to enforce a ton of policies anyway.

APPLICATION BOX

Concept: Setting values, expected behaviors, psychological safety, and accountability metrics

Organization: Alameda Health System Foundation

Alameda County is the fourth most diverse county in the nation. It sits to the east of the San Francisco Bay, and Oakland comprises the biggest portion of its residents.[25] As Chief of Staff Charlene Lobo Soriano puts it, if you get in a car accident on one side of the Bay Bridge, you're rushed to SF General Hospital; if you get in an accident on the other side of the bridge, you're taken to Alameda Health System's Highland Hospital. The Foundation offers Alameda patients a safety net to access needed care regardless of their ability to pay.

Lobo Soriano was brought in to create a learning environment, develop a more supportive atmosphere, and help the organization break free of silos. At the time, though, she didn't know all this was going to be accompanied by culture change. The first thing she did was talk to everyone. "What is it like working here for you? What do you want to stop, start, and continue? How can I as Chief of Staff go along with you?" Lobo Soriano asked.

From those conversations, she and the staff co-created the organizational values, naming these along with associated behaviors they all wanted to see in their coworkers. For instance, "act with integrity" is one of their values, exemplified by things like financial responsibility and clear and timely communication with colleagues. "Partner for impact" is another, which looks like partnering with smart outside organizations externally and with each other internally.

Now, 60 percent of their performance evaluation is based on behaviors: Are you collegial? Are you mission driven? Are you responsible with the finances?

Establishing psychological safety was a challenge, Lobo Soriano admits. "When you come into a space with a history of behaviors, that learned behavior impacts current practices," she explained. "To create space where we can unpack that together takes thoughtfulness, takes patience." Lobo Soriano led the staff through a strengths-finder test so they could understand how to work best with each other going forward in service to their value of partnership. Another value they established directly addressed the need for vulnerability (which this chapter covers next), defining the actions of "take risks together" and "talk it out together."

"We're trying to challenge people to *not* stay in their lane," she says. "We have one big lane. It needs to be okay to ask questions and not be berated for it." Crucial to this is giving people a choice of how and when to come into the office and setting boundaries about when and how to work. Hybrid work is closely related to psychological safety, she says, and she's careful to articulate boundaries, such as, "Just because someone sent an email at one o'clock in the morning doesn't mean you have to respond then. But if they message you on Teams during business hours, we are clear a response is expected within five to ten minutes."

Having clear expectations is a theme throughout Lobo Soriano's work at the Foundation. She talks a lot about naming processes and walking people through those processes. "It's one thing in the workplace to say, 'I have an open-door policy,' but how do you tell people what's appropriate and how to use that?" Oftentimes, it's being explicit: *I keep my door open between calls and am happy to take a five-minute break if you stop by to ask any questions.* When I asked about decolonizing power, she offered, "Decolonizing the space isn't to flatten the hierarchy, but to explain how to [most effectively] use that access to power and time. Access to power is easier when someone tells you the rules of the game." (She is referencing work by educationalist, researcher, and author Lisa Delpit.[26])

who pontificates verbally, but not in any substantive way. "Here's what should've happened . . ." "That idea won't work . . ." "You know what you should do . . ." We have this type on our staffs sometimes, too. And the whole idea is to create cultures where that behavior is not acceptable.

- **Stay armor free.** In other words, Brown says don't be so defensive—let that guard down at least a little. And also, give up the idea that "leaders have to be right" (which I used to care so much about). Instead, today's leaders have to let go of turf and carefully scripted rhetoric, which I think is both extra difficult amid so-called cancel culture (*what if I say something wrong?*), and simultaneously extra necessary when we're talking about the kind of vulnerability and courage our industry needs.

- **Name unsaid emotions.** During times of change, challenge, or uncertainty (like, I don't know, a pandemic, polarized political climate, war in Ukraine, recession, to name a few), Brown offers this advice in her best-selling book *Dare to Lead*: "Daring leaders might sit with their teams and say, 'These changes are coming in hard and fast, and I know there's a lot of anxiety—I'm feeling it too, and it's hard to work through. It's hard not to take it home, it's hard not to worry, and it's easy to want to look for someone to blame. I will share everything I can about the changes with you, as soon as I can.'"[27]

A vulnerable and courageous leader doesn't know all the answers, admits anxiety, acknowledges that it is easy to cast blame (i.e., names the tendency to armchair-quarterback), and is honest in their delivery. As someone who isn't the best at always naming my emotions, I know this is a skill to develop—but it's worth it.

- **Ask people what they need.** People process differently and grieve differently. Think of days like those on which the guilty verdict came out against Derek Chauvin for murdering George Floyd, the anti-Asian hate crimes occurred in Atlanta, Ye made his antisemitic comments, or yet another mass shooting happened. Some people want to talk, some don't. Some want or need the day off, while some prefer to use work as a distraction. It's okay to say, "We still need to produce work that makes us proud," as Brown writes, but also acknowledge what could get in the way of that work, along with any questions people have. And sometimes, because we are all wired differently, the most helpful thing we can ask, whether we're a supervisor or colleague or peer or friend, is simply, "What does support from me look like?"

- **Last, don't share just to share.** Being vulnerable doesn't mean we don't have professional boundaries, or that we overshare. It doesn't mean introverts have to speak up more than they feel comfortable doing. It means we have to *show* up.

All of this takes courage. Setting strong company culture requires bravery. Leadership (and I don't mean seniority; I mean leadership no matter your role or title) is not for the faint of heart.

CREATE INFRASTRUCTURE FOR CULTURE

Last, all of this work on company culture is only possible when we create infrastructure that allows us to prioritize it. In a report detailing results of a global study on how organizations attract and retain talent, one of the top findings was that, in today's hypercompetitive labor market, organizations should compete on culture rather than compensation.* Despite belt tightening, HR budgets across industries are going up—specifically in the areas of hiring, infrastructure, and EDI.[28] Hiring and EDI didn't surprise me, but infrastructure caught my attention. More and more companies are investing in the foundation for a strong culture. Here are three areas of investment most relevant to cultural institutions.

Invest in Onboarding, not "On-Boring"

Everything covered in this chapter necessitates onboarding, which offers a huge opportunity for welcoming new hires into the fold, establishing that sense of belonging, and outlining expectations and norms of the culture. While the most onboarding I've ever had was pretty much signing and returning the company handbook and going to lunch with my supervisor, Zappos sends the handbook

---

* This completely matches the Advisory Board for the Arts' research inside the field and is not to excuse suppressing salaries, as discussed in the last chapter. Still, knowing this is what employees care about is helpful when working within our always-tight budgets.

out in advance so employees can bring it signed on day one ready to begin.[29] And yes, they do take new hires out to lunch, too. But then, over a four-week process that every new employee undergoes—no matter how senior—Zappos also shares the company strategy (to give everyone a broader picture of how they fit into a larger purpose), reviews the company values, reinforces expectations and responsibilities for the employee's role, imparts any job-specific training, answers questions, introduces other team members, and goes over each team's current focus and roadmap—and then offers that "quitting bonus."

At cultural organizations, great onboarding should be required of everyone regardless of title, whether the employee is on staff, onstage, in the exhibits, front of house, back of house . . . everyone. And the benefits go beyond getting new hires up to speed: strong onboarding improves employee retention by 82 percent and improves productivity by more than 70 percent while those employees are there.[30]

The last piece of the onboarding process at Zappos is a feedback survey. Did the employee feel included and welcomed? Do they know what is expected of them? Are they having any difficulties four weeks in? This final step complements research from Adam Grant. As he writes in his book *Originals*, employers should shift from exit interviews to entry interviews. Too often, we ask employees for their thoughts on their way out. When we seek feedback upon arrival, not only do we help them feel valued, but we also enable them to contribute novel ideas.[31]

At one organization I worked with, we developed an onboarding component called the "Fresh Eyes Doc." It was a document where new hires could write down all their thoughts about coming into the organization as a newbie, including their thoughts on navigating the website, what info they were looking for as someone new to the company, and what helped them as they ramped up. This gave us irreplaceable intel about what newcomers of all types (not just employees, but sometimes people newer to the art form) were looking for, struggling with, and really enjoying as well. Once someone is indoctrinated, no matter the culture, this opportunity goes away because we forget what it's like to be new.*

---

* This is called "hindsight bias." It is the phenomenon wherein, after we learn something, we tend to forget what it's like to not know that thing. This is also why it's so hard to design experiences for newcomers; for most of us, it's been a long time since we were in those shoes, and we've learned so much about our art forms since. Same goes for employees.

Invest in Professional Development

Once someone is in the door and onboarded, it's our responsibility as employers to keep them growing. All too often, professional development is the first budget line that gets cut when things are tight, yet it's one of the job components high-performing people most desire.

I talk about growing revenue a lot in this book, but professional development is an expense line that we need to grow, too. High-performing organizations—those that are more agile, more innovative, and more financially successful than their peers—understand this. They've charted a 52 percent increase in the budget for talent development on average in recent years.[32] In my last several full-time roles, I've created a professional development stipend for everyone on the team. At a large institution that yearly allocation was a few thousand dollars per person; at a regional organization, the figure started at way less than that and grew over time (we just didn't have it at first, but I was determined to start somewhere). My rule is employees can use their professional development budget however they like as long as the pursuit meets a few criteria:

- **It has to relate to your contribution to the organization.** This can be broad, and that's intentional. I'm so amazed by what interesting and relevant opportunities people find, like the web developer who went to DrupalCon (Drupal was the content-management framework on the web-site backend), or the education manager who attended a conference outside the arts to learn to design better curriculum.

- **You have to report back in a future team meeting.** This can be a department meeting at a big organization and a full staff meeting at a small one. I want the attendee to internalize what they learned. Conferences in particular are a blitz of information, so to report back means you have to go back through your notes, find your key takeaways, and share them. That's an important exercise. It's also helpful for teammates to hear. It telegraphs to the group, "Oh, so-and-so is going to be working on this new thing or idea they learned." Plus it's a bonus when the person passes on the inspiration, excitement, and energy around the insights they gleaned. Another reason I require reporting back is accountability.

When you audibly commit to something, it helps drive accountability for yourself (generally true for any goal setting), which flows right into the final criterion.[33]

- **You must demonstrate accountability.** With great power comes great responsibility (Remember Spider-Man?). I have no problem including an evaluation metric in the performance review that measures if someone has applied what they learned from their self-selected professional development. It's fine if someone attended a conference or program, but I want to know how it helped their work afterward.

In short, here's what I don't want: for the employee to feel warm and fuzzy and inspired for about a week, and then go back to the grind without any change in performance. I want results from my investment.

For employees reading this wishing you had such a practice in place at your organization, you can still enact this strategy in reverse. Next time you are participating in any professional development (it doesn't have to be going to an expensive conference; it could even be the next webinar you watch), take the initiative to come back and do this report yourself. It signals to your team and your organization you take your growth very seriously and you are absolutely worth the investment going forward. Who knows—maybe next time someone else participates in a professional development opportunity, they'll come back and do the same—and now you're helping create a culture that values this.

Invest in Performance Evaluation/Feedback

The last building block of company culture infrastructure is performance feedback. If you remember from the beginning of the chapter, greater job accountability for everyone is one of the top culture attributes arts workers want. Some arts organizations have a structure for this, some don't. Either way, those structures, like those for hiring, are often not the most effective. Instead of setting aspirational annual goals and measuring progress toward those goals, zoom out. Job accountability (i.e., performance evaluation) is about measuring everyone's performance against all the other company-wide standards previously set. Your employee performance evaluation could include questions like:

- **Did the employee demonstrate behaviors that align with company values?** You'll be able to check against the list of the types of behaviors that reflect those values from the start of the chapter. When you assess those types of behaviors, it's often clear who embodies the values and who doesn't.

- **Did they establish psychological safety?** If you're doing a 360 review (meaning asking the employee's peers and subordinates to provide feedback), this is a key question, as it's difficult to assess that from the top-down alone. If not, roll it up into the behaviors question.

- **Did they deliver results? Was the work accurate? Did they do what they said they were going to do?** This includes evaluating all the great power/freedom components. Did they stay within their budget? Did they apply that top conference takeaway they raved about? Did their choices serve the organization's overall goals, or hinder them? If they're responsible for managing others, did they do all these things (communicate the expected behaviors and deliverables) with their direct reports?

The world's most prominent researcher on strengths and leadership at work, Marcus Buckingham, writes, "The best leaders realize that their people . . . do not need to be coerced into alignment through yearly goal setting." Instead, he attests that the most effective leaders infuse their team with meaning and purpose, which then allows and drives each team member to willfully set their own goals and execute their plan.[34] In the end, performance feedback is about how each employee is contributing to a healthier culture.

Kevin Oakes agrees: "Typically if you fix the culture, the performance follows. That's really the number one takeaway from the research." Zappos's Tony Hsieh said the same thing: "Our whole belief is that if you get the culture right, most of the other stuff like delivering great customer service or building a long-term enduring brand will just happen naturally on its own."[35] More than a billion dollars in annual revenue later—and growth from a dot-com shoe retailer to an online behemoth—that strategy really worked.

Last, when someone isn't contributing to a healthy culture in the ways outlined in this chapter, they need to be off the team. That may sound overly harsh, but that saying about one bad apple is true. In our places of work, we're not a family, we're a team. You can't choose your family, and you can't leave a family, at least not easily. But we can and should carefully choose our team, both as employers and employees. And when a team member doesn't perform accordingly, they get cut. There are of course steps we can take to try to resuscitate a team member before showing them the door, but in the end, our company health depends on it.

WHAT HAPPENS IN VEGAS SHOULDN'T STAY IN VEGAS

In 2018, Zappos decided to bring their world-class company culture and customer service to the entertainment industry: they announced a partnership in their hometown of Las Vegas to run the Planet Hollywood Theater. According to the press release announcing the deal, "The partnership will allow Zappos to show its Core Values and Culture in new and unexpected ways . . . The customer service company that just happens to sell shoes, clothing and accessories will take the concertgoer's customer journey to new heights in the entertainment world."[36]

As Zappos demonstrates, company culture translates to serving our community more effectively. And maybe the best news of all is that strengthening our company culture doesn't mean arts organizations have to sacrifice what we love about our long-standing traditions, as long as we bring others along on the journey—the final lesson of this chapter.

Back to Kevin Oakes's research at i4cp: they saw that 57 percent of culture change success stories focused on what to keep of the past culture while not ignoring the parts they could adapt. "You've got to listen to the workforce to hear what they think is unique and powerful about the org, but also what does need to change going forward," he explained as our conversation came to a close.

The view that change has to be modeled from the top is not wrong, I realized; it's just not complete. Others have to be a part of setting culture, too. "While this needs to be leader-led, you've got to get the cooperation of the workforce," Oakes concluded. "There's got to be a mentality of co-creation of the culture change." Zappos did this, too, deciding along the way to shift gears and refine, keeping what was working and updating what wasn't.

Edgar Villanueva of *Decolonizing Wealth* says it this way: "The issue is creating a culture of respect, curiosity, acceptance, and love. It's about fundamentally changing organizational culture, what constitutes acceptable behavior, and the definitions of success and leadership. It's about building ourselves a whole new table—one where we truly belong."

As a final offering, Villanueva adds, "We have to shift from our obsession with individual leaders to a focus on organizational design, which tends to be taken for granted and invisible in most of our institutions." Focusing on company culture is a group strategy. The results will follow.

8.

The 40-Year-Old ~~Virgin~~ Silo

Silos: They're detached, disconnected, and literally built to keep everything else out. They're good for grain, bad for business. Yet cultural institutions comprise department silos across marketing, fundraising, education, curation or programming, and finance, among others—a staff structure developed around forty years ago that's no longer helping us. And by "no longer helping," I mean actively hindering our bottom line. "As siloed mindsets and behavior increase, economic performance decreases," McKinsey reports.[1]

Arts organizations have embraced the current organizational structure since the 1970s and 1980s, when arts management became a profession. By the turn of the twenty-first century, arts management materialized as a bona fide subdiscipline of general management as measured by multiple factors, such as the number of publications about the subdiscipline, number of conferences, and evolving macro trends like marketing and consumer behavior during those decades.[2]

Over a similar period, the average number of concerts by orchestras nationwide increased by 110 percent, which in turn propelled the professionalism of arts marketing and fundraising, meaning these skills were now required for performing institutions.[3] The museum space saw the same explosive growth in the US and abroad, with an average of three new museums opening a week in the UK in the 1980s, and—while no exact counts exist—an estimated doubling of the size of professional staff during that decade.[4] From this confluence of factors was birthed the organizational structure that we largely know today.

To our credit as a cultural sector, we've tweaked and evolved over the decades, building up fundraising teams, digital marketing, social media channels, new presentation formats, arts management training programs and conferences, and most recently, streaming. But no matter how much we've refined and expanded roles, our fixed costs continue to rise and outpace the incremental revenue gains.

The reason this challenge persists is because of the evolving role of art in society. At one point, art was viewed as a substitute for religion—"museums [were] seen as the cathedrals of our time," the authors of a 2000 study write. Later, society viewed art as part of one's education, a component of any well-rounded citizen. At the dawn of the new millennium, though, an art-as-entertainment perspective emerged, and consuming art became squarely viewed as a leisure activity. This tectonic shift makes art consumption up to one's individual taste, free choice, and therefore "more or less like any other economic sector."[5] A quarter century later, and their thesis still holds up. Consumer behavior is an even more essential part of what we do today, and its importance is not waning. Arts organization structure is due for its next iteration: a customer-centric redesign, the strategy we'll unpack in this chapter.

———

Just a few decades before this shift, another consumer-facing industry more mature than arts management went through the same organizational and societal growing pains: credit cards. After debuting in the 1950s, credit cards saw monumental growth and widespread adoption in the 1960s. American Express was king at the time, leading in 1959 with the green plastic card we know today, debuting the premium platinum card in 1984, and instituting services for its affluent base, like twenty-four-hour customer support and travel assistance.[6] Still, by the 1990s, Amex began facing similar silo-led challenges.

With the rise in customer service came the very early days of CRM (customer relationship management) software, just as American Express was trying to understand who their customers were, why their customers did business with them, and which customers were the most important. Through an early sampling of consumer data, they started to see connections between things like travel, credit card use, and retirement funds in the Amex customer records—game-changing information. The problem was that those different parts of the customer journey were handled by different teams.

For example, although at the time Amex had the largest call center in the US if not the world, customer service agents had no idea when they picked up the phone if the customer was calling because they were past due on their bill, wanting to book travel, asking a question about a charge, or even what tier of card they held. Did the agent need to go into collection mode? Or was this a VIP who needed their problem solved right away?

"Each of the silos wanted to protect 'their' customer base and information in general, and specifically wanted to protect their most valuable customers," recalls Doug Marty, at the time a senior manager at Andersen Consulting (now Accenture), the firm that worked with Amex on these issues. Sometimes they found instances of green-card holders who spent more than platinum-card holders (Warren Buffett being a famous example), but they had no idea how to track and find these people in order to treat them like most valuable customers or upgrade them to a higher-tier card. "We found that Marketing and Operations were not all that wild about working with IT, a common challenge for the next twenty years. These silos went all the way to the top of the structure and took years to begin dismantling, all while smaller credit card start-ups were eating away at the customer base."

In the mid-1990s, Amex dropped in the rankings enough to jolt senior leadership to action. Soon after, Marty and his team began working with Amex on breaking down silos: consolidating call centers from somewhere around fifteen to four, building a system that helped route callers to the right personnel, and sending the most important or valuable customers to the front of the queue. Think about when you call a customer service 800 number today: by the time you reach an agent, they know what issue you're calling about and which card you use, and have the details of your account pulled up and ready to go. (Well, at least the good call centers do that.) That type of system came directly from this project with Marty's team.

These measures soon put American Express back on top, and today, the company is heralded for their customer-centric approach that attracts high-dollar individual and corporate clients alike. From the airport lounge to the plastic you use to pay for dinner (metal if you're a Gold or Platinum cardholder), to the concierge service you use to book your next hotel, American Express continues to find ways to weave in and out of their customer's lives backed by seamless integration across their many teams.

As his Amex work came to a close, in a twist of fate, Doug Marty went on to lead a cultural organization. Not unlike American Express, the Colonial Williamsburg Foundation is multifaceted: part outdoor museum, part historical society, part preservation and conservation, part arboretum, all existing as America continues to grapple with our colonial past. "When I changed my career direction entirely and joined the Colonial Williamsburg Foundation, I immediately began looking at the same challenge," he shared with me. "We had ticket buyers, donors, retail customers, hotel customers, and a catalog. All of those parts were assets to the organization, but all presented the same type of silos as my finance background."

In his first year in the role, he presented to the managers, directors, and board about building a combined database of all those constituents who spent money via the various channels and developing procedures around identifying, categorizing, and communicating with them. "We sold high-end furniture," Marty explained, "so if you're someone who buys a $12,000 sideboard, we want to talk to you." Technology had progressed enough by the mid-2000s that Marty's team had gotten this down to a science. They knew that if a customer had three positive transactions with different business units (e.g. hotel, ticket, retail), their propensity to donate went up considerably. If a customer had two exchanges, the team knew to find a way to get them to the third.

Remember Ballet Austin back in chapter one? They also say three is the magic number. If they can get a patron to attend three times, they become top donor prospects and likely patrons for life—a task that requires cross-silo fluidity from marketing single tickets to development fundraising efforts (and back again for future ticket and subscription sales). Whether one of America's oldest credit card companies, a big organization preserving old buildings and historical sites, or a classic art form, breaking down silos is the new way to work toward customer goals. The rest of this chapter covers three silo-busting solutions— declassifying groups, declassifying information, and reevaluating budgetary incentives that reinforce the current silos—followed by a new organizational model to consider so that we can more efficiently serve the customer and make the money we need.

DECLASSIFY GROUPS

Department lines delineate groups by definition, so working against this takes being intentional. As anthropologist Gillian Tett writes in her book, *The Silo Effect*, that means no name-calling. Like when we refer to "the idiots over in development," or something similar. That classifies. One organization privately called their artists "the children" to me. That's not just disparaging; it's silo-ing.

Brené Brown adopted the same rule of no name-calling on her team. People do stupid things, for example, but they are not stupid. Look, I'd be lying if I said I wasn't guilty of classifying other departments or groups of people I've worked with before. Work is frustrating, and disagreements with our colleagues come with the territory. But make declassifying part of your company values and the delineated behaviors that reflect those values if you must (honestly, why not?). If we want to break down our silo lines, we have to rewire our brains to think and speak this way.

The tests that a few sports-loving social psychologists conducted show us how this rewiring can be done. Their subjects were among the hardest-line people they could think of: Red Sox and Yankees fans. These diehard devotees couldn't stand their "obnoxious" and "arrogant" rivals, as they described them. In the first iteration of the experiment, the two groups were asked to reflect on their shared identity as both loving baseball, but that didn't work to change their deeply entrenched divisions. In other words, a common framing proved ineffective. But in another version of the experiment, when fans were asked instead to reframe altogether by thinking on the arbitrary aspects of their fandom, such as, "If I was Boston-born instead of a native New Yorker, I probably would love the Red Sox, not hate them," they were more likely to challenge their previously held stereotypes. They'd think things like *Yankees fans might have reasons for being so passionate. Red Sox fans are actually pretty admirable for their dogmatic loyalty.*[7]

Another study discovered the same thing: when people in different business or government departments were encouraged to reimagine the world by looking at an issue from the consumers' perspective rather than their normal viewpoint as producers, they often became more innovative and effective.[8] Reread that, but swap out "business or government" with the name of your organization.

When we refashion our lens by finding a different perspective—not quite the idea of "walk a mile in someone else's shoes," but more like "think how these shoes are somewhat arbitrary to begin with" (*what would I think here if I worked on the marketing team instead of artistic planning,* or *in curation versus education? How would I approach this differently if my whole career was in fundraising and not in operations? What if I was an administrator not an artist, or vice versa?*)—we open ourselves up to override our preexisting mental taxonomies for the groups in our orbit.

DECLASSIFY INFORMATION

The last chapter covered the importance of transparency as part of establishing psychological safety. It's also important for busting silos. Some people call this *procedural justice*—the idea that having a fair process by which decisions are made is not alone sufficient when convincing constituents to join you. Instead, what matters is the *perception* of a fair process and how that process is communicated. And in many instances, this perception of the process is more important than the outcome or decision itself.

The theory has been demonstrated in settings from workplace relationships to the criminal justice system. According to Yale Law School, individuals' perceptions of a decision being procedurally just are based on four central aspects of how they interact (or don't) with the information: whether they were treated with dignity and respect; whether they were given voice during the process; whether the decision maker was transparent and sincerely attempted neutrality; and whether the decision makers conveyed trustworthy motives.[9] Often at cultural organizations, decisions are made at the top—which sometimes is necessary—but the process doesn't always take into account the voices of everyone else affected by the decisions, doesn't demonstrate transparency or attempts at fairness, and therefore doesn't evoke trust.

One example to illustrate this came during the height of the pandemic. The Kennedy Center was given a $25 million government bailout grant . . . and then a few days later announced the furlough of the National Symphony musicians. Layoffs for 250 administrative staff soon followed.[10] People were outraged—community members, staffers, and the artists themselves. *How could you do this when you just got a giant wad of federal cash handed to you?* A Twitter firestorm ensued. *The Washington Post* reported on the layoffs and the backlash.[11]

But the thing is, that federal aid wasn't that much money in the context of the Kennedy Center's then–$300 million operating budget.[12] In fact, it amounted to about only one month's worth of expenses. And laying off artists and staff during lockdown was hardly an anomaly; it was happening everywhere.

Simultaneously, on the other side of the country, artists contracted by the Seattle Opera were also being furloughed, but were praising General Director Christina Scheppelmann amid the tears. One chorister even wrote online, "I can't imagine how hard it was to have to make a decision like this . . . I am confident that if they had any ability to keep the organization running and still pay us as artists after losing the largest show of their season, they would."[13] In almost identical situations, one organization was caught in the public crossfire while the other garnered public sympathy. What gives?

What Scheppelmann did was write a compassionate letter detailing the steps by which the decision was made, the voices who were part of the decision, the impacts to other parts of the organization beyond the artists, her own significant compensation cuts, and her empathy and sadness for the whole situation.[14] People believed her. They felt the process was just. Back at the Kennedy Center, even though some version of all those same things probably happened, the process felt unjust. And it turned into a PR mess.

Sometimes decisions need to be made by a small circle, especially during a crisis when we have to act fast. But other times, the stakes aren't near as high or acutely time sensitive, and we can bring more people in, like when we need to get our colleagues on board with a new strategy, or forge relationships within the community, or even pitch our own ideas to coworkers. In those cases, intentionally modeling transparency (this is what I'm/we're thinking, these are the options I/we are considering, here are the pros and cons of the options being evaluated) and providing opportunity for input (Have you considered X? Could you consider Y?) goes a long way toward establishing the perception of a fair process. Regardless of the scenario, when we declassify information as best we can, or at least explain the context and whose voices contributed (even when that means disclosing it was senior leadership team only and why), it helps people feel better—which is critical to de-siloing our work.

REEVALUATE BUDGET INCENTIVES

In many ways, siloed structures are self-perpetuating because they incentivize the wrong things. For example, separate revenue goals for marketing and development departments directly hinder collaborative work in serving the patron because both teams are extracting money from the same people. I know you're probably thinking, "But, Aubrey, that's how the budget is set up." And you're not wrong. Separate teams lend themselves to separate budget lines (see "self-perpetuating")—but there are other ways to craft a budget.

CEO of TRG Arts Jill Robinson recommends a budget reframing.[15] Just as Yankees and Red Sox fans were able to reimagine the others' goals and assumptions, the same is true for our ledger lines. Instead of the typical breakdown of earned revenue (ticket sales) versus contributed revenue (donations), Robinson asks, what if we looked at patron-generated revenue (tickets and individual donations) versus other sources (grants, corporate sponsorship, rentals, concessions, etc.). When you slice the numbers in this alternate way, it really underscores how critical our customers are and how marketing and development aren't on two different paths, but rather on one quest together.

For example, look at the top budget diagram on the opposite page, which is based on figures typical for an arts organization.

The traditional budget framing would be to say that, of all those various income sources, about 48 percent of revenue comes from earned income and 48 percent from contributed income (these days, more and more organizations have

TYPICAL ARTS REVENUE SOURCES

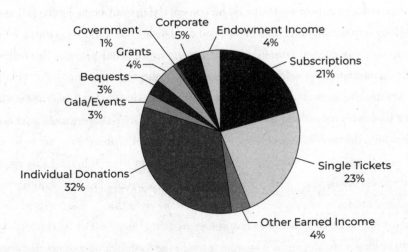

EXAMPLE OF A FAIRLY TYPICAL ORGANIZATION BUDGET BREAKDOWN

REVENUE ROLLUP: TWO DIFFERENT VIEWS

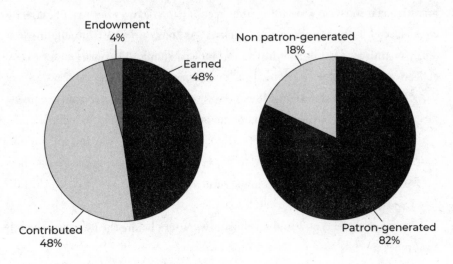

ROLLED UP INTO EARNED VS.
CONTRIBUTED REVENUE

ROLLED UP INTO PATRON VS.
NON-PATRON REVENUE

an even greater share coming from contributed income, but for the sake of this exercise, let's say the two sources are equal), with the remaining 4 percent being investment income from the endowment. But what if instead of slicing the revenue by tickets versus donations (like on the bottom left budget rollup), we sliced it by how much revenue comes from people versus institutions (like on the right)? We'd see that a whopping 82 percent of total revenue comes from patrons.

In our current model, the marketing folks are responsible for the earned share of the pie and the development folks are responsible for the contributed portion. Meanwhile, during board meetings, folks go on tangents about how we need to find more corporate sponsors (anyone witness that conversation before? Just me?), when the reality is, that's such a small piece of the equation. I'm not blaming the board here; the new reframing helps incentivize the right things. The Yankees fans aren't so bad after all. Customer revenue really is the biggest slice of the income pie. When we refashion our taxonomies, even in the form of a budget pie chart, we help break down preexisting silos.

Another example of reframing the budget to incentivize the right things (and, oh wow, this one is dry but necessary . . . so here we go) is the budget document itself. When we print out the QuickBooks file, or Excel doc, or ledger from whatever financial software we're using, the sheet of paper is row after row of perfectly equal spaced lines of revenue and expenses. As someone who is usually meticulously organized, I appreciate this. A lot. But that standard layout can play to our collective disadvantage.

Consider this real example: It was the very end of the season, and the organization had made every budget goal but one.

Single ticket sales: Check.

Subscription campaign: Nailed it.

Annual fund: On track for a home run.

Expenses: Right in line.

Upcoming gala that would take place two weeks before the fiscal year closed: Ruh roh!

I had the delicate task of telling the board they needed to up their game and help sell some gala tables. If the tables got filled with their networks, not only would the organization make the attendance numbers, they'd have more people bidding on the auction and raising the paddle for the fund-a-need, which (as we knew from past average gala spend per head) would get us to that final goal for the year and end the season in the black. Filling those tables was key to a happy fiscal-year ending.

A few months out, I presented at a board meeting and shared the budget document. And to my incredible frustration, the board kept diverting their attention to other line items. "But can we cut expenses on the production side?" one asked.

Not if we want a high production value event, I thought. *And don't even get me started on how cutting your way to health at our already very-lean organizations doesn't work . . . talk about the wrong incentive.*

"Yes, but can't the staff send some more grant proposals?" another said.

Wow, we're at 98 percent of the goal on grants and only 35 percent of the way on gala tickets. Isn't this obvious?!

I was growing exasperated. The organization needed their board members' help, and I was failing profoundly in focusing their attention. After the meeting, I had a call with my mentor and coach at the time, Kathryn Martin, and I complained about the board not understanding.

"You're showing them a bunch of budget lines all equally weighted," Kathryn said.

"But that's the budget," I protested, in a refrain that I'm sure sounds familiar.

"No, that's a budget *layout*," she pressed. "For every revenue goal they've made, roll it up [total it] into one line. For every expense on track, roll that up too if you want. What if you give that board a sheet of paper that has three lines on it? Revenue made, revenue outstanding [the gala], and expenses. That will be so clear where the opportunity lies."

"But . . . it's the budget!" I felt dejected and reticent.

It took a few more weeks of sluggish gala ticket sales before I adopted Kathryn's advice. At the next board meeting, we handed out a simplified budget.

One trustee spoke up: "Well, it looks like if we hit our gala targets, we end the season with a surplus."

I smiled. "What an astute observation!"

And it led into a board discussion of how to get it done—all of the organization, together, across departments and including the board. Fewer silos, more revenue. When we re-evaluate what we incentivize, it can make all the difference.

CONSIDER AN ORGANIZATIONAL REDESIGN

Most arts institutions are organized by practical job function. Marketing is different from development, which in turn sits apart from production, which is distinct from education, and so forth. On one hand, this makes sense: a function-specific structure produces deep specialization and expertise in each category. The finance people become very good at what they do, the development folks have their routine, production is dialed in . . . the trouble is, over time, deep specialization (good) results in deep separation (bad)—aka, silos.

Sometimes the best way to beat silos is to cut them off at the knees with a reorganization. In "The Silo Syndrome," McKinsey says, "In some cases, the best remedy will be a full-scale redesign of your company's operating model."[16] Creating new teams and new department lines can force the reframe: instead of thinking within the old parameters of the old teams, that default is removed, so everyone has to think anew.

In addition to the professionalization of the field over the past forty-plus years, two further developments now make the traditional functional structure insufficient. The first is the shift in consumer behavior mentioned at the start of this chapter. Because art is now viewed as a leisure activity, arts organizations face far more competition of greater variety. The second is that the entire world around us is increasingly complex and uncertain, especially compared to decades ago when the current structure arose. Our work and place in this world is not as simple now, requiring more of our teams and organizations.

Anthropologist Gillian Tett says rethinking is sometimes a matter of challenging inertia: "Most of the time, most of us simply accept the classification systems we have inherited." Just like the longtime Yankees or Red Sox fans, most of us with backgrounds from traditional cultural institutions accept the systems handed down to us. Yet if we want to achieve the kind of growth we need, a new organizational structure is the path forward. So let's step up to the plate.

A Model for a New Organization Structure

An expert in organizational design—one with years at Accenture's Organization Design practice—who also happens to be married to a musician in the Metropolitan Opera Orchestra, Julian Chender says that "functional org structures lend themselves to what we call *vertical* work." That's the type of work that's usually in service to a simpler or singular goal. In the case of the original cultural org structure, that singular goal was primarily producing great art. But when more is demanded of a company, a structure to support *horizontal* work across teams is needed.

For the best possible outcomes in our orgs, though, Chender says we need a structure with both vertical and horizontal components. Some of our work still has vertical elements (the fundraising people won't be curating the next exhibit, for example), but other elements of our work and goals need to or should affect everyone in the institution—obliterating silos—which are the horizontal components.

FUNCTIONAL ORGANIZATION STRUCTURE

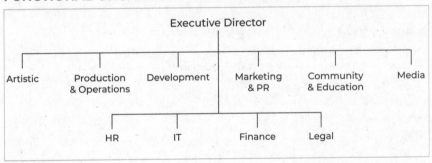

Vertical vs. Horizontal Work: In a functional organization structure, the design lends itself to vertical work. Smaller organizations likely don't have all these teams, but still have all these functions. Source: Adapted from Kates Kesler, © 11A Collaborative, 2022.

To determine what needs to be vertical versus horizontal, start with your over-arching strategy. If you have an existing strategic plan, ask yourself what goals apply to everyone (horizontal) and which require specific skills (vertical). For example, if you're using the main strategies in this book, your overarching goals are (1) to attract, engage, and retain paying customers by giving them a great experience while (2) reflecting the local community in all you do and (3) living out your company values.[17] Pieces of this work are vertical work (revenue, product, and infrastructure) and parts are horizontal (customer and community needs). An updated structure might look something like this:

A Modern Arts Organization Structure

REVENUE	PRODUCT	INFRASTRUCTURE
Customer and community needs: entertainment, belonging, safety, representation, shared values		
Content & Media	Artistic Administration	People Operations/HR
Customer Experience	Artists	Finance
Customer Retention	Artistic Production & Operations	IT
Customer Advancement		Data Science
Institutional Giving		Design/Creative
Education		

Each vertical component (revenue, product, infrastructure) requires specific skills and roles to execute its body of work. Each horizontal component (customer and community needs) requires active participation from all roles to execute the body of work.

Some of this is similar to what we know in typical nonprofit structures (e.g., we still have people selling tickets, raising money, and working in operations), and some of it means rethinking ownership of tasks. The idea is that this approach to a new structure can be carried out by arts organizations of varying sizes: while larger organizations have more people and roles and smaller organizations tend to have fewer people playing multiple roles, the skills and bodies of work necessary are largely the same.

Revenue

This new structure takes the teams formerly divided into marketing and development and refashions them around different parts of the patron journey. At a larger organization, these could each be their own team, while at a smaller organization, these functions could be served by fewer people across fewer teams.

Content and Media. This team includes people responsible for the website, streaming, digital ads, and social content for artists and staff, not just the brand account. This team uses strategies covered in chapter one (being newcomer facing with our marketing and newcomer focused online), as well as chapter four (digital content drives analog engagement). The goal of this team: optimizing the sales funnel.

Customer Experience. From the moment someone purchases a ticket, this team takes the handoff. They are responsible for all physical, in-person/analog activity including box office, guest services, front of house, ushers, and catering. The folks in charge of editorial material— the program book, signage, or other on-site handouts from chapter one (newcomer friendly in the venue)—could work in this department. The goal for this team: optimizing the experience surrounding the product.

Customer Retention. Executing the Long Haul Model from chapter two, this team is building the audience journey from first-attendance follow-up to repeat attendance to ultimately driving recurring revenue via subscriptions followed by low-level donations. Their goal: building loyalty and patron lifetime value to the organization.

Customer Advancement. Rather than overseeing mass communication relationships like the customer retention team (email blasts, digital content, postcards, brochures, bulk-mail appeal letters, et cetera), the Advancement role or team focuses on one-on-one donor relationships, meaning major gift prospects, major donors, and special events. Their goal: cultivating and securing larger gifts.

Institutional Giving. This team tackles corporate sponsorship, grants, and government donor relationships. If you think back to the budget pie charts earlier in this chapter, institutional support still comprises about 10 percent to 15 percent of the budget, give or take a few points depending on your organization. This team's goal: maximize this revenue.

Education. This team spearheads the work of filling in the arts-education gaps increasingly left by our public school system, whether serving children or adults. It's part of revenue because of the strategies covered in chapter four. This team's goal: driving both immediate revenue (e.g., "I purchased a class from the organization") and future sales ("I learned something that stimulates my future interest and proclivity to attend") via a workflow, such as an automated email after someone accesses online learning.[*]

All of this revenue vertical is about moving away from goals that pit our marketing and development teams against each other (even if inadvertently), and breaking down those old silos. We want to create a structure that works together to move the patron along a journey with us, from that first piece of content they see online to a ticket purchase, to a repeat visit, to an engaged regular attendee, then subscriber, to donor—all while the patron is learning more about the art form and deepening their connection along the way.

Product

Our "product" is our tangible, central deliverable: the art. This vertical concerns itself with optimizing our product in service to our mission—our strongest asset as cultural organizations—and consists of departments that perhaps were previously labeled "artistic planning" and "operations." While that part of the structure doesn't change too much, as you'll see, under this new model it does *not* include

---

[*] Also worth noting: In the old model, sometimes we literally call the work of the education team "community engagement," but in this new model, meeting community needs is part of the horizontal work for everyone. Here, the education team produces educational content as part of an ancillary revenue stream.

some of the aspects of our traditional product that are more closely aligned with infrastructure, like artistic personnel management.

The goal for all three of these teams is to produce excellent art that showcases the full spectrum of talent available and reflects the fullness of our communities.

Artists. The people in our institutions who create the art, including performers (orchestra members, singers, soloists, chorus, actors, dancers), artisans (hair, makeup, costumes, sets), directors (stage directors, music director, artistic director, choreographer), and curators (across art, animals, geology, botany, and so on). The goal: making the art.

Artistic Administration. So much of the programming strategy covered in chapter five falls under the purview of this team: season planning, contracting and commissioning artists, and curatorial and collection development. The goal of these folks: mapping out the who, what, when, where of the art we produce or present.

Artistic Production/Operations. This team keeps things moving. They're all about non-digital production and operations, stage management, exhibitions, touring, and the like. The goal: ensuring the art gets onstage and in the exhibits.

Infrastructure

Nothing gets done at any business without strong infrastructure—systems that support the organization's key functions. In some ways, the infrastructure teams are standard for arts organizations (HR and Finance, for example); in this new model, additional teams and roles that more holistically support the work of the institution also fall here:

People Operations (HR). This team oversees a smart and equitable hiring process consistent across the organization, as outlined in chapter six; compensation including tracking equal pay ranges across level bands; and performance evaluation. This includes artist personnel management liaising with artists and artisans, as well as staff personnel management coordinating employee support systems like healthcare and paid-time-off programs. The goal for this team: optimizing the employee life cycle, from recruitment to exit.

Finance. This team coordinates budget development, forecasting, accounting, payroll, and endowment management in partnership with the board. The budget framing discussed in this chapter largely falls here. The goal: optimizing how the organization manages and accesses money coming in and out while establishing controls that help rather than hamper business efficiency.

Information Technology (IT). The team responsible for developing and managing the tools to empower employees to do their best work, whether remotely, in the office, or a hybrid of both. This team also oversees the CRM database, ethical use of consumer data, data hygiene processes, cybersecurity, and compliance with payment card industry (PCI) security practices. The goal: optimizing employee workflows and collaboration company wide while managing security of sensitive information.

Analytics or Data Science. In a perfect world, everyone on staff is data driven, using the tools and programs needed related to their work. But in an organization that can support personnel specifically dedicated to more complex data work and modeling, I'd instill that position or team here in infrastructure. As we saw with American Express and the Colonial Williamsburg Foundation, using data across departments is usually the key to optimization. The goal: researching and discovering patterns in data that can be used to help achieve other departments' goals.

Creative Team. Typically the creative team (graphic design, copywriting, production of ads and materials) lives in the marketing department. But I've always seen that lead to other departments getting short shrift: the education folks trying to hone their amateur design skills to make the materials they need, the development people hiring outside designers to make sure those event invitations shine, or the production staff hurriedly printing a program insert with tonight's

casting change. And just about any time these other teams do ask for
the marketing team's support, it's through last-minute requests that
are not well integrated into a proper production timeline and riddled
with asks that start with "Could you just quickly . . ." (Note: nothing
is ever that "quick.")

A better setup for this work is more like an internal, centralized
creative agency serving everyone. So maybe what lives here is a creative director–type role and graphic design person or team, with the
other teams responsible for hiring their own copywriters. Or maybe
copywriting lives here, too, and every project starts with a true creative brief.* The org structure experts say to just experiment, ensuring
the department lines are different from what they were before so that
people can forge new brain paths that break down the silos.[18] The
goal: serving all organization-wide design needs to create a stellar
unified look and voice, regardless of the department or deliverables.

Again, in a large institution, each of these areas may have many people doing
this work, with their own department head and respective teams built out from
there—and maybe even additional teams like legal, archives, or venue management if you own your venue. In smaller companies, multiple areas fall under the
purview of just a few people. But the important thing is that these new vertical
components allow teams to think in terms of skill-specific work that rewrites the
old silo script,† so that we can next overlay the horizontal work that affects everybody in the organization.

---

* Quick definition of "creative brief" since it's not always used in cultural organizations (vs.
marketing agencies, which use them far more often): a short document that sums up a design
project's purpose, target audience, messaging, key dates (e.g., when the final deliverables or
project goes public), and other baseline details. The idea is to get all your thoughts about
the project in one place and achieve stakeholder alignment on the project before it begins.

† If you're wondering, *Won't this all eventually just create new and different silos?* you're not
wrong. Regardless of the organization's structure, if there are multiple teams, there runs the risk
of silos. This is why de-siloing is a perennial issue for all kinds of companies, and maybe also
why some reorg so often. Most important is to stay vigilant and intentional about breaking silos
down, no matter which of the tactics in this chapter you choose to embrace.

APPLICATION BOX

Concept: A model for a new organization structure

Organization: Dayton Performing Arts Alliance

The Dayton Performing Arts Alliance revamped its entire structure, moving from separate marketing and fundraising teams to redrawn department lines around mass communication versus one-on-one relationships. The resident companies of the Alliance include the Dayton Symphony, Opera, and Ballet, and the customer is the throughline (the horizontal work) connecting all their vertical teams, says president and CEO Patrick Nugent.

This means ticket sales and a low-level annual fund are now under the same umbrella of a full-time director-level position over "patron engagement." This director oversees the patron journey from their second purchase to subscriber to annual fund donor. Then, there's the head of development and their team, who diligently pursue individual relationships, from pre–major donor to significant gifts at the top of the giving pyramid. Additionally, the Alliance completed the revenue vertical by creating a director of acquisition role, who presides over new customers, with junior staff support for all three teams. During the reorg, Nugent moved a development officer to the newly formed patron engagement team to help with bridging the customer pathway from subscriber to donor. He also hired a firm specifically to help train the remaining major gifts officers.

"Everyone on the team now knows and believes developing the customer journey is the way forward." In service of this goal, after the staff restructure, Nugent added $200,000 to the budget to jump-start this work. Additionally, he brought on a new vice president for learning and community engagement, who is responsible for traditional education efforts plus monetizing adult education. There's also a new chief information officer who oversees all things data, including patron segmentation for all their Long Haul Model work.

This restructure process began with a staff retreat where they talked through the work ahead, the customer throughline, and their apprehensions around the changes afoot. Together, they agreed on

the path forward. What Nugent's team did in this retreat was brilliantly move from common framing (we're all arts fans), to reframing
(we're all here to make our community arts fans).

The way the Dayton Performing Arts Alliance began focusing on
its customers captured the attention of city government. Now, the
arts are part of the civic plan to entice people to move there. "What
we're doing here is part of the value proposition to live in Dayton,"
Nugent shared with me. "It's a big goal, but I believe the arts are a
necessary part of that goal, and we're taking seriously how to best
see it through with every position in the entire organization."

Overlay the Horizontal Work

Once the vertical work structure is determined, it's time to overlay the horizontal
work—the goals to which everyone in the organization must contribute in some
way. Earlier in the chapter, we identified customer and community needs as the
horizontal work—the underlying institutional-wide focus across every team.

Take the community need for representation, for example. Every person in
the institution is either advancing this work or not. This work means HR is examining staff makeup at every level of seniority and ensuring equitable pay ranges
across each level band (chapter six). It means our artistic personnel are working
to create fairer audition practices, developing more inclusive artist rosters—guest
artists, soloists, conductors, casting—and expanding our repertoire, always working to make sure we're reflecting as much of the community as possible (chapters
five and six). It means our content teams are using digital offerings to provide
access to and stimulate interest in our in-person product (chapter three) in a
way that's approachable and welcoming (chapter one). It means our advancement
folks are not assuming BIPOC attendees and donors have lower levels of income
(chapters two and five).[19] Every role within each vertical function is contributing
to this work.

When it comes to customer needs, such as offering a sense of belonging, horizontal work means our advertising people are choosing images that reflect the
customer (such as audience shots rather than just the conductor, as per chapter

one). It means our IT people are doubling down on protecting our customers' data (chapter three). The education team is developing entry-level training, teaching, and studying opportunities that bring in new revenue while filling in the knowledge gap left by our schools (chapter four). Artistic and production teams are helping to break down the fourth wall, and our finance people are developing budgets that prioritize all this work.

How do we make sure these things are happening across an entire institution, though? It's one thing to say this is what *should* be happening. It's another to execute organization-wide. Organization design research shows that, in addition to tools like declassifying groups and information, plus reevaluating budget framing, the key to ensuring horizontal work succeeds is to incentivize it. Experts offer a few ways to do that.

Evaluate Management Processes and Tools

How many times has an artist contract (soloist, actor, guest conductor, opera singer, etc.) been negotiated by the operations team without them ever talking to the development team (who definitely wants that superstar to do a donor reception when they come to town), or education team (who definitely wants that performer to attend a school visit), or marketing team (who definitely wants to film a behind-the-scenes video with them for social media)? The answer: Regularly.

These are customer and community needs—"customer" in this case being the donors and "community" being the schools and social media followers—so clearly the horizontal work requires a different process than the current way of the operations folks handling the entire artist contract. It's fairer for the artist, too, if these needs are communicated up front. That's how they'll understand the totality of what's being asked of them. A prominent soloist was telling me how frustrated they get when they don't hear from these other teams until well after the contract is negotiated, when this could have been rectified fairly easily by having a joint planning call with all those parties during the contracting process.

So many digital tools for project management exist now that help embed this type of work across teams. We have incredibly powerful and economical programs available to us that didn't exist even a decade ago to help with updating our processes and routines for cross-department, horizontal work. Let's use them.

Add Integrator Roles

One organization I worked with decided to get serious about horizontal work across teams, so they created a role that facilitated just that. That person attended multiple departments' meetings, reported to two different managers,* and—unlike some arrangements I've seen where a staff person attends multiple department meetings but has zero power or authority—the employee was given autonomy to make some decisions on behalf of the teams with whom they were collaborating. Perhaps the most common integrator role outside the arts is a chief of staff, and more and more cultural organizations are bringing these types of positions into the fold.

Support Hybrid Work

As the last chapter mentioned, at a cultural institution, we know some people have to be on-site because we offer an in-person, physical experience as our primary product. But when more than half of administrative employees say they prefer to work for an arts organization that has flexible work components over one that has a reputation for high artistic quality, it's not helping horizontal work to say that everyone needs to be physically present.[20] The forward-looking answer isn't a one-size-fits-all institutional policy (remember from the last chapter—we want less of those). Rather, it could involve reframing and reforming the systems we inherited so our brains allow new ideas to surface, as well as some trial and error—much like the de-siloing recipe overall.

Determine Aligned Metrics

Think back to the budget example earlier in the chapter. Traditional departmental revenue goals drive over-solicitation and upsell frenzy on both the marketing and development teams while the operations, artistic, and education teams have no real revenue responsibility at all. Instead, in service to the horizontal work of meeting customer needs, try evaluating performance not on departmental revenue

---

* This "two boss" arrangement is also called a matrix approach, and they laid out a whole system to help mitigate inherent challenges with this type of dual-supervisor reporting structure.

alone but also on metrics that measure customer loyalty and retention across all departments—including how teams like production, IT, and artistic helped, too. Measure on things like if the artistic planning people worked with marketing on what program was occurring for the subscriber appreciation days. Or if IT helped with the streaming infrastructure so the donors got their behind-the-scenes exclusive access.

When looking at the need for representation, every first-round candidate pool for every open role on every team should be measured for how diverse it is. If it's not representative of the community or has only token (singular) candidates from different backgrounds or identities, the hiring manager should go back to the application stack. This metric should be part of performance evaluation for all employees in supervisory roles.

In other words, what gets measured gets managed.

When American Express finally figured all this silo stuff out in the late 1990s, it wasn't a rebound straight to the top of Credit Card Mountain. It was bumpy. Some things didn't work like they'd imagined. But they persisted through the friction of change, leaning on the fact that they knew the old way wasn't working.

At the time, Y2K was on the horizon (remember when all the computers in the universe were supposed to crumble into mass chaos at the stroke of the year 2000?), so they used that as a catalyst for their de-siloing work: The excuse of *We gotta get these computers talking to each other* helped them declassify groups. Additionally, a new company president was coming on board, which Doug Marty's team was able to leverage as well, ensuring buy-in came from the top. They didn't just have a CEO attending some meetings, but one participating in the changes. The new president, Kenneth Chenault, held all-hands meetings quarterly, where they regularly talked company wide about their evolution, which declassified information. They also launched an internal PR campaign to disseminate messaging around the new ways of doing business, demonstrating procedural justice. Along the way, some people left. But the ones who stayed got it and latched on to the new centralized customer strategy.

And so it is, too, with cultural organizations. Some people will embrace updated systems and some people may want to abort, both of which are okay. What's not okay, or at least not best serving us anymore, is keeping the same old structure the same old siloed way. Our world and our profession have come way too far in the last forty years.

9.

Not Throwing Away My Shot

Companies That Advocate, Outperform

"Talk less, smile more," sings Aaron Burr in the musical *Hamilton*. "Don't let them know what you're against or what you're for," he croons to his friend-turned-archrival Alexander Hamilton. As *Hamilton*'s millions of fans know, Burr's vanilla, milquetoast reluctance to take a firm stand on anything ultimately led to his political defeat.

Today, politics extends to brand management—and as the twin pandemics of coronavirus and systemic racism have made clear, organizational statements alone are not enough. Not only do consumers expect companies to take action in support of their positions; research shows that nonprofits actually generate more revenue when they advocate for their beliefs.[1]

Advocacy is a broad term. It's really more of an umbrella term that can include activism (such as pitching media stories, building awareness, or registering voters) and lobbying (working to change public policy or obtain government funding). But in short, advocacy is taking any action on behalf of our values. This chapter unpacks it all, and shows how vocal businesses separate from the pack, galvanizing unwavering devotees who support them through thick and thin because they've done something most companies only feign: tapped people's values.

We've known this is true in the for-profit sector for some time. We think of companies like Patagonia, which is known for taking a public stand on issues of environmental responsibility and abortion rights, suing President Trump in 2017 alongside several Native American tribes for his attempt to shrink national monuments in Utah, and—the week after I initially drafted this very chapter—giving away the company altogether to fight climate change and protect undeveloped land.[2] At the time of their announcement, company revenues had sustained at over a billion dollars a year for the prior three years.[3]

But this trend goes back further than that. The entire B Corp, or Benefit Corporation, movement began back in 2007 when around eighty companies were first certified for their social and environmental performance and public transparency. Before that, basketball shoemaker AND1 was a 1990s poster child for a socially responsible business that also turned mega-profits. Before being acquired in 2011, the firm offered employees shared ownership, strong parental leave benefits, on-site yoga classes and a basketball court, and enhanced conditions for their supply chain workers—all while donating 5 percent of profits to charity and its annual revenue exceeding $250 million in the age of competing with Air Jordans for shelf space. Nike definitely wasn't doing all that at the time.[4]

Even though companies have been advocating for their values for a few decades now, the rise in so-called conscious capitalism is still a massive shift in the business landscape, which can conjure fear. "The problem right now is you have businesses that are afraid," said Marc Elias, a voting rights lawyer who has worked with many corporations on their activism efforts. "It's really unfortunate," he told the *Los Angeles Times*, "because now is not the time for businesses to offer thoughts and prayers."[5]

Organizations now have a broader responsibility than they've taken on in the past, and declarations without accompanying action are no longer enough for consumers. Elias, Patagonia, AND1, and hundreds of B Corporations were ahead of the curve, proving to the rest of us that demonstrating values externally goes hand in hand with revenue growth. Beyond that, there are four big reasons to assuage our fears: consumers want brands to take action, the risk of backlash isn't as severe as we may think, it actually hurts our organization when we don't act on behalf of our values, and the size and economic impact of our industry demonstrates how much collective power we have to move the needle.

CONSUMERS WANT ADVOCACY

A global survey of more than 30,000 people globally concluded that nearly two-thirds of consumers want brands to stand for something.[6] When the majority of consumers feel this way, given that they are the biggest source of funding for most cultural institutions (see previous chapter on how much of our total revenue is patron generated), we cannot ignore that trend. In fact this trend is rising, according to a separate multiyear study, with almost seven out of ten high-income consumers identifying as "belief-driven" buyers—those who say they choose, switch, avoid, or boycott a brand based on its stand on societal issues. That's up from five out of ten in previous years.[7]

In chapter seven, I talked about the need for companies to establish core values, which is an internally facing first step toward strengthening company culture. When your organization is ready to level up, use those same values to inform your external activism. That way, when the next big incident happens—whether political, social, economic, environmental, or racial—you have established these values as guide rails for how the organization responds, or in some cases, makes the choice clear not to respond. (Not everything has to be a priority for every organization.) That's why our company values are a north star by which to navigate.

Consumers understand this as well. According to Gartner, 62 percent of US consumers agree that "companies should only express support for issues or causes that are consistent with the values of the company."[8] And once a company acts, consumers act (with their wallets). When Patagonia stitched tags into all their shorts that read "VOTE THE ASSHOLES OUT" ahead of the 2020 presidential election, their day-after-Thanksgiving sales were quadruple their normal Black Friday revenue, with a third of customers being new.[9] To be clear, Patagonia's extreme advocacy was possible because it was built on years of taking action in alignment with their values.[10] This was not a one-off gimmick. So while I'm not recommending VOTE THE ASSHOLES OUT ticket stock anytime soon for arts organizations, we do need to build up trust in our activism, because over time, that can reap big rewards.

Another example of consumer behavior trending toward action is what happened when Senator Lindsey Graham introduced legislation for a national abortion ban on the heels of the Supreme Court's decision to overturn *Roe v. Wade*. Aside from widespread outrage, voter registration by women skyrocketed and President Biden's dismal approval rating improved so drastically that the 2022 midterms defied the trends of previous election cycles. Voter turnout soared in many places, and the giant "red wave" swing to the opposing party didn't materialize that voting year.[11] These two examples herald a much larger trend that holds no matter where you personally stand on contentious issues: on the whole, people generally act according to their values.

We'll talk more about the legal parameters (what's lawfully allowed for nonprofits and what's not) around organizational advocacy later in the chapter, but for now, the point is that expansive trends like this present institutions with the opportunity to align with patrons, which deepens their trust in and loyalty to our work. Things as simple as setting up a voter registration table in your lobby, for example, or hosting a Get Out the Vote crew in front of your entrance can serve as starting places. The majority of consumers want our activism.

As Alexander Hamilton pledges his support for Thomas Jefferson, he raps about how the two have never agreed on anything, with opposing views on something like seventy-five different issues—yet he still endorses the candidate. "When all is said and all is done, Jefferson has beliefs. Burr has none." Don't be like Burr. Standing for nothing results in just that: nothing.

THE BACKLASH AGAINST ADVOCACY ISN'T REAL

The second reason not to fear amping up organizational advocacy is the backlash is . . . not really real. Only one in three consumers will actually boycott a brand according to one study. Of those same respondents, significantly more said they'd be turned off by a poor purchase experience than anything they see in a brand's advocacy (once again, it all goes back to the customer experience).[12]

In 2014, CVS grabbed headlines—but didn't lose revenue—when they made the then jaw-dropping decision to stop selling cigarettes in their nearly ten thousand stores nationwide because it didn't fit their healthcare mission. When the announcement went out, smokers and analysts alike went berserk. The move was projected to cost the company $2 billion in lost revenue.[13] Walgreens, Rite Aid, and other drugstores all stayed with the herd, prioritizing profit over people's lives (until the FDA forced Walgreens's hand in 2019, asking a federal judge to bar Walgreens from selling tobacco products, alleging the company was selling tobacco to minors).[14] Which company do you think enjoyed better headlines as a result of these choices? Plus, CVS's predicted billions of dollars in losses didn't happen. Smokers didn't move their business to other retailers as people had predicted; they stopped buying cigarettes everywhere.[15] And CVS's revenue has grown year over year *every single year* since.[16]

CVS shows us that we shouldn't assume too much about our customers without the data to back it up—as does Ben & Jerry's. With flavors like "Save Our Swirled" (with the "O" as a globe) raising awareness for climate change and "I Dough, I Dough" (with the "O's" as wedding rings) following the Supreme Court's decision on marriage equality, you might think the ice cream maker's base leans left politically. Yet, head of global activism strategy Christopher Miller says not so fast. "We sell more ice cream to Walmart than any other retailer," he told *Harvard Business Review* about their efforts, "so I don't think you can look at our consumer base and say they're more or less liberal than people who buy Häagen-Dazs."[17] The message: We just don't know where our customers stand a lot of times, and overgeneralizing doesn't give us the answer.

Ultimately, if your organization does take a stance on an issue it holds as a core value, and there is a threat of backlash, take a breath and maintain the course. You're sticking to your established beliefs, and most people reward that integrity, while some who disagree often at least respect it. Consumers don't fall for brands' insincerity but are positively influenced by their authenticity, especially when those messages are consistent through their C-suite, senior leaders, and employees.[18] Maybe you can't win 'em all by acting on your values, but you can definitely win more patrons.

And if you really want a boss move, you could take a page from the Patagonia playbook. After the company made a donation to Planned Parenthood and cranky calls to their customer service line commenced, they told callers who complained they were donating an additional $5 for each of those calls they received. The calls stopped pretty quickly after that.[19]

IT HURTS US WHEN WE DON'T ADVOCATE

The third reason cultural institutions should overcome any fears over raising our company voice is the downside for *not* taking action. When the coronavirus took hold and lockdown began, hundreds of thousands of cultural jobs were lost, by artists and administrators alike. Then, as a whole industry, we effectively rallied together and advocated to secure federal funding like the arts in America haven't seen before: Shuttered Venue Operators Grants, forgivable Paycheck Protection Program loans, American Rescue Plan awards, tax credits, and state and local relief grants. Our industry received amounts of government dollars unprecedented in recent history. A lot of organizations balanced budgets in 2020 and 2021 for the first time in years with no substantial earned income at all due to the increased funding, both public and private. I can't tell you how many executive leaders have said to me "the pandemic saved us" in reference to the bailout dollars.

But if one side of the pandemic advocacy coin, where legislators passed the relief funding measures, was victory, the other side—how those same officials offered astonishingly little support and few guidelines for bringing the arts back—felt like defeat. The result: We became a politically neglected sector that was the first to close and the last to reopen, sidelined while our counterparts in restaurants and retail were ushered back to business. They got outdoor dining and sidewalk shopping while, in many regions, we were forced to remain closed—even though we regularly produce events like outdoor concerts and open-air exhibits. We know how to gather large groups of people in a controlled environment—we do it all the time! Yet no dice. Even some movie theaters reopened while cultural organizations were passed over for the green light.[20] Folks could sit in a theater and watch the big screen but not a performance. The disparity is enraging, and yet, some of that's on us as a field.

Being able to balance the budget of an arts organization while simultaneously being unable to deliver the *art* isn't exactly the best advocacy win. But it is a substantial advocacy beginning. It shows that we have the collective power to garner both needed funding and attention from our elected officials.

A study out of Georgetown University sought to capture what differentiates the most effective nonprofits who have demonstrated reach, growth, and impact over multiple years from the average ones. Modeling the methodology of Jim Collins's *Good to Great* and *Built to Last* to the nonprofit sector, the researchers evaluated hundreds of nonprofits across all types of services and programs. Their number one finding across every top-performing nonprofit was that the most impactful ones all engaged in and reaped the benefits of advocacy—far and away beyond who had the best fundraisers or the largest budgets.[21]

Often in the nonprofit sector, we tend to outsource the advocacy heavy lifting to places like Americans for the Arts, each artistic discipline's member service organizations, and state advocacy agencies, instead of taking this on at our individual cultural institutions. Those organizations do wonderful, needed work, to be clear, but we miss an opportunity when we separate this work entirely from our direct-to-consumer services and programs.

"High-impact nonprofits engage in both direct service *and* advocacy," the Georgetown research offers. "The organizations we studied conduct programs on the ground and simultaneously advocate for policy change at the local, state, or national level."[22] Cultural organizations see firsthand what's working and not working with our constituents; we can use that to identify policy or funding needs. And then instead of fully handing off that work to industry member service organizations, we have direct access to mobilize our patron base. That in turn helps us raise our organizational profile, establish ourselves as a leader in the community, and gain credibility with elected officials and community members alike. And when these efforts result in successful change (a new law is passed, new funding received, new policy developed), that goes right back to supporting our programs and services. It hurts us when we don't advocate, and wow, does it help us when we do.

SIZE AND IMPACT OF THE INDUSTRY

A final reason why cultural organizations should feel unafraid to advocate externally is the sheer size of our industry. Coming out of the pandemic, the arts are a

$1 trillion industry.[23] That's 4.4 percent of the United States' GDP—bigger than agriculture, air transportation, or warehousing[24]—and yet almost no American would know this.*

If we in the arts won't advocate for ourselves, who will? Cultural organizations exist in almost every county, together employing 5.1 million creative workers.[25] Another 3.3 million board members serve these institutions. And every single one of these organizations has an audience base of loyal supporters—a base that is also growing with the help of the strategies in this book. We are big, and we can claim our power and economic impact.

Looking at agriculture, think about the "Got Milk?" campaign. The Backstreet Boys with those white-lipped smiles, or supermodel Kate Moss wearing the famous mustache and not much else, or the campaign's very first commercial, where the guy couldn't win the radio quiz show because his mouth was full of peanut butter and he had no milk to wash it down (by the way, that winning question was "Who shot Alexander Hamilton?"). If milk mustaches can be made cool and ubiquitous, arts and culture absolutely can be, too. Also noteworthy is that the dairy industry's success came when they moved away from milk "doing your body good," in a perfect example of shifting the marketing from product-centric to customer-centric.[26] Stop extolling the virtues of why the product is inherently good (milk is healthy and gives you strong bones, the soloist is a virtuoso, the playwright is a genius), and instead focus on what you can become when you consume it (gorgeous and popular and capable of winning quiz shows and part of something bigger than yourself when you're surrounded by fellow audience members who feel the same way). And our sector is bigger than agriculture—the opportunity is before us.

As an industry, we've dipped our toe into the waters of advocating for our work locally and nationally and seen the benefits. Now we're called to continue to wade

---

* I learned the stats are very similar in the UK, which I think is so cool and interesting. Pre-pandemic, the arts (creative industries, as they call them) were a £116 billion industry, which was 4 percent of the UK's GDP (just like in the US)—bigger than fishing and energy, and almost as big as construction.

in, whether that's via clever branding, lifting our brand voice, or both. And when we lift our brand voice, remember that taking a stand on important issues is hardly a new concept in the arts: art is historically a vehicle for statements, for advocating in the present and for the future. Neutral is out. Bold is in. Much like how an audacious, unapologetic rap-battle musical turned into a cultural phenomenon.

ADVOCACY TIPS: DO'S AND DON'TS

We don't always know how to advocate or what's allowed (read: legal) for non-profits. But that shouldn't stop us—not least because, again, advocacy is a broad term, so there's a lot that falls under its purview, from speaking out to taking direct action in order to influence legislation.

Bolder Advocacy is a national organization led by lawyers and nonprofit experts that empowers and educates nonprofits on how to advocate. A few years ago, I was able to learn directly from Sara Matlin, Bolder Advocacy's senior bilingual counsel. Here are some of her top recommendations.

Know the Law

Charities cannot engage in partisan political activity, which is any activity directed toward the success or failure of a partisan candidate, political party, or partisan political group. Matlin says the best way to translate this is that nonprofits can generally support *policies, not people*.

Ben & Jerry's takes this approach. CEO Matthew McCarthy says, "It may come as a surprise, but Ben & Jerry's is not partisan. Even in the divisive 2020 election, there was no 'Vote Biden' post or press release from us . . . We are political but not in supporting any candidates."[27]

The important takeaway is *always focus on the issues*. Let's say, for example, you disapprove of a proposed policy of a legislator (whether in office already or while they are campaigning). Under the law, you can't call the person a racist or sexist (or whatever the criticism may be) because that doesn't affect policy. However, calling a *policy* racist or sexist can absolutely influence said policy—and that is legal for us to do. Policies, not people. Causes, not candidates.

Understand the Rules Around Lobbying

A lot of times when we think of lobbying, we think of men with greasy, slicked-back hair in suits paying for legislation deals (or is that just me?). But that's not really accurate. Lobbying is simply an attempt to influence legislation. It includes expressing views about a proposed law (no, we don't want a change in tax code to discourage charitable giving) or about federal or state budgets (why yes, we do want more funding for arts and culture in next year's coffers). It can entail a meeting with the legislator, an email or phone call to the official's office, a tweet where you tag the official, or any other direct channel. Lobbying also includes communications meant to steer public opinion around legislation (sign the petition, contact your senator's office).

All of these types of lobbying are permissible for nonprofits under the law, as long as it's an "insubstantial part" of a 501(c)(3) organization's activities. So if you're spending *some* time and money on lobbying activities, that's okay. If it's arguably more than 5 percent of the budget, experts say slow your roll (but honestly, 5 percent is a pretty hefty cap to meet given that a lot of us currently spend zero on these types of things). And remember, not all advocacy is lobbying, and this "insubstantial" test specifically refers to activities meant to influence legislation. You've probably got a lot more wiggle room than you think.

Use the Tools Already in Your Wheelhouse

Cultural nonprofits have enviable communications tools at our disposal: multiple social media channels, email lists, and sizable databases. We can invite our base to send letters, make calls, share posts, and the like. And we can use those same channels even when we don't have an action item, but simply want to raise our voice.

Jan Masaoka, CEO of CalNonprofits (the California Association of Nonprofits), said in a training session, "When a legislator is driving around and sees two hundred bumper stickers that say '*I go to the ballet and I vote*,' they pay attention." Think of ideas like this to show the magnitude of your base. Our size and scope give us so much power. Even smaller arts organizations have greater reach than other types of companies. Our platforms can help us mobilize others, and we can use that power for good to effect much broader change.

Major League Baseball used their platform for good in 2022. Normally on game day, teams would use their social media accounts to share player stats, real-time score updates, and postgame highlights. Instead, in the aftermath of the Uvalde, Texas, mass school shooting, the New York Yankees and Tampa Bay Rays used their social channels to advocate for change to gun laws during a game that took place two days after the murders. The teams didn't just issue statements condemning gun violence; they shared poignant fact after fact about gun violence in America with their millions of followers across Twitter and Instagram.

New York Yankees ✓
@Yankees

Firearms were the leading cause of death for American children and teens in 2020.

4:02 PM · May 26, 2022 · Twitter Web App

25.6K Retweets   **1,876** Quote Tweets   **128.1K** Likes

28

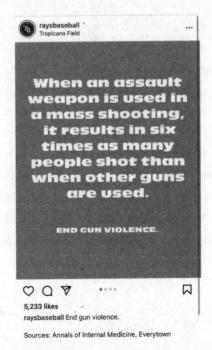

raysbaseball
Tropicana Field

When an assault weapon is used in a mass shooting, it results in six times as many people shot than when other guns are used.

END GUN VIOLENCE.

5,233 likes
raysbaseball End gun violence.

Sources: Annals of Internal Medicine, Everytown   29

For arts organizations, sometimes our best platform available is our art itself. In 2021, the Smithsonian National Museum of Natural History, usually a science museum showcasing dinosaur bones and geological rocks, debuted a photography exhibit co-curated with the Smithsonian American Art Museum focusing on climate change. The provocative images depicted environmental devastation, including an aerial shot of tar-filled oil slicks slicing across the Gulf of Mexico like black lightning striking a rich turquoise canvas; and another overhead shot of an open pit gold mine in Nevada emanating intense, beautiful shades of emerald and Kelly green that you then learn are created by toxic mercury released during the ore extraction. As co-curator Scott Wing told the *Washington Post*, "The thing that you shouldn't conclude is that you can ignore your relationship to the environment."[30] So, arts orgs, take this as our sign to stop ignoring our surroundings; there are *so many issues* affecting our nation right now that are urgent, personal to people on our staffs and in our audience, and too important to ignore.

Get to Know Your Local Officials

Invite your local officials to events (performances, exhibit openings, galas). These relationships matter regardless of your organization's or community's size. Officials getting to see and experience what we do forms a stronger bond than a letter or phone call from us any day. (And in other countries where even more government funding is on the line, these relationships matter just as much if not more as they do in the US.)

Board members can really help here. At one gala for the California Symphony, we strategically assigned a board member the reconnaissance mission of getting to know a city council member who was likely to be the next mayor. We sat the two next to each other, and the following Monday I got an excited phone call from my trustee: "Councilmember Wylie loves the symphony.* She's been coming to performances for years, but the biggest issue on her agenda isn't the arts. It's the

---

* Name changed to protect the councilmember who didn't know about our recon plan. Or maybe she put it together, as she is a smart politician.

parks department and what they are doing with community spaces." Interesting—because guess which organization was then ready to offer to help activate community space.

With that nugget of information, we were able to help our local legislator, deepen the relationship, and call on her when we needed the support in return, like when we needed the city-owned venue to give us different concert dates, for example.

"When you meet with elected officials, ask them what's at the top of their desk. What are their priorities?" says Heather Noonan, vice president for advocacy at the League of American Orchestras. "That gives you intel and context on what they're concerned with, and you can try to find connections of how your work fits into that." Noonan adds that we shouldn't make assumptions about what a politician will or won't support. And she shared stories about moderate Republicans who were just as supportive of the National Endowment for the Arts as some of their Democratic counterparts—a linchpin to the survival of the NEA when it was under threat of elimination back in 2017. Don't guess; talk about it.

Also, Noonan says, as you're talking, remember it's not just about the data. "A lot of legislators have heard all the data. So bring that, but bring the story, too, about the people or a person who was impacted. That's how you connect the data to their heart." Side note: This is exactly how the research says we are supposed to write fundraising appeal letters as well.[31]

One time Noonan was working in Washington, DC, to meet with Congress and the US Fish and Wildlife Service about an executive order signed that severely limited all transport and trade of ivory. The only problem is that many old musical instruments still played today have components made from ivory, so professional musicians who travel for work (think superstar soloists or orchestras on tour) risked having their lifeline—their instrument—confiscated. No one was in DC that day to debate that using poached ivory is a horrific practice that must be stopped. Rather, they were sharing the ways the verbiage of the order had unintended consequences for owners of instruments made sometimes a hundred years ago or more. To brilliantly illustrate this issue, Noonan brought a professional violinist with her. The artist talked about their instrument and how it was made in an approachable, human way.

Then, the legislators asked if they would play something. "You could feel the sound vibration in the room, and it was maybe the only thing we needed to do that day," Noonan reflected, "We sometimes forget how much the art speaks for itself." Those legislators instantly became the biggest champions for that issue. Today, the ivory travel ban has a protective clause for musical instruments made before a certain date.

One last point on this subject of knowing our elected officials. What we do—producing art, adding cultural vibrancy and economic impact to our communities—is inherently nonpartisan. Whether we're inviting a local city official to the gala, writing the governor's office to petition for greater funding, or making noise for reopening guidelines if we ever (god forbid) have another shutdown, we have nonpartisanship in our corner no matter who is in office. So remember to extend our voice by reaching across the aisle.

Reward Good Behavior

If and when legislators do what you want, make some noise about it and reward the good behavior. Heather Noonan asked me to make sure to credit the Fish and Wildlife Service for helping make the instrument ivory clause happen for exactly this reason. "We always want to publicly praise the good work," she said. There's also the Monterey Bay Aquarium, which hosts an annual Ocean Champions award for legislators and officials. It's a black-tie event; they send out a press release to the award recipient's district, shining the spotlight on what the winner has done, and shower recipients with praise on social media.[32]

Another example that combines rewarding good behavior with some of the other tips comes from Austin Soundwaves, a Texas-based creative-youth development organization. As we know, when early arts education gets cut, it impedes the whole system—not only curbing the development of future artists and audiences but also damaging test scores across the board. So, Austin Soundwaves created a music education inventory on their website that's a sort of report card for all the local public school art programs. If you're a parent or resident, for instance, you can click on a school and see what arts programs that school offers, whether they offer afterschool programs or only in-school electives, and the student–teacher ratio. Through that work, Austin Soundwaves can now demonstrate things like how wealthier schools have more arts teachers. They've been able to use that data to get parents to rally at school board meetings against cutting arts funding and in favor of more equally distributing it.

Austin Soundwaves executive director Patrick Slevin didn't stop there, though. He then envisioned awarding principals doing the desired work. "Instead of shaming the Austin School District, let's lift up those who are doing it right," he told me. With the results they started seeing from other advocacy efforts, Slevin decided they needed to mobilize year-round—not only because of the benefits of the activism but also because he believes it will help them create more brand recognition in the region.

Banging the drum even about small successes is an important part of advocacy and activism. At the Ocean Champions dinner, the recipients like the praise and attention, plus other legislators see the attention others are getting and want that for themselves, too. At Austin Soundwaves, shining the spotlight on a principal or school board official who prioritizes arts programming makes parents want their kids at that school, which the principal loves. With the League of American Orchestras, the results they achieved were national legislation change and kudos to the government and NGO partners like the World Wildlife Fund who helped make it happen. When you praise the folks helping with your advocacy wins, make sure to share the victory lap with your base, too. Doling out praise is free, and we're sending the message that we are always paying attention to the decisions around us and that we value our community allies.

Don't Advocate Because You Think You're "Supposed" To

The sixth and final tip for advocating is to stick to your values. What doesn't work is trying to piggyback on the hot issue du jour or go big a few times to make a splash because we think that's what we're supposed to do as nonprofit corporate citizens. Matthew McCarthy, the Ben & Jerry's CEO, is adamant on this point: "What you don't want to do is try to appropriate a value that you suspect your customers have. It's important that your position be rooted in something you deeply believe."[33]

Without those deeply held beliefs, this work gets hard—like land mine hard. One example is in 2021 when Tulsa Opera pulled their performances of composer Daniel Bernard Roumain's work, *They Still Want to Kill Us*, which the opera had commissioned for the centennial anniversary of the 1921 Tulsa Race Massacre. Upon receiving the libretto, company leadership deemed some of the lyrics too sensitive, requested he change them, and then canceled the premiere when Roumain stood by the text. Opera Philadelphia picked up the baton and spearheaded a consortium effort to produce the work, while Tulsa Opera received considerable public backlash.[34]

On one hand, not a good look for the opera company. On the other, the lyrics clearly made some folks uncomfortable—yet this was by design. So what do you do when you're not sure what's "too risqué," "pushing the envelope too far," or unclear whose comfort to center? When you are appropriating values or doing what you think you "should" be doing, even if you're well intentioned, the waters get murky to answer those questions. But when your organization has unwavering conviction about its values, the questions get much easier to answer.

APPLICATION BOX

Concept: Taking a Public Stand

Organization: Louisville Public Media

Daniel Gilliam is the director of radio for Louisville Public Media, a weekday afternoon host, and program director at 90.5 WUOL, the classical music station. During his show on the afternoon of October 15, 2020, Gilliam did something he had never before done on air. "I want to tell you about a listener letter we received yesterday," he began. "You're used to hearing praise and love from our fellow members, especially during the fund drives. We don't usually share the negative letters, but this one deserves mention: because it's racist."

He explained that this longtime donor took such issue with the fact that more music by Black composers had been programmed that they were withdrawing their support. Gilliam went on to denounce racism, acknowledged the station's role in a racist system, "acting as gatekeepers to music and culture for a large audience," and restated that the station will continually strive to amplify diverse voices of all types. And he left no room for interpretation among listeners: "If you share the views of this letter writer, who is cowardly, anonymous, and sympathize with their views, please stop giving Louisville Public Media and WUOL your money."

After Gilliam aired his statement, Louisville Public Media also posted it on its website, which was then shared to Facebook.[35] "I wanted this message not just on air to only that limited audience," Gilliam told me. "I wanted it on the record as something we believed." For the remaining hours of his show that day, Gilliam played only music by Black composers.

Call it advocacy, call it standing up for values, but whatever you call it, the proof is in the pudding. The Facebook post went viral. Donations started coming in from all over the country, from places Gilliam hadn't thought would ever be interested in supporting a Louisville station. Yes, they received a few cranky comments on social media. But they also received zero negative response from listeners or donors. Instead, affirmation came pouring in, with listener comments such as "F—— that former racist donor," "I was a monthly sustainer for several years, then let it drop . . . I've been meaning to go back to contributing and just didn't get around to it . . . I am purposely choosing now," and "I want to buy out the membership of the racist listener and thank you for your principled stand."

The station was not soliciting donations that day. It was not running a pledge drive. But in the end, WUOL received six times the normal amount of donations that week, all because they unapologetically drew a line in accordance with their beliefs. As one other listener wrote in their comments, "May others see this and walk in your footsteps."

It all comes back to company values and the actions that support them (chapter seven). Having those values in place spreads the roadmap of what matters most before us, and we can measure ideas for activism against that terrain. Then it's also much clearer when an issue doesn't need our attention. Sometimes it's just as refreshing to sit one out when an issue falls outside our guide rails, because we have clarity on who we are as institutions.

When we use our mission-driven work as a vehicle to raise our voice, to advocate, it draws more people into our orbit because we've elevated the conversation to a whole new level. We're building a stronger future with people who, beyond buying tickets or donating, also die-hard love us, not because we're solely producing art "of the highest excellence" but rather because they see their beliefs reflected in it.

10.
The Art Is Not the Problem

Brand Relevance

If you google "most relevant brands," the usual suspects top about every list out there: Apple (I wrote this on a MacBook Air with my iPhone by my side, except when I took breaks and went on a walk with AirPods in my ears and my Apple Watch counting my steps), Spotify (how does it *know* what I want to listen to next?!), and Google (I mean, it appears twice in this same sentence alone, as both noun and verb).

These brands are irreplaceable in millions, if not billions, of people's lives, likely including yours (I'd be shocked if someone reading this hadn't depended on at least one of those brands at some point). Global consultancy Prophet is known for their annual ranking of most relevant brands, and several other companies you probably can't live without are also on their list:

- **Android**. Despite Apple's dominance at the top, Android commands over 70 percent of the operating system market share worldwide, so if you're not on team Mac, chances are Android is pretty important to you.

- **Peloton**. There's a reason the company is the inspiration for chapter three, and despite their occasional bumpy rides, they still set the standard for growing a base of rabid fan subscribers.
- **Instant Pot**. It's fast, it's reliable, and as the *New York Times* says, people "may like their blenders, cherish their slow cookers, and need their food processors, but the Instant Pot . . . sends even mild-mannered cooks into fits of passion."
- **Calm**. The number one app (over 120 million downloads!) for sleep, meditation, and relaxation, Calm is beloved for its celebrity-narrated Sleep Stories and has outpaced other mindfulness apps in revenue.[1]

The most relevant brands are not all tech companies. Nor are they all start-ups or mega-conglomerates. They are newer brands and long-timers alike. They occupy multiple categories: from gaming to automotive, media and entertainment to finance. But what these brands have in common is their significant place with consumers. In fact, Prophet says relevance is *the* most reliable indicator of a brand's long-term success.

At cultural organizations, we talk about "relevance" all the time as we seek a path forward in a changing world. It's a big buzzword—but what does "relevance" actually mean? Across their years of benchmarking, Prophet has found four themes emerge as pillars of relevance. The most relevant brands in their rankings meet those criteria every year with unwavering rigor.

This final chapter looks at Prophet's four principles of relevance—being customer obsessed, ruthlessly pragmatic, distinctively inspired, and pervasively innovative—then examines what happens when we achieve—or don't achieve—those goals.* These principles will help you solidify your brand equity—that *je ne sais quoi* that makes our cultural institutions more memorable, recognizable, and beloved by the communities we serve.

---

* All of the for-profit brands mentioned throughout this chapter come from the top 50 ranking of Prophet's 2022 Brand Relevance Index.

CUSTOMER OBSESSED

Relevant companies meet the needs of their customers, point blank. Whether that's through our KitchenAid mixer making baking so much easier, our favorite Pixar film tapping into our emotions, or the can't-get-it-anywhere-else Trader Joe's Mandarin Orange Chicken, these brands understand what their customers want, and we adore them for it. At cultural organizations, we often *think* we understand what our customers want, like when the donors love the wine at the intermission reception—or don't love a new piece of art. For this group, though, we probably do know exactly how they're feeling and what they want. Because we talk to donors. A lot. But if you think back to chapter one and the iceberg that is our databases, donors are at the tippity-top, making up a very small percentage of patrons.

Being customer obsessed means we need to do this type of listening work *for the remaining 99 percent of our accounts* who have come only once or twice in the last few years, and particularly for the massive amount of underwater folks who came at one point and then went cold. High percentages of patrons going cold is the market telling us we are not relevant.

For any organization reading this and thinking that the survey outreach you do is sufficient for being customer obsessed, consider that survey response bias means only the most engaged people are completing the survey, so you're not getting good intel from where we need it most: that substantial "un-loyal" group.

Yet, finding people who are less connected to us and talking with them directly can be tough. Finding those newer people, reaching out and asking about their experience and how they feel about us, and then taking action on the feedback usually requires more work, empathy, and emotional labor. Because the average customer experience with and understanding of our art form is usually vastly different from our own, meeting their needs may require doing things in a different way than your team or org normally operates or revising how you tackle problem-solving. Fortunately, not only is every strategy in this book designed to activate and empower us all to do this better, when you use them to obsess over your customers, the relevance of your institution will skyrocket.

APPLICATION BOX

Concept: Be customer obsessed

Organization: Women's Business Development Center

Headquartered in Chicago, the Women's Business Development Center (WBDC) has helped over one hundred thousand women business owners advance their companies. The nonprofit works with culinary artists, teaching artists, and also accountants, marketers, college prep advisers—you name it—to empower them to realize economic sustainability through programs and services such as coaching, contracting assistance, microloans, and business development. They teach in English and Spanish (shout-out to chapter five), advocate nationally for policy changes that support women and other diverse communities (checkmark for chapter nine, too), and focus on maximizing economic impact (i.e., they have measurable results).

Of everything WBDC does, Lindsay Mueller, managing director of program innovations, says the entrepreneurial "aha moments" always come for their clients when they talk about being customer obsessed and understanding who is their target customer. A jack of all trades, Mueller graduated with an arts management degree in theater, spent years with the Deaf community as an American Sign Language interpreter, and worked on Obama's presidential campaign before returning to the nonprofit space. "Across all sectors and types of people I've served, including the women in our programs, the impact grows when the target is beyond what's right in front of them," Mueller said. "For example, if they [the entrepreneur] are offering test prep, the actual client isn't the Ivy League kid; it's the mom of the Ivy League kid, who has to be convinced to pay for it. 'Who is the customer and what do they want?' We teach them to obsess over this, talk to their constituents to understand this, and it leads to breakthroughs in their business model every single time."

RUTHLESSLY PRAGMATIC

Prophet defines pragmatic brands as those that constantly experiment, fail fast (i.e., quickly identify what's not working and abort) when an experiment doesn't pan out, and use those data to make smart bets and take bold steps going forward. Those things are pragmatic because they are the model of learning and iterative design: we test an idea, analyze the results, then refine the idea before doing it again or launching it in a bigger way.

Too often at cultural organizations, we either go hard on new ideas without the data to back them up, or quit before we've been able to give an idea proper time to prototype or fully develop. Witness how many institutions rolled out big paywalled streaming platforms in 2020 only to walk them back by 2022. Or consider the experiment in many venues circa 2010 with "Twitter seats"—a designated area where phones and social media were allowed during the performance—but it "didn't work" (as in, didn't drive tons of new sales immediately), so phones are still prohibited entirely.

Generally, when people or institutions have big problems, we want equally grand solutions (so no shame if you advocated for Your Org TV+ or Tweet Seats). But the opposite path forward is usually better: small, intentional steps forward producing disproportionate gains. Organizations that develop a disciplined mindset for testing small ideas and doubling down when those ideas prove they may work will excel going forward.[2]

This concept of pragmatic iteration—small steps—may be the most important takeaway from the whole book. Rome wasn't built in a day, right? Brands that do this well are Amazon, which iterated their way to one-click purchases and next-day delivery; Zelle, which surpassed competitors like Venmo and PayPal because of a small but important seamless integration with your bank instead of requiring you to download a separate app; and Bose, which continuously makes small improvements to appearance, durability, and setup.

Good products alone aren't enough for these companies—or for cultural organizations. Iterating and experimenting to optimize for practicality and ease of use is key. Ways to do this include A/B testing ads, switching the header photo on a website landing page because the bounce rate for that page is too high,* removing the number of fields on the donation form to increase the conversion rate, trying out new lighting onstage, getting intermission-drinks preordering down to a science (yes, even when you're tied to a third-party caterer) because you've tweaked it just so. All of these are the way forward. Ruthlessly pragmatic brands pull away from their competitors because of how rigorously they pursue making those products easy for us to embrace, one micro step toward relevance at a time.

DISTINCTIVELY INSPIRED THROUGH FORMING EMOTIONAL CONNECTIONS

Brands that form emotional connections with their customers and fulfill a larger purpose are inspired. This is where it gets so good for arts organizations. It's in our arts' DNA to inspire. LEGO and TED are known for inspiring, too: they help us dream and think about what could be—that other-world or future version of ourselves we envision and are empowered to create.

Arts and culture are enormously powerful and moving and exquisitely beautiful all at the same time. Art makes us feel things—like awe.[3] "Awe is central to the experience of religion, politics, nature, and art," according to a landmark paper on the science of awe. The psychologist authors found that awe-inspiring experiences expand our perception of time, help people feel connected to others, and even make us more generous.[4] A follow-up paper affirmed this: "If you've hiked among giant sequoias, stood in front of the Taj Mahal, or observed a particularly virtuosic musical performance, you may have experienced the mysterious and complex emotion known as 'awe.'"[5]

Of the four pillars of relevance, inspiring others is the one we intrinsically do best. Brands everywhere are dying to figure out to how to deliver what our institutions do day in and day out. The art is not the problem. We've got this pillar in our corner.

---

* Some quick definitions for the non-digital-marketing folks: A/B testing is when some portion of the target audience is shown one version of the ad while another portion of the target audience is shown another version in order to test which version of the ad—A or B—performs better (e.g., higher clicks, more sales completed). Bounce rate is the percentage of website visitors who navigate away (i.e., leave) after viewing only one page.

There's a reason why the most relevant brands check all four boxes, though. Arts organizations may be strong in delivering emotion and fulfilling a larger purpose—a mission—but that alone is not enough. That's why these other areas are so important to building the sustainable future the arts need.

PERVASIVELY INNOVATIVE

Innovative companies focus less on what newfangled ideas they can bring to bear, and more on what's *not* going to change. Similar to the tech company "disrupters" discussed in chapter three, solving for ongoing human needs, whether via digital content or product improvements, is a path to innovation.

The British electronics maker Dyson spent two decades improving its vacuum cleaner and accompanying chic design to the point where they accomplished something exceptionally rare: realizing high profit margins on hardware. They then proceeded to scrap all that research and develop cordless vacuums that do the same job on battery, knowing consumers just about always want sleek appliance upgrades.[6] Beyond Meat focused on the reduced environmental impact of their meatless meat—something way more people than just vegetarians care about.[7] It landed them deals with TGI Fridays, Pizza Hut, and Peet's Coffee, among others.[8] And IKEA, knowing that everyone loves a bargain, optimizes on price through a lot more than just flat packaging and at-home assembly; sometimes they even set the price *first*, then have designers and suppliers create within that parameter.[9]

People will always want electronics that work better and faster and look prettier. (Like, say, someone who really wants the Dyson Supersonic hair dryer for their birthday, as a totally hypothetical example, and not at all a hint to their loved ones who might be reading this.) They will always want to eat tasty food that doesn't destroy the planet (even the most die-hard meat lovers don't want Earth's impending doom, though they might deny it's in progress). And, as long as people have homes, they'll need furniture (and for the folks that are *so over* self-assembly, IKEA acquired TaskRabbit to help you outsource that).[10] Innovative brands earn their reputations through how they regularly pursue new ways to address *ongoing* needs.

When it comes to balancing "innovation" with "tradition" and "legacy" (a whole other category of words used a lot in our field), Prophet says that "while history and past performance should influence an organization's decisions, free-thinking companies don't allow that legacy to squash new ideas."[11] Innovating around the constants we see in consumer needs is the right approach, such as how Amazon often centers its advancements on what people are always going to want: low prices, good selection, and fast and easy delivery.[12] Arts organizations can optimize a lot around basic customer needs (like saving time, finding information, and having control) by making it effortless for patrons to buy tickets, get information about upcoming shows/events/exhibits, and choose the dates they want in their subscription instead of being coerced into a fixed package.[13]

We in the arts and culture space already have a product that excels at inspiring others. Yet innovation in our field is also about asking how we can further enhance that emotional connection and escape consumers will always be seeking. Sometimes our programs can achieve those goals just by, say, updating the programming and commissioning new work (as in chapter five). But we can also do things like modify the way information is presented, such as updating things like object labels on a wall or glossy program books. We can solve for desires like wanting to see the artists better through things like IMAG (image magnification) screens next to the stage or getting patrons back from the bathroom faster at intermission by identifying bottlenecks (is it only one floor or all floors? Near the entrance only? Just the women's bathroom?) and addressing them (options range from posting better signage all the way to making all stalls gender neutral to cycle people through faster).

There are so many areas where patron needs are never going to change, that our innovation will not be wasted. We only stand to gain from addressing patrons' needs. Innovation will help us get there.

APPLICATION BOX

Concept: The four pillars of relevance

Organization: Mississippi Museum of Art

In 2016, the Mississippi Museum of Art knew they needed a new approach. They wanted to be more open (not just in terms of operating hours), make more space (not just physically), and ultimately become more relevant to the people and history of Mississippi (not just White people). "We needed to alter what we had been," Monique Davis explained to me. "Jackson is 85 percent Black, but our visitorship did not match this. White folks felt comfortable here, but the same wasn't true for everyone else."

In response to these concerns, the museum formed the Center for Art & Public Exchange (CAPE), a sort of community think tank that began as a laboratory to explore these issues and test solutions. Davis moved from her role over membership and community engagement to become managing director of CAPE, then began leading their journey to build all four pillars of relevance. Here is how CAPE pursued each:

Customer obsessed: First, CAPE went to the community. They asked what tools people needed to make sense of the artwork, focusing on feedback from underrepresented groups and zip codes they believed were top targets for museum visitors due to their proximity to the building. CAPE also enacted a "Welcome Audit," in which participants carried clipboards around the building and marked down emojis indicating how they felt everywhere they went, from the parking lot to the bathroom, while commenting on signage, food service, and just about every other museum feature.

Davis and her team found that people wanted to know about the process of making art (How is this made?), for the museum to humanize the artists (Why is this person interesting or important?), and to have places for conversation (Where can I talk about this with others I'm with?). Over three years of this user experience research, the museum began updating seemingly simple things, providing better signage, writing newer labels to tell the stories of the art and artists, and adding conversation nooks, among other changes. The CAPE team met regularly with senior leadership and curatorial teams, and the museum's executive director was present at most of those meetings, showing the commitment to this work.

Ruthlessly pragmatic: CAPE, known as the R&D lab of the museum, started small before going big. For example, at first, CAPE's Community Advisory Council was a pilot program; it's now moved institution wide. Similarly, the CAPE team trialed inviting community members to co-create instead of just giving feedback, and now that's moving organization wide as well. Davis's team is also proto-typing a team-building model with corporations that teaches story-telling and deep listening while looking at a work of art. It's a new, not typical EDI activity for the corporations, Davis explained, and for the museum it's a new consulting-revenue stream (aligning with chapter four on vertical integration). The museum is constantly experiment-ing and using that data to make smart bets going forward. What doesn't work (like a longitudinal study that didn't garner the commu-nity trust CAPE had anticipated) gets cut or refined for future testing. What does work goes institution wide.

Distinctively inspired: Davis exhaled, "The mission statement ... is fine. What underpins that though is to be that third place, where peo-ple can convene and have compassionate civil discourse." She showed me a piece of art in their collection, Titus Kaphar's *Darker Than Cot-ton*, an oil painting depicting an enslaved Black woman's face mirrored against an eighteenth-century male land and slave owner peeling off the canvas—a piece that sparks conversation. Before, the label would have said things like "oil on canvas," the artist's birth year (b. 1976), and that it was part of the collection. Now the museum also describes why the woman's features were greatly magnified compared to his, for example, and what the artist was trying to achieve. Stenciled on the wall are also questions, including, "How does this painting make you feel?" Sticky notes are available to post your answer.

Pervasively innovative: Visitors at an art museum always have questions. Pre-COVID, the museum asked visitors to write their ques-tions on index cards or those sticky notes, and then drop them in a box next to the displayed work or post them nearby. What they found, Davis said, was that "people want stories, not the scholarship of it." The team would then update the label accordingly, then con-tinue editing it as more common questions came in—the very defini-tion of iteration. "We don't get it all right; we're just doing it, and other people can do it. You just have to want to."

The results of this work include exactly what they sought to achieve: a change in their visitor demographic and expanded atten-dance. Along with that came more press and publicity, which in turn resulted in greater brand awareness, and even more visitors. They're now helping to create new exhibits on a national tour to "major" insti-tutions. And they've also garnered increased funding from several large foundations underwriting more and more of their work.

Davis insists they didn't reinvent the wheel. "We're not creating something that's brand new, we're just doing it very intentionally. We're doing it on a human-centered focus. We're just making prog-ress. Museums need to care more about the people than they do their objects." The museum now has a toolkit on their website for other organizations wanting to adopt this kind of relevance-inducing approach. And even though she swears there's no secret sauce, her final words to me—about the institution's shift in mindset over the last seven-plus years of this work—sure sounded like one: "People's lived experience is just as important as all the scholarship."

If this work were easy and straightforward, all brands across all industries, including cultural organizations, would be doing it. But it's not easy, and there-fore, some brands toil to the top of our own personal can't-live-without rankings, while others fade away.

As the buzzword of "relevance" permeates administrative job descriptions and updated mission statements, it's imperative to keep in mind that no matter how hard we try, the customer decides if we are relevant, not us—not grant makers, not executive directors, not board members, not staff members, and not artists. As Nina Simon, former museum executive, says in *The Art of Relevance*, "People choose for themselves what is relevant . . . Our work is only relevant when people tell us it is."[14] They'll tell us with their social media and word of mouth, with whether they spend their time with or without us, and most of all with their wallets.

WHAT HAPPENS WHEN WE'RE NOT RELEVANT

The benefits of relevance are generally obvious: customers give us free marketing with their posts online, this positive organic endorsement results in five times more sales than direct advertising, buzz about the organization swells, our patron base grows, donations increase.[15] But when a brand doesn't obsess over their customers, relentlessly pursue data, offer an inspiring emotional connection, or pervasively innovate—when a brand doesn't adapt—well, they become a cautionary tale.

For instance, HBO (now Max) has fallen off the Prophet index, proving that a quality entertainment product alone isn't enough, even if it's inspiring, because all four areas of focus must be constantly addressed.*[16] Folgers, which was once the best part of waking up and ranked accordingly, has been replaced on the list by rival Keurig. Other "maladaptors" include Pandora (knocked out by Spotify, which keeps rising every year with new features driven by a customized-just-for-you homepage that I swear is wizardry but is actually smart algorithm, nice design, and a growing body of exclusive content), PayPal (replaced by other DIY financial services like Afterpay, Zelle, and even TurboTax), and The North Face (succumbing to athleisure mega-lord Lululemon, which totally nailed vertical integration, by the way, and cemented their place on the ranking with their purchase of home personal-training device Mirror).[17]

The stories of these brands aren't over—being, say, the fifty-first most relevant brand doesn't exactly equal demise—so I'm not counting them out just yet. But the final bell has tolled for companies like Polaroid (bankrupt in 2001), Black-Berry (stopped supporting legacy phones in 2022), and Sears (down to a handful of stores), all brands who once ruled their respective consumer worlds. All three had a fantastic product or service, but fell behind due to their inflexible way of delivering that product.

Humans will always have a need for belonging, emotional fulfillment, being a part of something bigger than ourselves, and even for awe. As arts organizations, we are now competing with all forms of entertainment and leisure as a category, with escapism, with other ways people find human connection, and with increasingly stuffed schedules and shrinking attention spans. But with such a compelling asset as our incredible artists—so many truly exceptional talents—we have the opportunity to build a sustainable future even as the world around us and its

---

* HBO fell off in 2018, dropping fifty-eight places in the rankings that year. Meanwhile Netflix enabled customers to binge (customer obsessed), created an algorithm to serve up what you might want to watch next (ruthlessly pragmatic, pervasively innovative), and invested in a quality product that emotionally resonates (distinctively inspired). HBO has been playing catch-up with Netflix ever since.

people have changed so much in recent years. Our industry's story is nowhere near over.

ONE BIG DIFFERENCE

While I think we have more in common with the corporate world than we sometimes realize, there's one big way we diverge: arts organizations are nonprofits. We don't have to post quarterly earnings, subject our plans to analyst projections, or tether ourselves to profit growth every three months. We don't serve shareholders; we serve a mission. We have one legally required public-facing financial report in the annual tax return, a reflection of our work—our relevance—in our community, which means we can execute these strategies at a manageable pace.

All of this is a come-full-circle reminder of a concept first mentioned in the Introduction: the flywheel. If you recall, the idea is there's no one thing that makes a business successful; not a single big bet, no silver bullet program, no one-stop solution to growth. But when organizations engage with multiple strategies, executed over time, iterating baby-step improvements as we go, they set in motion a flywheel of forward momentum. And the revenue follows, which in turn frees us to better fund the art, not sacrifice it. With this fuel, we are liberated to program without overrelying on blockbusters, commission new work we believe in, expand our audience to reflect our communities, pay our artists and our staffs what they deserve, and claim the power of our economic impact. If irrelevance is a bitch, momentum is a boss.

A final benefit of relevance is that consumers aren't tied to a product, but instead root for the brand as a whole. This is the holy grail paradigm shift. When we achieve this shift, instead of centering all our marketing efforts around the next event, we create a future where consumers want whatever we put on the stage or in the exhibits because they trust us. They know that no matter what's on, they will learn something, feel unintimidated while doing so, feel prepared, feel welcomed— feel *better* somehow—than if they didn't come at all. This is brand loyalty.

We have the tools to build this relevant future. A future that lifts us up, rather than bogs us down. A reality of wind in our sails instead of the choppy seas of chasing sales goals one week at a time. A blue ocean of patrons and donors instead of an iceberg of gone-cold accounts that wrecks us. An atmosphere of air in our lungs instead of the suffocation of cutting expenses that have already been chipped away, or the anxiety of striving for a slim chance at a new major gift, or the pain of contorting to win a new grant for which we're not totally a fit. A liberating force that lets us plan our operations and programs calmly and confidently instead of bending to the latest operational pivot.

The art is not what's keeping us from relevance; it's what offers us the gateway to it. This future is ours to claim, and we've all likely done pieces of this work already. We are smart and savvy, equipped and capable. And when we run it like a business, we will unleash the full power of arts and culture in the world ahead.

Epilogue

Where Are We Now?

Shortly after I finished writing this book, a friend sent me a podcast, encouraging me to take a listen. It was *No Stupid Questions*, hosted by Stephen Dubner (of *Freakonomics* fame) and Angela Duckworth, a psychologist, University of Pennsylvania professor, best-selling author, and MacArthur Fellow. The topic was, "Is it okay to hate highbrow culture?"

They interrogated why some things, like opera or visual art museums, are described as "highbrow," but not music from Taylor Swift or the Twilight novels. Their ultimate definition? "It's highbrow when not a lot of people like it," concluded Dubner.[1] Ouch. Then Duckworth concurred. More ouch.

Dubner and Duckworth are arguably a reasonable barometer for the taste of what some would call intellectual elites. They are both highly educated at prestigious universities, esteemed in their respective disciplines, and incredibly successful by any measure. On paper, they're both decent contenders for the profile of a potential arts-organization audience member or visitor (a profile this book contends we need to expand).

What surprised me wasn't how much they admitted they didn't know about the arts, both performing and visual, but how completely unashamed they were about this. They literally did not care. To be fair, Dubner has an MFA, so was perhaps a little more interested, but get Duckworth going on the Twilight series, and a whole dialogue about Team Edward or Team Jacob ensues. And this, I realized, represents the big shift in how arts and culture is viewed more broadly in this country. Whereas appreciating "highbrow" culture used to be a sign of intelligence, an indicator of a well-adapted member of society—or at least a conversation starter at a dinner party—today it is not.

If you disagree, look no further than the current state of ticket sales and donations. Across artistic disciplines, paid capacity for the first season back after the pandemic closure (2021–2022) slid almost 20 percent from before lockdown. Ticket revenue totaled less than two-thirds pre-pandemic levels. New attendees were down by a third and returning patrons dropped by almost as much.[2] And for some organizations, subscription sales for the 2022–2023 season dropped as much as 51 percent.[3]

As of this writing, attendance hasn't rebounded, we're still behind with subscription and membership numbers, and many longtime older attendees are still saying they're not planning on going out. Theaters from coast to coast are laying off staffs, shrinking their seasons (same for many opera companies, too), and some even halting production altogether.[4]

Meanwhile, sports arenas are packed; dining and retail spending continues to soar; Las Vegas tourism and the accompanying gambling hit a record high;[5] and summer music festivals, rock and pop concerts, and all those Instagram-ready museums are overflowing (looking at you, Museum of Ice Cream and Van Gogh: The Immersive Experience). People do want to go out . . . they're just not coming to our venues.

What these trends indicate, in Dubner's words, is that "not a lot of people like it." And while something being less-than-popular might not be the actual definition of "highbrow," and we might balk at being called that, apparently the stigma of elitism still exists. Alas, the challenges before us are not real or perceived. They are real *and* perceived.

Trends can be reversed, though, and challenges solved—that's why each chapter features case studies of organizations who are doing it. Ballet Austin began by inviting patrons to arrive an hour early and then filled that wait. Mongoose education software got you to come to a campus football game rather than asking you to apply straight to college. The Museum of the Shenandoah Valley tried out a sixty-second cooking video. Composer Sakari Dixon Vanderveer didn't quit her day job when she first rolled out a three-week trial run of her composing course. The library at the University of San Francisco turned to a Stephen King novel for their first step. The American Alliance of Museums started by asking *why is our staff so homogenous*, and updated a few bullet points on a job description. And the inciting question for Alameda Health System Foundation was, "What's it like working here for you?"

Change can be hard, I know. Upending centuries of "tradition" is an apple-cart some folks don't want to topple. But iteration is how we grow—take a small step, assess, learn, repeat. We are continuing to evolve, as people and organizations, just as art itself does. The future is ours to compose, paint, sculpt, birth, plant, and produce.

I didn't use the word "innovation" much in this book (except in one section in the final chapter). I did use words like "data" and "research," though—a lot. That's because what's in these pages is known, proven, and vetted. And in addition to the arts organizations I just named, other sectors have done tons of trial and error for us—we can and should borrow from outside the industry. Now is the time for cultural organizations to run like the businesses they are. We are companies that do tremendously important work, serving people literally around the world, with no age, demographic, or geographical limit to how many we can impact.

We don't need to wait for permission, we don't need to wait for someone or someplace else to move first, nor for more resources, human or financial. We are not promised tomorrow. We are, however, promised the opportunity to use our art as a vehicle to make our mark on this world, and I'm so glad to be on this exciting journey with you to do just that. Let's get this business going.

If you want more tools and training on
some of the strategies in this book, visit
www.aubreybergauer.com/RunItLikeABusiness.

If you want like-minded, forward-thinking
people alongside you in this business, explore
the Changing the Narrative Community at
www.aubreybergauer.com/community.

ACKNOWLEDGMENTS

Writing a book is like writing into the void. Hours and hours alone, pouring words into pages and pages *that no one sees for a very long time.* These are people who were with me in the void, and I'm so grateful for all their help in bringing this book to you.

To Stephen Rubin—you're known as a titan of publishing, but I came to know you first as an exemplary board member. You love classical music and the institutions you've served; give generously of your time, talent, and treasure; show up at every opportunity; and deliver on every commitment. I count it a privilege and real honor to have worked with you at the San Francisco Conservatory of Music. And when I shared my idea for a book and first proposal draft with you, you gave me some tough yet practical (and sorely needed) advice. When I circled back again a few months later with updated proposal in hand, you told me the person I needed to contact who would be the best possible agent, and you were right. I can't thank you enough for the support and grace you showed me, and for pointing me to the right path for this project from its onset.

Irene Goodman, when I first reached out to you on Steve's advice, I wasn't sure why he was so adamant you were the agent for me, as all my website stalking pointed you toward other genres—fiction! thrillers! mysteries!—none of which this book was or is. But you took the call, and I promptly learned of all the many New York arts institutions you patronize, and also that you have a husband who runs a gallery. I fell in love. Not just because you know the arts firsthand as a longtime audience member and supporter, or because of your astounding, success-ful track record and reputation over three decades in this business, but because of how you immediately championed the concept. What you said to me on that call would become a bit of a mantra you repeated to me over the months that fol-lowed: "The world needs this book." You were the first person who believed in this project in that way, and you kept reminding me of it every time I was fearful or hesitant to put my thoughts out there. You also were the first to push me to write about multiple artistic disciplines (I probably didn't do it enough, but I know the writing was richer when I did). And you got the deal with the right-fit publisher in BenBella. I stan you and your career, and it has been truly a pleasure and honor to work with you.

To the team at BenBella, I was immediately drawn to the plethora of amaz-ingly talented people there—smart, driven, and fiercely dedicated—and almost all of whom happen to be women (for the record, Glenn Yeffeth, you are a delight, too).

And how do I begin to thank Alyn Wallace, my editor, who from the moment I internet-stalked *her* before *our* first call, I found to be just as fun as she is bril-liant. Both these things have proven 100 percent true, and I've so enjoyed getting to know you through our long comment threads in the manuscript (and definitely through your amazing Instagram dance videos, too). Thank you for making my writing better, helping me find clarity when it was lacking, and making me feel like you had my back—sensitive to my concerns, always making me feel heard, and always having a menu of solutions. You are so tremendously talented and good at your job. And also, I cherish our mutual disappointment that Microsoft Word comments don't support emojis (update: we figured it out as we were editing this paragraph). I'll end by saying how badly I want to work with you again (maybe not on a book, because holy cow, this was a lot of work, but on something . . .) mark my words.

To everyone whose organization I mentioned and who shared your stories with me, I learned so much from you and now see how you are doing the needed work to push your organization and the field forward. Specifically, for all the application box examples and case studies: thank you to Cookie Ruiz for your leadership at Ballet Austin and for letting me come see it all in person; to Mike Kochczynski, who, while I know you're not at Mongoose anymore, so wonderfully drew the parallels to the Long Haul Model and took the time to share them with me; to Jonathan Bennett for applying these concepts outside the arts in Canada; to Zenetta Drew for your brilliant, strategic mind leading the Dallas Black Dance Theatre to become just as much of a virtual powerhouse as it is in the theater; to the Museum of the Shenandoah Valley for responding to my cold outreach when I stumbled upon your great videos online; to Jennifer Rosenfeld for pretty much everything and everyone in chapter four (I affectionately and informally have been calling that the Jennifer Rosenfeld chapter to folks), and to Sakari Dixon Vanderveer for hopping on a call with me upon Jennifer's recommendation; to Salvador Acevedo, to whom I can't express enough how much I appreciate and am grateful for your help, care, time, authenticity, and research, which taught me so much; to Shawn P. Calhoun at the University of San Francisco, who has championed my work online for years now—I'm so glad this book provided the excuse to finally meet and allow me to champion yours; to Katherine McNamee for so wonderfully writing about all you've done at the American Alliance of Museums, which allowed me to discover and connect with you and learn even more about all the steps you've taken there; to Charlene Lobo Soriano for sharing so vulnerably about the journey at the Alameda Health System Foundation (plus another thank-you to Shawn Calhoun for sending me your way); to Patrick Nugent for that one day when you posted on LinkedIn about your staff retreat and taking on the Long Haul Model in your own way in Dayton—and for staying in touch with all the updates as you go; to Daniel Gilliam for using your role and radio station platform to make an undeniable, no-holds-barred, wide-reaching denouncement of racism, which captured my attention from across the country; to Patrick Slevin for sharing what you've built at Austin Soundwaves (and taking me for some much-needed Tex-Mex); to Heather Noonan for your exceptional advocacy work on behalf of orchestras in this country for years, and for modeling how we can join in with you; to Lindsay Mueller for helping thousands of women entrepreneurs in Chicago (and this woman in San Francisco); to Lydia Jasper for responding to my social media post and putting me in touch with Monique Davis; and to Monique for what you've accomplished in Mississippi, embodying everything this book is about and more, long before we ever met.

Also thank you to Hannah Grannemann and to Ryan Dumas for pointing me toward several other organizations doing great work, and an extra thank-you to Hannah for teaching all your students so many of these concepts as well.

Linda Hsieh Logston, you didn't know this, but you sent me that *No Stupid Questions* podcast episode at just the right moment—thank you.

Frank Capek and Amy Webb, you were the people that first helped me consider user experience research for an orchestra, an undertaking that changed how I think about audience development forevermore. And as fate would have it, Frank, you connected me with Cookie Ruiz years ago, and you have so generously stayed in touch with advice and thought-provoking idea exchanges ever since.

To Paula Wilson, you lent another set of eyes, experience, and expertise when you reviewed the EDI material. When we first met, it was because you reached out for advice as you were about to graduate; now I'm the one reaching out to you.

A heartfelt thank-you to Bill Armstrong—you set the bar as a board chair who shares a similar vision to mine for what an orchestra can do, giving freedom and sharing wisdom in equal parts to achieve that vision. We pretty much always scheduled as many meetings as possible over wine, true to this day.

And Matteo Cusini, it's not lost on me that you checked in on how the book was going just about every single day (that's a *lot* of days). I've never felt that kind of ongoing support from anyone before. Thank you.

Last, to you, dear reader. These pages are now out of the void and into your hands. I'm not proclaiming myself an expert on everything in this book, but I do know my lived experience and learning journey, and am grateful for the opportunity to share it with you. I'd love to hear how you and your organization take it from here; drop me a line or two online if you'd like. Because if you've actually read this far, I count you along for the journey, too.

ENDNOTES

INTRODUCTION

1. "Spanx Plans to Open Its Own Stores," SRS Real Estate Partners, May 9, 2013, https://srsre.com/media/spanx-plans-to-open-its-own-stores; Eliza Haverstock, "Sara Blakely Is A Billionaire (Again) After Selling a Majority of Spanx to Blackstone," *Forbes*, Oct 20, 2021, https://www.forbes.com/sites/elizahaverstock/2021/10/20/sara-blakely-is-a-billionaire-again-after-selling-a-majority-of-spanx-to-blackstone/?sh=5f6be0e47d5c.
2. Bohne Silber and Tim Triplett, "A Decade of Arts Engagement: Findings from the Survey of Public Participation in the Arts, 2002–2012," National Endowment for the Arts, January 2015, https://www.arts.gov/sites/default/files/2012-sppa-feb2015.pdf.
3. Oliver Wyman in partnership with the League of American Orchestras, "Reimagining the Orchestra Subscription Model," November 2015, https://www.oliverwyman.com/content/dam/oliver-wyman/global/en/2015/nov/Reimagining-the-Orchestra-Subscription-Model-Fall-2015.pdf.
4. Colleen Dilenschneider, "Population Up, Cultural Organization Attendance Down. What Gives? (DATA)," *Know Your Own Bone*, February 27, 2019, https://www.colleendilen.com/2019/02/27/population-up-cultural-organization-attendance-down-what-gives-data/.
5. Zannie Voss, Manuel Lasaga, and Teresa Eyring, "Theatres at the Crossroads: Overcoming Downtrends & Protecting Your Organization Through Future Downturns," National Center for Arts Research, September 2019, https://culturaldata.org/pages/theatres-at-the-crossroads/.

6. Colleen Dilenschneider, "How Often Do People Really Revisit Cultural Organizations? (DATA)," *Know Your Own Bone*, May 15, 2019, https://www.colleendilen.com/2019/05/15/how-often-do-people-really-visit-cultural-organizations-data/.

7. Voss et al., "Theatres at the Crossroads."

8. Oliver Wyman in partnership with the League of American Orchestras, "Reimagining the Orchestra Subscription Model."

9. US Bureau of Labor Statistics, "Consumer Price Index Historical Table, U.S. City Average," https://www.bls.gov/regions/midwest/data/consumerpriceindex historical_us_table.pdf.

10. Michelle Obama, "Remarks by the First Lady at Opening of the Whitney Museum," Whitney Museum New York, April 30, 2015, https://obamawhite house.archives.gov/the-press-office/2015/04/30/remarks-first-lady-opening -whitney-museum.

11. Silber and Triplett, "A Decade of Arts Engagement," 19; National Endowment for the Arts, "U.S. Patterns of Arts Participation: A Full Report from the 2017 Survey of Public Participation in the Arts," 41.

12. Glenn B. Voss and Karthik Babu Nattamai Kannan, "When Will Arts Attendance Return? How Vaccination Rates May Impact Performing Arts Ticket Sales Through March 2022," Southern Methodist University, Spring 2022, https://culturaldata.org/pages/attendance-prediction-spring2022/; WolfBrown, "Audience Outlook Monitor: Executive Briefing for June 2022," June 27, 2022, 20.

13. Arts Consulting Group, "Recent Trends in Philanthropic Giving in the United States and Canada: Annual Reports on Key Metrics," *Arts Insights*, accessed October 5, 2022, https://artsconsulting.com/arts-insights/recent-trends-in -philanthropic-giving-in-the-united-states-and-canada-2022/.

14. Ruth McCambridge, "Speculations on the Roots of the Loss of Small U.S. Donors: What Nonprofits Can Do," *Nonprofit Quarterly*, December 6, 2019, https://nonprofitquarterly.org/speculations-on-the-roots-of-the-loss-of-small-u-s -donors-what-nonprofits-can-do/.

15. Paul Clolery, "U.S. Philanthropy Plummeted $17 Billion As Donors Disappeared," *The Nonprofit Times*, June 20, 2023, https://thenonprofittimes.com/npt _articles/u-s-philanthropy-plummeted-17-billion-as-donors-disappeared/.

16. The NCAA reports that each year, 1.2 percent of college athletes join the NBA and 1.6 percent join the NFL. "Estimated Probability of Competing in Professional Athletics," 2019, https://www.ncaa.org/sports/2015/3/6/estimated-probability-of -competing-in-professional-athletics.aspx. For major orchestras (the top twenty ensembles by budget size), nearly 8,000 music performance majors graduate each year and would need to win 96 auditions in order to tie the NCAA rate of 1.2

percent. Far fewer auditions take place each year, and of the auditions that do occur, the applicant pool also includes already-graduated musicians also vying for each role. Music graduation data from "2022 Music Degree Guide," 2022, https://www.collegefactual.com/majors/visual-and-performing-arts/music/.

17. Christina Gough, "Total Revenue of All National Football League Teams from 2001 to 2020," Statista, July 27, 2022, https://www.statista.com/statistics /193457/total-league-revenue-of-the-nfl-since-2005/#:~:text=In%202020%2C %20the%2032%20teams,of%2012.2%20billion%20U.S.%20dollars.

18. Tom Peters, "McKinsey's Work on Opioid Sales Represents a New Low," *Financial Times*, February 15, 2021, https://www.ft.com/content/82e98478-f099-44ac -b014-3f9b15fe6bc6.

19. Jim Collins, *Good to Great* (New York: Harper Business, 2011).

CHAPTER 1

1. Mark Matousek, "United Airlines Has a Long History of Infuriating Customers—Here Are Its Worst Customer Service Incidents," *Insider*, March 16, 2018, https://www.businessinsider.com/united-airlines-worst-customer-service -incidents-2018-3; Alex Abad-Santosalex, "Why United Airlines Can Get Away with Treating Its Customers Like Garbage," *Vox*, April 11, 2017, https://www.vox .com/culture/2017/4/11/15246632/united-airlines-drag-man-off-plane.

2. Kate Puentes, "15 Reasons People Love Going to Costco More Than Regular Grocery Stores," *Yahoo! Money*, December 18, 2022, https://money.yahoo.com /15-reasons-people-love-going-011000346.html.

3. Oliver Wyman analysis of all orchestras box office data (2006 national averages) in partnership with the League of American Orchestras, "Turning First-Timers into Life-Timers: Addressing the True Drivers of Churn," Presentation at the League of American Orchestras annual conference, June 12, 2008, 8.

4. David Brownlee and Eric Nelson, "COVID-19 Sector Benchmark: Insight Report 9: March 2022," TRG Arts & Purple Seven, March 10, 2022, 1–2.

5. Cindy Blanco, "2020 Duolingo Language Report: Global Overview," Duolingo, December 15, 2020, https://blog.duolingo.com/global-language-report-2020/.

6. Conor Walsh, "Back from the Brink: What Duolingo Learned About Its Resurrected Users," Duolingo blog, August 30, 2017, https://blog.duolingo.com/back -from-the-brink-what-duolingo-learned-about-its-resurrected-users/.

7. Conor Walsh, "Back from the Brink."

8. Lavanya Aprameya, "Improving Duolingo, One Experiment at a Time," Duolingo blog, January 10, 2020, https://blog.duolingo.com/improving-duolingo-one -experiment-at-a-time/.

9. Aubrey Bergauer, "Introducing Orchestra X: If You Don't Know a Lot (or Any-thing at All) About Orchestras, You Are Exactly Who We're Looking for," *Medium*, August 16, 2016, https://aubreybergauer.medium.com/https-medium -com-californiasymphony-introducing-orchestra-x-a2fbe9a1bf4c.

10. Aubrey Bergauer, "Orchestra X: The Results," *Medium*, November 21, 2016, https://aubreybergauer.medium.com/orchestra-x-the-results-ec12e48f28fb.

11. Dan Benoni and Louis-Xavier Lavallee, "8 User Retention Tactics Tested on 300 Million Users," Growth.Design Case Studies, accessed September 1, 2021, https://growth.design/case-studies/duolingo-user-retention.

12. UXDX Conference, "Lessons from a Cellist (or, What Product People Can Learn from User Research) Conor Walsh, Duolingo," YouTube video, 6:40, January 11, 2020, https://www.youtube.com/watch?v=S41WTcfdy8Q.

13. Conor Walsh, "Back from the Brink"; "Lessons from a Cellist (or, what prod-uct people can learn from user research) Conor Walsh, Duolingo," YouTube video, 21:43, posted by "UXDX Conference," January 11, 2020, https:// www.youtube.com/watch?v=S41WTcfdy8Q.

14. "Arts Industry Digital Marketing Benchmark Study: Findings from a Survey of 180 Arts Organizations by Capacity Interactive," November 2018, 59.

15. Alan Brown, "Activating Your Audience," WSAC Arts Participation Leadership Initiative, Seattle, WA, August 26, 2010, slide 8.

16. Ted Bauer, "The NeuroScience of Storytelling," *Your Brain at Work*, NeuroLead-ership Institute, September 30, 2021, https://neuroleadership.com/your-brain -at-work/the-neuroscience-of-storytelling/; Paul Zak, "How Stories Change the Brain," *Greater Good Magazine*, December 17, 2013, https://greatergood.berkeley .edu/article/item/how_stories_change_brain.

17. Charity Stebbins, "Educational Content Makes Consumers 131% More Likely to Buy [RESEARCH]," *Spotlight Conductor*, July 6, 2017, https://www.conductor .com/blog/2017/07/winning-customers-educational-content/.

18. Stebbins, "Educational Content."

19. Zoe Chance, "Faculty Viewpoints: Advice for a Better 2021—According to the Research," *Yale Insights*, December 21, 2020, https://insights.som.yale.edu /insights/advice-for-better-2021-according-to-the-research; Yale Center for Cus-tomer Insights, "The Pursuit of Influence," July 5, 2022, https://som.yale.edu /story/0/pursuit-influence.

20. Eric Bornemann, associate director of marketing, Los Angeles Opera, email mes-sage to the author, June 23, 2022.

21. Glyn Roberts, Festival Director, Castlemaine State Festival, email message to the author, February 3, 2021.

CHAPTER 2

1. Glenda Toma, "The Farmer's Dog Raises $39 Million in the Largest Series B Round for a Pet Startup," *Forbes*, January 15, 2019, https://www.forbes.com/sites /glendatoma/2019/01/15/the-farmers-dog-raises-39-million-in-the-largest-series -b-round-for-a-pet-startup/?sh=56abe43553ac.
2. SUBTA (Subscription Trade Association), SUBTA 2019 Annual Report, October 2019, https://subta.com/wp-content/uploads/2019/10/2019_SUBTA_Annual _Report.pdf.
3. Zannie Giraud Voss et al., *Orchestra Facts: 2006–2014 A Study of Orchestra Finances and Operations, Commissioned by the League of American Orchestras*, November 2016, https://americanorchestras.org/orchestra-facts/.
4. Colleen Dilenschneider, "Crunching the Numbers—Just How Valuable Are Your Members? (DATA)," *Know Your Own Bone*, Impacts Experience, April 9, 2019, https://www.colleendilen.com/2019/04/09/crunching-the-numbers-just -how-valuable-are-your-members-data/.
5. Association for Fundraising Professionals, "Fundraising Effectiveness Project: Giving Increases Significantly in 2020, Even as Donor Retention Rates Shrink," March 15, 2021, https://afpglobal.org/fundraising-effectiveness-project-giving -increases-significantly-2020-even-donor-retention-rates.
6. NICE Satmetrix, "Net Promoter Benchmarks," *NICE Satmetrix 2018 Consumer Net Promoter Benchmark Study*, 2018.
7. Namita Desai, "Reimagining the Subscription Model," Oliver Wyman in partnership with the League of American Orchestras, 33.
8. TRG, "Launching Loyalty from a Second Date with Patrons: A Case Study with Seattle Repertory Theatre," (webinar), November 20, 2013, https://www .slideshare.net/TRGArts/srt-webinar-slides-d4finalforslideshare.
9. Colleen Dilenschneider, "Cultural Organizations Are Still Not Reaching New Audiences (DATA)," *Know Your Own Bone*, Impacts Experience, November 8, 2017, https://www.colleendilen.com/2017/11/08/cultural-organizations-still-not -reaching-new-audiences-data/.
10. TRG Arts + Purple Seven, "Lemonade and Loyalty: An Introduction to Subscription," September 23, 2022, https://trgarts.com/blog/lemonade-and-loyalty -an-introduction-to-subscription.html.
11. If someone is a renewing subscriber who also donates, their renewal rate is also around 90 percent Eric Nelson, "Audience Development: How to Effectively Grow Your Patron Base," presentation at 2019 National Arts Marketing and Ticketing Conference, fall 2019, slide 7, https://namt.org/app/uploads/TRG -Eric-Nelson-Presentation-Generational-Patron-Trends-NAMT-Fall-2019.pdf.

12. Colleen Dilenschneider, "Why Donors Stop Giving Money to Cultural Organizations (DATA)," *Know Your Own Bone*, Impacts Experience, April 20, 2016, https://www.colleendilen.com/2016/04/20/why-donors-stop-giving-money-to-cultural-organizations-data/.

13. Holly Hall, "Economists Spurn Conventional Wisdom to Boost Fundraising," *The Chronicle of Philanthropy*, September 22, 2013, https://www.philanthropy.com/article/economists-spurn-conventional-wisdom-to-boost-fundraising/.

14. Stephen Shankland, "Adobe Launches Creative Cloud Subscription Service," *CNET*, May 11, 2012, https://www.cnet.com/tech/tech-industry/adobe-launches-creative-cloud-subscription-service/; Adobe Press Release, "Adobe Reports Record Revenue in Q1 Fiscal 2023," March 15, 2023, https://news.adobe.com/news/news-details/2023/Adobe-Reports-Record-Revenue-in-Q1-Fiscal-2023/default.aspx.

15. Stephen Shankland, "Adobe Kills Creative Suite, Goes Subscription-Only," *CNET*, May 6, 2013, https://seekingalpha.com/article/4105909-adobes-cloud-based-subscription-will-continue-to-grow-revenue.

16. Erica Waasdorp, "The Success of Charity: Water's Monthly Donor Community," *NonProfit Pro*, January 18, 2021, https://www.nonprofitpro.com/post/the-success-of-charity-waters-monthly-donor-community/.

17. Louis Diez, "How Muhlenberg College Broke into the Top 100 for Alumni Giving Participation," unpublished manuscript, September 1, 2022, https://docs.google.com/document/d/1t_OVHtuMQfyJX1TDZEdJFa0yeAELMrTMz0OYLd3tTio/edit?usp=sharing, 7.

18. Prescott & Associates, "Churning Butter into Gold: Patron Growth Initiative," League of American Orchestras National Conference, June 2011, 17.

CHAPTER 3

1. Desai, "Reimagining the Subscription Model"; US Bureau of Labor Statistics, "Consumer Price Index Historical Table, U.S. City Average," https://www.bls.gov/regions/midwest/data/consumerpriceindexhistorical_us_table.pdf.

2. Aubrey Bergauer, "The Subscription Economy (& What the Arts Can Learn From It)," interview with Robbie Kellman Baxter, YouTube video, 28:16, March 19, 2022, https://youtu.be/Yj2UMK9OWUY.

3. Scott Galloway, *Post Corona* (New York: Portfolio, 2020), 73.

4. CapacityInteractive, "Google's Digital Path to Ticket Purchase Study," Conference presentation by Luke Rodehorst, YouTube video, 11:54, April 29, 2019, https://www.youtube.com/watch?v=0fSci-HxBV4.

5. Angela Watercutter, "Amazon Will Buy MGM for over $8 Billion. Your Move, Netflix," *Wired*, May 26, 2021, https://www.wired.com/story/amazon-mgm-acquisition-streaming/.

6. Tanya Treptow et al., "Taking Another Listen: Audience Research with People of Color to Help Make Classical Music Radio More Welcoming," summary report, April 2023, 21; Ruth Hartt, "Can Arts Organizations Survive the Longest-Running Disruption in History? Opera Australia Has Cracked the Code," *Culture for Hire*, June 12, 2021, https://www.cultureforhire.com/articles /disrupting-classical-musics-disruption; Keith Jopling, Mark Mulligan, and Zach Fuller, "The Classical Music Market: Streaming's Next Genre?" *MIDIA*, June 12, 2019, https://www.midiaresearch.com/reports/the-classical-music -market.

7. Christina Gough, "Quarterly Revenue of Peloton Worldwide from 1st Quarter 2019 to 4th Quarter 2022," Statista, September 27, 2022, https://www.statista .com/statistics/974087/peloton-quarterly-revenue/.

8. Christina Gough, "Peloton Global Quarterly Subscriptions 2019–2022," Statista, September 27, 2022, https://www.statista.com/statistics/1203121 /peloton-quarterly-subscriptions/.

9. Sarah Whitten, "Peloton Slapped with $150 Million Lawsuit for Using Songs by Drake, Lady Gaga Without Permission," *CNBC*, March 19, 2019, https:// www.cnbc.com/2019/03/19/peloton-hit-with-150-million-suit-for-using-songs -by-drake-lady-gaga.html.

10. Daniel Victor, "Peloton Recalls Treadmills After Injuries and a Child's Death," *New York Times*, May 5, 2021, https://www.nytimes.com/2021/05/05/business /peloton-recall-tread-plus.html.

11. Stephanie Farrell and Ayushi Gupta, "Peloton Marketing Strategy: Uncovering Key Lessons For Rapid Growth," *No Good*, January 14, 2022, https://nogood.io /2022/01/14/peloton-marketing-strategy/.

12. Courtney Rubin, "'The Netflix of Wellness': Inside the Hollywoodization of Peloton," *The Hollywood Reporter*, June 14, 2021, https://www.hollywoodreporter .com/business/business-news/hollywoodization-of-peloton-1234964386/.

13. Jason Wise, "How Many Peloton Users in 2022 Are There?" *Earthweb*, June 14, 2022, https://earthweb.com/how-many-peloton-users/.

14. David Curry, "Peloton Revenue and Usage Statistics (2022)," Business of Apps, November 4, 2022, https://www.businessofapps.com/data/peloton-statistics/.

15. Peloton Interactive, Inc., "FORM S-1 REGISTRATION STATEMENT," US Securities and Exchange Commission, August 27, 2019, https://www.sec.gov /Archives/edgar/data/1639825/000119312519230923/d738839ds1.htm.

16. Rachel Moore, "COVID-19 Impacted the Technology & Performing Arts Relationship: Are the Arts Ready?" *CSQ*, May 4, 2021, https://csq.com/2021 /05/c-suite-thought-leader-rachel-moore-covid-19-impacted-the-technology -performing-arts-relationship/#.YrJUbuzMLt1.

CHAPTER 4

1. Carnegie Corporation of New York, "Andrew Carnegie's Story," 2015, https://www.carnegie.org/interactives/foundersstory/#!/.
2. Carnegie Corporation of New York, "Andrew Carnegie's Story," 2015, https://www.carnegie.org/interactives/foundersstory/#!/#wealthiest-man-world.
3. Scott Galloway, *Post Corona*, 66–68; Abby McCain, "15 Largest Web Hosting Companies in the World," Zippia, March 8, 2021, https://www.zippia.com/advice/largest-web-hosting-companies/.
4. Scott Galloway, *Post Corona*, 103.
5. Jordan Crook, "Peloton Acquires Music Startup Neurotic Media," *TechCrunch*, June 27, 2018, https://techcrunch.com/2018/06/27/peloton-acquires-music-startup-neurotic-media/.
6. WolfBrown, "Audience Outlook Monitor."
7. California Symphony website, accessed July 13, 2023, https://www.californiasymphony.org/fresh-look/ and https://www.californiasymphony.org/fresh-look-rewind-2022/.
8. Richmond Symphony School of Music, accessed October 10, 2022, https://richmondsymphonysom.com/.
9. Jennifer Rosenfeld, "Case Study: Beth Morrison Projects' Producer Academy," LinkedIn, October 29, 2020, https://www.linkedin.com/pulse/case-study-beth-morrison-projects-producer-academy-jennifer-rosenfeld/.
10. BMP: Producer Academy, "Our Story," Beth Morrison Projects website, accessed April 6, 2023, https://bethmorrisonprojects.org/bmp-producer-academy/.
11. "Carnegie Technical Schools," Carnegie Mellon University, accessed April 6, 2023, https://www.cmu.edu/about/history.html.
12. Statista Research Department, "Size of the Global E-learning Market in 2019 and 2026, by Segment," Statista, July 6, 2022, https://www.statista.com/statistics/1130331/e-learning-market-size-segment-worldwide/; Christopher Pappas, "The Top eLearning Statistics and Facts for 2015 You Need to Know," eLearning Industry, January 25, 2015, https://elearningindustry.com/elearning-statistics-and-facts-for-2015; Jesse Maida, "E-learning Market Size to Grow by USD 1.72 Trillion at a CAGR of 16.35%; Increasing Adoption of Microlearning to Emerge as Key Driver," Technavio Research, *PR Newswire*, May 13, 2022, https://www.prnewswire.com/news-releases/e-learning-market-size-to-grow-by--usd-1-72-trillion-at-a-cagr-of-16-35-increasing-adoption-of-microlearning-to-emerge-as-key-driver--technavio-301546203.html.

13. Forbes Technology Council, "10 Industries on the Cusp of Technological Disruption," *Forbes*, February 5, 2019, https://www.forbes.com/sites/forbestechcouncil/2019/02/05/10-industries-on-the-cusp-of-technological-disruption/?sh=170174fd5d47.

14. Abigail Johnson Hess, "Google Announces 100,000 Scholarships for Online Certificates in Data Analytics, Project Management and UX," *CNBC*, July 13, 2020, https://www.cnbc.com/2020/07/13/google-announces-certificates-in-data-project-management-and-ux.html.

15. Austen Allred, "BloomTech to Launch New Backend Engineering Program, Jointly Developed with Amazon," Bloom Institute of Technology, April 13, 2021, https://www.bloomtech.com/article/bloomtech-launches-backend-engineering-program-amazon.

CHAPTER 5

1. Erica Gonzales, "82 Million of Us Burn for *Bridgerton*," *Harper's Bazaar*, January 28, 2021, https://www.harpersbazaar.com/culture/film-tv/a35122184/bridgerton-viewers-netflix/.

2. Joanna Robinson, "How *Bridgerton* Officially Became Netflix's Biggest Hit Ever," *Vanity Fair*, January 27, 2021, https://www.vanityfair.com/hollywood/2021/01/bridgerton-netflix-biggest-hit-highest-ratings-female-audiences-romance.

3. Bohne Silber and Tim Triplett, "A Decade of Arts Engagement: Findings from the Survey of Public Participation in the Arts, 2002–2012," National Endowment for the Arts, January 2015, 12 (performing arts) and 20 (visual arts).

4. United States Census Bureau, "DPO5 | ACS Demographic and Housing Estimates," 2020: ACS 5-Year Estimates Data Profiles, accessed June 17, 2023, https://data.census.gov/cedsci/table?q=United%20States&g=0100000US&tid=ACSDP5Y2020.DP05.

5. Actors' Equity Association, "Diversity Report: 2016–2019 in Review," 6.

6. Chad M. Topaz et al., "Diversity of Artists in Major U.S. Museums," *PLoS One*, March 20, 2019, https://journals.plos.org/plosone/article?id=10.1371/journal.pone.0212852.

7. Operabase, "Statistics," https://www.operabase.com/statistics/en.

8. Joseph Carman, "Behind Ballet's Diversity Problem, *Pointe*, May 20, 2014, https://pointemagazine.com/behind-ballets-diversity-problem/; Olivia Goldhill and Sarah Marsh, "Where Are the Black Ballet Dancers?" *Guardian*, September 4, 2012, https://www.theguardian.com/stage/2012/sep/04/black-ballet-dancers;

Stacia L. Brown, "Where Are the Black Ballerinas?" *Washington Post*, May 5, 2014, https://www.washingtonpost.com/news/act-four/wp/2014/05/05/where-are-the-black-ballerinas/.

9. James Doeser, "Racial/Ethnic and Gender Diversity in the Orchestra Field," League of American Orchestras, September 21, 2016, 4; Rob Deemer and Cory Meals, "Orchestra Repertoire Report 2022," Institute for Composer Diversity, May 31, 2022, 11.

10. National Endowment for the Arts, "A Decade of Arts Engagement," 12.

11. Erik Larson, "New Research: Diversity + Inclusion = Better Decision Making at Work," *Forbes*, September 21, 2017, https://www.forbes.com/sites/eriklarson/2017/09/21/new-research-diversity-inclusion-better-decision-making-at-work/?sh=480cfe734cbf; Sundiatu Dixon-Fyle et al., "Diversity Wins: How Inclusion Matters," McKinsey, May 19, 2020, https://www.mckinsey.com/featured-insights/diversity-and-inclusion/diversity-wins-how-inclusion-matters; Moira Alexander, "5 Ways Diversity and Inclusion Help Teams Perform Better," *CIO*, September 3, 2021, https://www.cio.com/article/189194/5-ways-diversity-and-inclusion-help-teams-perform-better.html; David Rock and Heidi Grant, "Why Diverse Teams Are Smarter," *Harvard Business Review*, November 4, 2016, https://hbr.org/2016/11/why-diverse-teams-are-smarter.

12. Mark Brown, "Arts Bodies Threatened with Funding Cuts over Lack of Diversity," *The Guardian*, February 17, 2020, https://www.theguardian.com/culture/2020/feb/18/arts-bodies-threatened-with-funding-cuts-over-lack-of-diversity.

13. Jonathan Dunn et al., "Black Representation in Film and TV: The Challenges and Impact of Increasing Diversity," McKinsey, March 11, 2021, https://www.mckinsey.com/Featured-Insights/Diversity-and-Inclusion/Black-representation-in-film-and-TV-The-challenges-and-impact-of-increasing-diversity.

14. Dunn et al., "Black Representation."

15. Silber and Triplett, "A Decade of Arts Engagement," 12; Wikipedia, s.v. "Demographics of San Francisco," last modified April 3, 2023, https://en.wikipedia.org/wiki/Demographics_of_San_Francisco.

16. Silber and Triplett, "A Decade of Arts Engagement," 12; Wikipedia, s.v. "Nashville, Tennessee: Demographics," last modified June 17, 2023, https://en.wikipedia.org/wiki/Nashville,_Tennessee#Demographics.

17. Conference session with Salvador Acevedo, Association of California Symphony Orchestras, August 2017.

18. Demicia Inman, "Lil Nas X's 'Old Town Road' Is First Song in History to Reach 15x-Platinum Status," *Vibe*, September 21, 2021, https://www.vibe.com/music/music-news/lil-nas-x-old-town-road-first-song-history-15x-platinum-1234629385/.

19. Salvador Acevedo, Verna Bhargava, and Steven Diller, "Latin Xperience in the Arts," *Scansion*, 2017, 3.

20. We See You W.A.T., "BIPOC Demands for White American Theatre," 3.

21. Drew Desilver, Michael Lipka, and Dalia Fahmy, "10 Things We Know About Race and Policing in the U.S.," Pew Research Center, June 3, 2020, https://www .pewresearch.org/fact-tank/2020/06/03/10-things-we-know-about-race-and -policing-in-the-u-s/.

22. Pew Research, "Bilingualism Fact Sheet," March 19, 2004, https://www .pewresearch.org/hispanic/2004/03/19/bilingualism/.

23. Camila Guerrero, "Why Might Bilingual Spanish Speakers Choose to Speak in English?" Slover Linett Audience Research, July 13, 2022, https://sloverlinett .com/news-notes/why-might-bilingual-spanish-speakers-choose-to-speak-in -english/.

24. Acevedo, Bhargava, and Diller, "Latin Xperience in the Arts," 9.

25. Peter Yen, Sushiritto website, https://www.sushirrito.com/about/.

CHAPTER 6

1. Jeffrey Dastin, "Amazon Scraps Secret AI Recruiting Tool That Showed Bias Against Women," *Reuters*, October 10, 2018, https://www.reuters.com/article/us -amazon-com-jobs-automation-insight/amazon-scraps-secret-ai-recruiting-tool -that-showed-bias-against-women-idUSKCN1MK08G.

2. Joshua Barone, "Opera Can No Longer Ignore Its Race Problem," *New York Times*, July 16, 2020, https://www.nytimes.com/2020/07/16/arts/music/opera -race-representation.html.

3. Dunn et al., "Black Representation in Film and TV."

4. OperaAmerica, "Field-Wide Opera Demographic Report 2021," June 21, 2022, 2.

5. Mariët Westermann, Roger Schonfeld, and Liam Sweeney, "Art Museum Staff Demographic Survey," 2018, 6–9.

6. Aubrey Bergauer, "Orchestra CEOs: The Smaller the Budget, the More Likely Female," *Medium*, March 15, 2021, https://aubreybergauer.medium.com /orchestra-ceos-the-smaller-the-budget-the-more-likely-female-6e9771b2c7ce.

7. Susan Seliger and Shauna Lani Shames, "The White House Project: Benchmarking Women's Leadership," 2009, 12.

8. Lean In and McKinsey & Company, "Women in the Workplace 2022," 2022, 7.

9. Maxwell Huppert, "5 Must-Do's for Writing Inclusive Job Descriptions," LinkedIn Talent Blog, April 9, 2018, https://www.linkedin.com/business/talent/blog /talent-acquisition/must-dos-for-writing-inclusive-job-descriptions; Danielle Gaucher, Justin Friesen, and Aaron C. Kay, "Evidence That Gendered Wording

in Job Advertisements Exists and Sustains Gender Inequality," *Journal of Personality and Social Psychology* 101, no. 1 (2011): 109–128, https://www.sussex.ac.uk/webteam/gateway/file.php?name=gendered-wording-in-job-adverts.pdf&site=7.

10. "Women in the Workforce: The Gender Pay Gap Is Greater for Certain Racial and Ethnic Groups and Varies by Education Level," U.S. Government Accountability Office, December 15, 2022, https://www.gao.gov/products/gao-23-106041.

11. Andreas Leibbrandt and John A. List, "Do Equal Employment Opportunity Statements Backfire? Evidence from a Natural Field Experiment on Job-Entry Decisions," National Bureau of Economic Research, September 2018, https://www.nber.org/papers/w25035.

12. Quinetta Roberson, "How to Build an Inclusive Workplace," *WorkLife with Adam Grant* (podcast), April 19, 2021, 38:28, https://www.ted.com/podcasts/worklife/building-an-anti-racist-workplace-transcript.

13. Karin Kimbrough, "The Great Reshuffle in 2022: Top Trends to Watch," Linked In, January 21, 2022, https://www.linkedin.com/pulse/great-reshuffle-2022-top-trends-watch-karin-kimbrough/.

14. Stefanie K. Johnson, David R. Hekman, and Elsa T. Chan, "If There's Only One Woman in Your Candidate Pool, There's Statistically No Chance She'll Be Hired," *Harvard Business Review*, April 26, 2016, https://hbr.org/2016/04/if-theres-only-one-woman-in-your-candidate-pool-theres-statistically-no-chance-shell-be-hired.

15. We See You W.A.T., "BIPOC Demands for White American Theatre," 7.

16. Eve Fine and Jo Handelsman, *Searching for Excellence & Diversity: A Guide for Search Committees—National Edition* (Madison: University of Wisconsin, Women in Science and Engineering Leadership Institute, 2012).

17. John W. McCoy, "Behaviorally Anchored Rating Scale: A Full Guide with Examples," Academy to Innovate HR, page visited April 11, 2023, https://www.aihr.com/blog/behaviorally-anchored-rating-scale/.

18. Atta Tarki, Tyler Cowen, and Alexandra Ham, "It's Time to Streamline the Hiring Process," *Harvard Business Review*, July 11, 2022, https://hbr.org/2022/07/its-time-to-streamline-the-hiring-process; Disha Sharma, "10 Effective Ways To Reduce Time To Hire: 9. Improve Your Job Listing," Harver, January 2, 2020, https://harver.com/blog/reduce-time-to-hire/#JobListing; George Oehlert, "Why Consistency Matters in Hiring," LinkedIn, August 18, 2020, https://www.linkedin.com/pulse/why-consistency-matters-hiring-george-oehlert/.

19. Laszlo Bock, *Work Rules!* (New York: Twelve, 2015), 93.

20. "Lift Every Voice: A Conversation Hosted by J'Nai Bridges," Facebook live video, 54:58–55:34, posted by LA Opera, June 5, 2020, https://fb.watch/ffpu7xRUnu/.

21. Bock, *Work Rules!*, 240.

22. Cobi Krieger and Bronwyn Mauldin, "Make or Break: Race and Ethnicity in Entry-Level Compensation for Arts Administrators in Los Angeles County," Los Angeles County Department of Arts and Culture with the Center for Business and Management of the Arts at Claremont Graduate University, May 2021, 4.

23. Zachary Small and Eileen Kinsella, "Most Art Gallery Assistants Earn Far Less Than a Living Wage, According to Our Exclusive Dealer Salary Survey," *Artnet*, June 1, 2021, https://news.artnet.com/market/artnet-news-gallery-assistants-living-wage-1974343.

24. Hakim Bishara, "Wexner Center for the Arts Workers Move to Unionize," *Hyperallergic*, March 8, 2022, https://hyperallergic.com/715579/wexner-center-for-the-arts-workers-move-to-unionize/.

25. "A Nationwide Movement," Cultural Workers United homepage, last modified November 2, 2022, https://www.culturalworkersunited.org/.

26. Elaine Velie, "New Database Shows Which Museum Job Boards Post Salaries," *Hyperallergic*, July 13, 2022, https://hyperallergic.com/745875/new-database-shows-which-museum-job-boards-post-salaries/.

27. Aubrey Bergauer, "Attracting Talent: What Arts Employees Want + How Orgs Can Meet Those Needs," interview with Karen Freeman, LinkedIn Live, YouTube video, timestamp 14:00, September 15, 2022, https://youtu.be/cc4ays5JLW4.

CHAPTER 7

1. Trish Christoffersen, "20 Years, 20 Milestones: How Zappos Grew Out of Just Shoes," Zappos, June 5, 2019, https://web.archive.org/web/20201212203407/https://www.zappos.com/about/stories/zappos-20th-birthday.

2. Trish Christoffersen, "These Are the Books Zappos Wants Its Employees (And You) to Read," Zappos, June 15, 2020, https://www.zappos.com/about/stories/zappos-library.

3. Elizabeth Medina, "Job Satisfaction and Employee Turnover Intention: What Does Organizational Culture Have to Do with It?" (master's thesis, Columbia University Academic Commons, 2013), https://academiccommons.columbia.edu/doi/10.7916/D8DV1S08, 10.

4. Marc Kaplan et al., "Shape Culture: Drive Strategy," *Deloitte Insights*, February 29, 2016, https://www2.deloitte.com/us/en/insights/focus/human-capital-trends/2016/impact-of-culture-on-business-strategy.html?id=us:2el:3dc:dup3020:awa:cons:hct16.

5. Aubrey Bergauer, "Attracting Talent."

6. Ade Onibada, "Brands Have Been Speaking Out About Racism and This One Meme Captures Just How Hollow Some of Them Are," *BuzzFeed News*, June 1, 2020, https://www.buzzfeednews.com/article/adeonibada/generic-brands-george-floyd-protest-statement; Fernando Duarte, "Black Lives Matter: Do Companies Really Support the Cause?" *BBC*, June 12, 2020, https://www.bbc.com/worklife/article/20200612-black-lives-matter-do-companies-really-support-the-cause.

7. Patrick Lencioni, "'Six Critical Questions' by Patrick Lencioni," YouTube video, 1:03, May 29, 2014, https://youtu.be/TXDKo6zT6U8.

8. Centers for Disease Control and Prevention, "Disability Impacts All of Us" (infographic), September 16, 2020, https://www.cdc.gov/ncbddd/disabilityandhealth/infographic-disability-impacts-all.html.

9. Jonathan Emmett et al., "COVID-19 and the Employee Experience: How Leaders Can Seize the Moment," McKinsey & Company, June 29, 2020, https://www.mckinsey.com/capabilities/people-and-organizational-performance/our-insights/covid-19-and-the-employee-experience-how-leaders-can-seize-the-moment.

10. Adam Grant, *Originals* (New York: Penguin Books, 2016), 253.

11. Zappos, "Zappos 10 Core Values," Zappos Insights page, accessed September 23, 2022, https://web.archive.org/web/20220808215731/https://www.zapposinsights.com/about/core-values.

12. Jim Collins and Morten T. Hansen, *Great by Choice: Uncertainty, Chaos, and Luck—Why Some Thrive Despite Them All* (New York: Harper Business, 2011).

13. Zannie Giraurd Voss, Daniel M. Cable, and Glenn B. Voss, "Organizational Identity and Firm Performance: What Happens When Leaders Disagree About 'Who We Are?'" *Organization Science* 17, no. 6 (2006): 677–775, https://doi.org/10.1287/orsc.1060.0218.

14. Julia Rozovsky, "The Five Keys to a Successful Google Team," *re:Work*, November 17, 2015, https://rework.withgoogle.com/blog/five-keys-to-a-successful-google-team/.

15. Marcus Buckingham and Ashley Goodall, *Nine Lies About Work* (Boston: Harvard Business Review Press, 2019), appendix A, 276.

16. Aubrey Bergauer, "Company Culture and How to Renovate It," interview with Kevin Oakes, LinkedIn Live, YouTube video, February 1, 2022, 14:09, https://youtu.be/I5mUX_vHvaM.

17. Buckingham and Goodall, *Nine Lies About Work*, 142.

18. Buckingham and Goodall, *Nine Lies About Work*, appendix A, 276.

19. Edgar Villanueva, *Decolonizing Wealth* (Oakland, CA: Berret-Koehler, 2018), 125.

20. Aimee Groth, "Zappos Is Going Holacratic: No Job Titles, No Managers, No Hierarchy," *Quartz*, December 30, 2013, updated July 21, 2022, https://qz.com/161210/zappos-is-going-holacratic-no-job-titles-no-managers-no-hierarchy/.

21. Kevin Oakes, "Company Culture and How to Renovate It," interview by Aubrey Bergauer, LinkedIn Live, YouTube video, February 1, 2022, 28:20, https://youtu .be/I5mUX_vHvaM.

22. Reed Hastings and Patty McCord, "Culture" (slide deck), Netflix, August 1, 2009, https://www.slideshare.net/reed2001/culture-1798664.

23. Patty McCord, *Powerful* (San Francisco: Silicon Guild, 2018), loc. 334.

24. Aubrey Bergauer, "Q&A with Patty McCord, Former Netflix Chief Talent Officer," interview for ACSO, YouTube video, timestamps 3:49 and 16:40, September 12, 2019, https://youtu.be/VwUBoOdXevY.

25. Svati Kirsten Narula, "The 5 U.S. Counties Where Racial Diversity Is Highest—and Lowest," *The Atlantic*, April 29, 2014, https://www.theatlantic.com/national /archive/2014/04/mapping-racial-diversity-by-county/361388/.

26. Lisa Delpit, "The Silenced Dialogue: Power and Pedagogy in Educating Other People's Children," *Harvard Educational Review* 53, no. 3 (1988): 282.

27. Brené Brown, *Dare to Lead* (New York: Random House, 2018), 35.

28. Katheryn Brekken, Kevin Oakes, and Kevin Martin, "The Talent Imperative," i4cp and *Fortune*, 5.

29. Trish Christoffersen, "Memorable Onboarding for New Hires, the Zappos Way," Zappos, January 28, 2020, https://web.archive.org/web/20210116135200 /https://www.zappos.com/about/stories/memorable-onboarding-new-hires.

30. Madeline Laurano, "The True Cost of a Bad Hire," Brandon Hall Group for Glassdoor, August 2015, 12.

31. Grant, *Originals*, 251.

32. "The Talent Imperative," webinar detailing findings in study of the same name, i4cp and *Fortune*, slide titled "Estimated HR Department Budget Changes for the Coming Year as Compared to the Previous Year," June 29, 2022.

33. Jeff Grabmeier, "Share Your Goals—but Be Careful Whom You Tell," *Ohio State News*, The Ohio State University, September 3, 2019, https://news.osu.edu/share -your-goals--but-be-careful-whom-you-tell/.

34. Buckingham and Goodall, *Nine Lies About Work*, 86.

35. Tony Hsieh, "Corner Office: Zappos CEO Tony Hsieh," interview by Kai Ryssdal, *Marketplace*, American Public Media, August 19, 2010, https:// www.marketplace.org/2010/08/19/zappos-ceo-tony-hsieh-full-interview -transcript/.

36. Caesars Entertainment, "Zappos and Caesars Entertainment Partnership Turns Concert Experience Up to Eleven," PRNewswire, February 26, 2018, https://www.prnewswire.com/news-releases/zappos-and-caesars-entertainment -partnership-turns-concert-experience-up-to-eleven-300603853.html.

CHAPTER 8

1. "The Silo Syndrome," *McKinsey Quarterly*, accessed September 16, 2022, https://www.mckinsey.com/business-functions/people-and-organizational-performance/our-insights/five-fifty-the-silo-syndrome.

2. Yves Evrard and François Colbert, "Arts Management: A New Discipline Entering the Millennium?" *International Journal of Arts Management* 2, no. 2 (2000): 4–13.

3. Thomas Wolf, "What a Cannoli Maker Can Teach Us About Classical Music Audiences," *The Nightingale's Sonata* (blog), June 7, 2021, https://www.nightingalessonata.com/blog/2021/6/3/what-a-cannoli-maker-can-teach-us-about-classical-music-audiences-by-thomas-wolf.

4. Patrick J. Boylan, *The Museum Profession* (Malden, MA & Oxford: Blackwell Publishing, 2010 2nd Edition), pp. 415.

5. Evrard and Colbert, "Arts Management."

6. Stella Shon et al., "The Complete History of Credit Cards, from Antiquity to Today," *The Points Guy*, September 6, 2021, https://thepointsguy.com/guide/history-of-credit-cards/.

7. Adam Grant, *Think Again: The Power of Knowing What You Don't Know* (New York: Penguin, 2021), 115–135.

8. Gillian Tett, *The Silo Effect* (New York: Simon & Schuster, 2015).

9. The Justice Collaboratory, "Procedural Justice," Yale Law School, December 11, 2019, https://law.yale.edu/justice-collaboratory/procedural-justice.

10. Peggy McGlone and Michael Andor Brodeur, "After $25 Million Stimulus, Stunned NSO Players Receive One-Week Notice from Kennedy Center," *Washington Post*, March 28, 2020, https://www.washingtonpost.com/lifestyle/style/after-25-million-stimulus-stunned-nso-players-receive-one-week-notice-from-kennedy-center/2020/03/28/9c27603e-7118-11ea-aa80-c2470c6b2034_story.html.

11. McGlone and Brodeur, "After $25 Million Stimulus"; Peggy McGlone, "Kennedy Center Furloughs 250 in Wake of $25 Million Federal Grant," *Washington Post*, March 31, 2020, https://www.washingtonpost.com/entertainment/music/kennedy-center-announces-250-more-layoffs-in-wake-of-25-million-federal-grant/2020/03/31/461d21ec-72b7-11ea-a9bd-9f8b593300d0_story.html; *The Washington Post* (@washingtonpost), "After $25 million stimulus, stunned National Symphony Orchestra players receive one-week notice from Kennedy Center," Twitter, March 28, 2020, 2:11 p.m., https://twitter.com/washingtonpost/status/1244009137664647168.

12. Kennedy Center IRS Form 990 filing for fiscal year 2019. Total revenue reported: $326,464,245.

13. Zach Finkelstein, "In Graceful Letter to Artists, Seattle Opera Cancels Rest of Season, Citing Force Majeure," *The Middleclass Artist*, March 26, 2020, https://www.middleclassartist.com/post/in-graceful-letter-to-artists-seattle-opera-cancels-rest-of-season-citing-force-majeure.

14. Finkelstein, "In Graceful Letter to Artists."

15. TRG Arts, "6 Metrics Arts Leaders Should Track, #1: Patron-Generated Revenue," YouTube video, 1:48, September 15, 2015, https://youtu.be/AnTzeEpfDR8.

16. "The Silo Syndrome."

17. Aubrey Bergauer, "Organizational Design," interview with Julian Chender, LinkedIn Live, YouTube video, March 23, 2022, 31:04, https://youtu.be/viWhWa9YJXY.

18. HBS Working Knowledge, "Is Your Org Chart Stuck In A Rut? Try A Scientific Experiment," *Forbes*, July 5, 2016, https://www.forbes.com/sites/hbsworkingknowledge/2016/07/05/is-your-org-chart-stuck-in-a-rut-try-a-scientific-experiment/; Ethan Bernstein, "The Organization Lab (o-Lab): How Might We Create the Next Iteration of Our Organizations?" *Medium*, March 15, 2016, https://medium.com/@ethanbernstein/the-organization-lab-how-might-we-create-the-next-iteration-of-our-organizations-22a90695fea4.

19. Colleen Dilenschneider, "Median Income of Cultural Attendees by Ethnicity: Another Reason Not to Judge Visitors by Appearance (DATA)," *Know Your Own Bone*, November 10, 2021, https://www.colleendilen.com/2021/11/10/cultural-entities-dont-confuse-affordability-with-diversity-data/.

20. Aubrey Bergauer, "Attracting Talent: What Arts Employees Want + How Orgs Can Meet Those Needs," interview with Karen Freeman, LinkedIn Live, YouTube video, timestamp 25:23, September 15, 2022, https://youtu.be/cc4ays5JLW4.

CHAPTER 9

1. Leslie R. Crutchfield and Heather McLeod Grant, *Forces for Good: The Six Practices of High-Impact Nonprofits* (New York: Jossey-Bass, 2012).

2. Patagonia, "Hey, How's That Lawsuit Against the President Doing?" accessed June 17, 2023, https://www.patagonia.com/stories/hey-hows-that-lawsuit-against-the-president-going/story-72248.html; David Gelles, "Billionaire No More: Patagonia Founder Gives Away the Company," *New York Times*, September 14, 2022, https://www.nytimes.com/2022/09/14/climate/patagonia-climate-philanthropy-chouinard.html.

3. Statista, "Patagonia Inc.," accessed October 11, 2022, https://www.statista.com/companies/c/25207154/patagonia-inc.

4. Kevin Foley, "The Certified B Corporation: A Definition and Brief History of How It All Started?" *Valley to Summit*, May 27, 2019, https://www.valleytosummit.net/the-certified-b-corporation-a-definition-and-brief-history-of-how-it-all-started.

5. Andrea Chang, "Patagonia Shows Corporate Activism Is Simpler Than It Looks," *Los Angeles Times*, May 9, 2021, https://www.latimes.com/business/story/2021-05-09/patagonia-shows-corporate-activism-is-simpler-than-it-looks.

6. Rachel Barton, Kevin Quiring, and Bill Theofilou, "From Me to We: The Rise of the Purpose-Led Brand," Accenture, December 5, 2018, Accenture.com/us-en/insights/strategy/brand-purpose.

7. Tonia E. Ries and David M. Bersoff, "2019 Edelman Trust Barometer Special Report: In Brands We Trust?" 2019, 2.

8. Kate Muhl, "Brands That Stand for Something, Take a Stand!" *Gartner Blog*, July 3, 2019, https://blogs.gartner.com/kate-muhl/brands-stand-something-take-stand/.

9. Chang, "Patagonia Shows Corporate Activism."

10. USC Annenberg Center for Public Relations, "The Future of Corporate Activism," March 2022, 24, https://issuu.com/uscannenberg/docs/usc_cpr_global_communication_report_2022/24.

11. Francesca Paris and Nate Cohn, "After Roe's End, Women Surged in Signing Up to Vote in Some States," *New York Times*, August 25, 2022, https://www.nytimes.com/interactive/2022/08/25/upshot/female-voters-dobbs.html; "How unpopular is Joe Biden?" FiveThirtyEight, accessed April 16, 2023, https://projects.fivethirtyeight.com/biden-approval-rating/; Susan Milligan, "The Red Wave That Wasn't," *USA Today*, Nov. 9, 2022, https://www.usnews.com/news/elections/articles/2022-11-09/the-red-wave-that-wasnt.

12. Katarina Stankovic, "Chart of the Week: Do Consumers Actually Care About Corporate Social Responsibility?" GWI, September 10, 2019, https://blog.gwi.com/chart-of-the-week/corporate-social-responsibility/.

13. Susan Berfield, "CVS Cigarette Ban Will Drive Away $2 Billion in Sales," *Bloomberg*, August 6, 2014, https://www.bloomberg.com/news/articles/2014-08-06/cvs-cigarette-ban-2-billion-in-lost-sales-and-not-just-tobbaco#xj4y7vzkg.

14. Sarah Owermohle, "FDA Blocks Walgreens and Circle K Tobacco Sales," *Politico*, February 7, 2019, https://www.politico.com/story/2019/02/07/fda-tobacco-sales-1155248.

15. Bruce Japsen, "After CVS Stopped Cigarette Sales, Smokers Stopped Buying Elsewhere, Too," *Forbes*, February 20, 2017, https://www.forbes.com /sites/brucejapsen/2017/02/20/after-cvs-stopped-cigarette-sales-smokers-stopped -buying-elsewhere-too/?sh=70b65d11c8f5.

16. "CVS Health Revenue 2010-2022," *Macrotrends*, https://www.macrotrends.net /stocks/charts/CVS/cvs-health/revenue.

17. Alison Beard, "Why Ben & Jerry's Speaks Out," *Harvard Business Review*, January 13, 2021, https://hbr.org/2021/01/why-ben-jerrys-speaks-out.

18. Rachel Barton, "To Affinity and Beyond: From Me to We, the Rise of the Purpose-Led Brand," Engage for Good, Accenture Strategy, December 5, 2018, https://engageforgood.com/accenture-strategy-from-me-to-we-the-rise-of-the -purpose-led-brand/, 11.

19. Chang, "Patagonia Shows Corporate Activism."

20. Sarah Whitten, "AMC, Regal and Cinemark Prepare to Reopen in the U.S. After Five-Month Shutdown," *CNBC*, August 20, 2020, https://www.cnbc.com/2020 /08/20/coronavirus-amc-regal-and-cinemark-prepare-to-reopen-in-the-us-after -five-month-shutdown.html; Associated Press, "San Francisco to Reopen Indoor Dining, Movie Theaters Wednesday After Coronavirus Cases Fall," *KTLA5*, March 2, 2021, https://ktla.com/news/california/san-francisco-poised-to-reopen -indoor-dining-movie-theaters-after-coronavirus-cases-fall/; Sarah Cascone, "As One of the First Major Museums to Reopen in California, the de Young Says It Is 'Ready to Provide Succor' to San Franciscans," *Artnet*, September 15, 2020, https://news.artnet.com/art-world/de-young-reopening-california-1908364.

21. Crutchfield and Grant, *Forces for Good.*

22. Crutchfield and Grant, *Forces for Good.*

23. National Endowment for the Arts, "New Data Show Economic Activity of the U.S. Arts & Cultural Sector in 2021: Data Reveal Some Industry Gains amid the Ongoing Impact of COVID-19," March 15, 2023, https://www.arts.gov/news /press-releases/2023/new-data-show-economic-activity-us-arts-cultural-sector -2021; U.S. Bureau of Economic Analysis website, GDP by Industry 2021 Totals, last modified March 30, 2023, https://www.bea.gov/.

24. Eren Waitzman, "Impact of Government Policy on the Creative Sector," House of Lords Library, UK Parliament, October 28, 2021, https://lordslibrary.parliament .uk/impact-of-government-policy-on-the-creative-sector/.

25. Press Release, "Americans for the Arts and over 775 Cultural Organizations and Creative Workers Come Together to Propose Plan for Putting Creative Workers to Work After Pandemic," Americans for the Arts, September 10, 2020, https://

www.americansforthearts.org/news-room/press-releases/americans-for-the-arts
-and-over-775-cultural-organizations-and-creative-workers-come-together-to.

26. Matthew Daddona, "Got Milk? How the Iconic Campaign Came to Be, 25 Years Ago," *Fast Company*, June 13, 2018, https://www.fastcompany.com/40556502 /got-milk-how-the-iconic-campaign-came-to-be-25-years-ago.

27. Beard, "Why Ben & Jerry's Speaks Out."

28. New York Yankees (@Yankees), "Firearms were the leading cause of death for American children and teens in 2020," Twitter, May 26, 2022, 4:02 p.m., https://twitter.com/Yankees/status/1529961238788202522?s=20&t=DYJP zhBVl1AYpA4z_wg6gg.

29. Tampa Bay Rays (@raysbaseball), "End gun violence. Sources: Annals of Internal Medicine, Everytown Research," Instagram, May 27, 2022, https://www .instagram.com/p/CeCwbfVudBv/.

30. Mark Jenkins, "A Smithsonian Museum Turns to Art, Not Science, to Hammer Home a warning About Mother Nature," *Washington Post*, July 6, 2021, https:// www.washingtonpost.com/goingoutguide/museums/national-museum-natural -history-unsettled-nature-art-review/2021/07/03/2e557b02-d505-11eb-ae54 -515e2f63d37d_story.html.

31. Stanford Graduate School of Business, "Jennifer Aaker: Harnessing the Power of Stories," YouTube video, timestamp 4:28, March 13, 2013, https://youtu.be /9X0weDMh9C4.

32. "Advocacy: How the Monterey Bay Aquarium Does It," Conference session with Ken Peterson and Kera Panni, Monterey Bay Aquarium, Association of California Symphony Orchestras, August 9, 2019.

33. Beard, "Why Ben & Jerry's Speaks Out."

34. Logan Martell, "Arts Organizations Partner for World Premiere of Daniel Roumain's 'They Still Want to Kill Us,'" *Opera Wire*, May 11, 2021, https://operawire .com/arts-organizations-partner-for-world-premiere-of-daniel-roumains-they -still-want-to-kill-us/.

35. Daniel Gilliam, "Statement to a Racist Listener," *90.5 WUOL Blog*, October 15, 2020, https://wuol.org/statement-to-a-racist-listener/.

CHAPTER 10

1. Christine Brandt Jones et al., "Prophet Brand Relevance Index," December 2022, 15; Federica Laricchia, "Mobile Operating Systems' Market Share Worldwide from 1st Quarter 2009 to 4th Quarter 2022," Statista, January 17, 2023, https://www.statista.com/statistics/272698/global-market-share-held-by-mobile -operating-systems-since-2009/; Melissa Clark, "The Instant Pot: Here's Why

Cooks Love It," *New York Times*, January 31, 2017, https://www.nytimes.com /2017/01/31/dining/instant-pot-electric-pressure-cooker-recipes.html; David Curry, "Calm Revenue and Usage Statistics (2023)," Business of Apps, January 9, 2023, https://www.businessofapps.com/data/calm-statistics/.

2. Chip Heath and Dan Heath, *Switch: How to Change Things When Change Is Hard* (New York: Crown Business, 2010), 129.

3. Aubrey Bergauer, "Orchestra X: The Results."

4. Dacher Keltner and Jonathan Haidt, "Approaching Awe, a Moral, Spiritual, and Aesthetic Emotion," *Cognition and Emotion* 17 (2003): 297–314.

5. Allen Summer, "The Science of Awe: White Paper Prepared for the John Templeton Foundation by the Greater Good Science Center at UC Berkeley, Executive Summary," 1.

6. Brian Bennett, "Dyson Says It's Done Making Corded Vacuums," *CNET*, March 6, 2018, https://www.cnet.com/home/kitchen-and-household/dyson-says-its-done -making-corded-vacuums/.

7. "A Burger with Benefits: Beyond Meat Releases Impact Report Quantifying the Environmental Benefits of the Beyond Burger," Beyond Meat Company Press Release, September 26, 2018, https://investors.beyondmeat.com/news-releases /news-release-details/burger-benefits-beyond-meatr-releases-impact-report -quantifying.

8. Alicia Kelso, "With Beyond Meat Partnership, Pizza Hut Is the First Major Pizza Chain to Launch Plant-Based Toppings Nationwide," *Forbes*, November 10, 2010, https://www.forbes.com/sites/aliciakelso/2020/11/10/with-beyond-meat -partnership-pizza-hut-is-the-first-major-pizza-chain-to-launch-plant-based -toppings-nationwide/?sh=52ddac8b18a7; Carmen Reinicke, "These Are Beyond Meat's 16 Highest-Profile Partnerships in the Food Industry," *Markets Insider*, October 28, 2019, https://markets.businessinsider.com/news/stocks/10-most -high-profile-beyond-meat-partnerships-in-food-industry-2019-7-1028381863; Peet's Coffee, "Peet's Coffee Partners with Beyond Meat and JUST Egg to Roll Out the Everything Plant-Based Breakfast Sandwich Nationwide," press release, March 3, 2021, https://www.prnewswire.com/news-releases/peets-coffee -partners-with-beyond-meat-and-just-egg-to-roll-out-the-everything-plant -based-breakfast-sandwich-nationwide-301239585.html.

9. Jessica Tyler, "Here Are IKEA's Secrets to Keeping Its Prices Low," *Business Insider*, October 12, 2018, https://www.businessinsider.com/why-ikea-is-so -cheap-2018-10.

10. Megan Rose Dickey, "IKEA Has Bought TaskRabbit," *TechCrunch*, September 28, 2017, https://techcrunch.com/2017/09/28/ikea-buys-taskrabbit/.

11. Scott Davis, "Three Ways Innovation Can Keep Your Brand Relentlessly Relevant," Prophet Blog, May 3, 2017, https://prophet.com/2017/05/3-ways-innovation-drives-brand-relevance/.

12. Mark Schaefer, *The Marketing Rebellion* (Louisville, KY: Schaefer Marketing Solutions, 2019).

13. Erin Hueffner, "7 Common Types of Customer Needs (+ How to Meet Them)," ZenDesk Blog, April 12, 2023, https://www.zendesk.com/blog/customer-needs/.

14. Nina Simon, *The Art of Relevance* (Santa Cruz, CA: Museum 2.0, 2016).

15. Georgi Todorov, "Word of Mouth Marketing: 49 Statistics to Help You Boost Your Bottom Line," Semrush (blog), March 22, 2021, https://www.semrush.com/blog/word-of-mouth-stats/.

16. "Prophet Brand Relevance Index," 2018, 21.

17. Christine Brandt Jones et al., "Prophet Brand Relevance Index 2022," 15; Davis et al., "Prophet Brand Relevance Index 2021," 2021, 14; Jesse Purewall, "Prophet Brand Relevance Index 2019," September 2019, 15; "Prophet Brand Relevance Index," 2018, 12.

EPILOGUE

1. Angela Duckworth and Stephen Dubner, "Is It Okay to Hate Highbrow Culture?" *No Stupid Questions* (Freakonomics Radio), Aug 28, 2022, 8:20.

2. Jennifer Sowinski et al., "Trends in Audience Behavior: Reopening Season Trends," JCA Arts Marketing, August 2022, 5, 8, 13.

3. Jennifer Sowinski Nemeth et al., "Trends in Audience Behavior: Subscription Sales," JCA Arts Marketing, January 2023.

4. Isaac Butler, "American Theater Is Imploding Before Our Eyes," *New York Times*, July 19, 2023, https://www.nytimes.com/2023/07/19/opinion/theater-collapse-bailout.html.

5. Christopher Browne, "Commercial Gaming Revenue Reaches $14.8B in Q2 2022, Sets All-Time Quarterly High," American Gaming Association press release, August 11, 2022, https://www.americangaming.org/new/commercial-gaming-revenue-reaches-14-8b-in-q2-2022-sets-all-time-quarterly-high/.

INDEX

ABOUT THE AUTHOR

Hailed as "the Steve Jobs of classical music" (*Observer*) and "the Sheryl Sandberg of the symphony" (*LA Review of Books*), Aubrey Bergauer is known for her results-driven, customer-centric, data-obsessed pursuit of changing the narrative for the performing arts. A "dynamic administrator" with an "unquenchable drive for canny innovation" (*San Francisco Chronicle*), she's held offstage roles managing millions of dollars in revenue at major institutions, including the Seattle Symphony, Seattle Opera, Bumbershoot Music & Arts Festival, and San Francisco Conservatory of Music. As chief executive of the California Symphony, Bergauer propelled the organization to double the size of its audience and nearly quadruple its donor base.

Bergauer helps organizations and individuals transform from scarcity to opportunity, make more money, and grow their base of fans and supporters. Her ability to cast and communicate vision moves large teams forward and brings stakeholders together, earning her "a reputation for coming up with great ideas and then realizing them" (*San Francisco Classical Voice*). With a track record for strategically increasing revenue and relevance, leveraging digital content and technology, and prioritizing diversity and inclusion onstage and off, Bergauer sees a better way forward for classical music and knows how to achieve it.

A graduate of Rice University, her work and leadership have been covered in national publications including the *Wall Street Journal, Entrepreneur, Thrive Global*, and Southwest Airlines magazine, and she is a frequent speaker spanning TEDx, Adobe's Magento, universities, and industry conferences in the US and abroad.

www.aubreybergauer.com
@aubreybergauer on LinkedIn, Instagram, X, Facebook, and YouTube